LEADING AT THE EDGE

True Tales from Canadian Police in Peacebuilding and Peacekeeping Missions around the World

BEN J.S. MAURE, M.S.C.

LEADING AT THE EDGE
2nd Edition, Black and White
Copyright (c) 2021 by Ben J.S. Maure, M.S.C.
1st Edition, Colour Copyright (c) 2020 by Ben J.S. Maure, M.S.C.

All rights reserved. No part of this book may be reproduced or transmitted in any form by any means, electronic or mechanical, including photocopying and recording, or by any information storage and retrieval system, except as may be expressly permitted in writing from the author. The views and opinions expressed in this book are those of the author and do not necessarily reflect the official policy or position of the RCMP. Any content provided is not intended to malign any religion, ethnic group, club, organization, company, or individual.

ISBN:
978-0-9950343-0-3 (1st Edition, Paperback)
978-0-9950343-1-0 (1st Edition, eBook)
978-0-9950343-2-7 (2nd Edition, Paperback)

Front cover photo: RCMP Police Officer Gregor Aitken during a foot patrol in Kandahar City, Afghanistan

Typeset and cover design by Edge of Water Designs, www.edgeofwater.com

PRAISE FOR LEADING AT THE EDGE

"Peacekeeping forces really do (on average) keep the peace, and their valour and courage should earn them the medals, parades, and statues bestowed on other military heroes. In this engaging book, Ben Maure shows the human side of two of Canada's great contributions to the world: the Mounties and peacekeeping forces."
– **Professor Steven Pinker, Johnstone Professor of Psychology, Harvard University,** and author of *The Better Angels of Our Nature and Enlightenment Now*

"Instead of lecturing about the reality of international police operations, [Ben Maure] shares his personal experience and introduces the reader to the everyday reality of the globalization of security. For students of this crucial transition in world history where security moves from nations to the entire globe, this book offers not just analysis, but also unique personal experience." – **Timo Kivimäki, Professor of International Relations, University of Bath**

"Leading at the Edge is a rich and original account of Canadian police officers' experiences of international conflict during the last three decades. Canada's police pride themselves in being highly expeditionary, able to deploy and help restore the rule of law in the most challenging of operational environments. Maure's work provides valuable insights that should inform future international peace support missions."
– **Dr. Edward Burke, Assistant Professor in International Relations, University of Nottingham**

"*Leading at the Edge* comes just when it is needed, providing a marvellous antidote to cynicism about the effectiveness—and even the need—for international peacekeeping … Especially notable is that rather than viewing such activities from a distant, geopolitical perspective, *Leading at the Edge* invites us to experience and understand the human costs and courage that is involved. Bravo!" – **David P. Barash, Professor Emeritus, University of Washington, and author of** *Strength Through Peace*

A useful and informative account of international police support for post-conflict democratic transitions, filled with anecdotes and insights on the challenge of establishing locally-based and accountable police protection for communities threatened by armed conflict and criminal violence. – **David Cortright, Kroc Institute for International Peace Studies, University of Notre Dame**

"Out of the spectre of human revitalization in the troubled places of the world, Insp. Maure has created an insightful chronicle of what it means to be a police peacekeeper … The historical vignettes he has assembled and his accounting of some of the most important missions in the modern era is a seminal piece of the peacekeeping literature of our time." – **Len Babin, Former RCMP Superintendent, Canadian Police Contingent Commander, MINUGUA 1998**

"If you have ever wondered what it is like to be a police officer who is dropped into a foreign country, vibrating with ethnic or economic tension, then this is the book for you. Maure's writing captures the essence, the texture, the sensations, and the minutiae of unimaginable details involved in going to a strange country to try to bring peace and order." – **Professor Michael R. Sanchez, PhD, University of Texas Rio Grande Valley, Former Director of Personnel and Administration of UN Police in Kosovo**

"This is an outstanding book. Through his ten empathetic biographies, Ben Maure illuminates the range of crucial roles which police can effectively play." – **Professor John Langmore, Melbourne University, Former Australian MP And UN Director**

"Written from the perspective of someone who has been there, this book provides the reader with an insider's keen insight into the successes and challenges associated with peacekeeping and peacebuilding ... This is a compelling book that brings to life the roles and contributions that Canadian peacekeepers and peacemakers make around the world." – **Irwin M. Cohen, PhD, Associate Professor, Director of Centre for Public Safety and Criminal Justice Research, University of the Fraser Valley**

"What I love about this book is that it is both factually informative and contains personal narratives of Canadian peace officers ... Ben Maure has crafted a unique picture of United Nations policing, allowing readers to gain a deeper understanding of world politics and global conflict." – **Garry Gray, PhD, Associate Professor, University of Victoria**

"This book restores the letters of nobility to our profession, so often forgotten or neglected ... It will be an inspiration for many people, police or not." – **Fady Dagher, Directeur du Service de police de l'agglomération de Longueuil**

"RCMP veteran Ben Maure takes readers on an exhilarating and engaging odyssey to the far nooks and crannies of the globe ... He delivers the history of these countries' struggles, and his accounts put many of today's international tensions in their proper perspectives, allowing the reader to better understand the present and, perhaps, anticipate the future." – **Steve Pomper, Author of De-Policing America: A Street Cop's View of the Anti-Police State**

"Though written from a Canadian perspective, this book is globally helpful for everybody who is interested in the particularities, problems, progress, and projects of civilian-military or civilian-peace operations. Ben Maure is a great storyteller who artistically features officers who went out to contribute their share to a peaceful world. His stories invite the reader to connect with the human beings in mission, with their ethics and values, expectations and ambitions, hopes and fears, with their success and frustration." – **Professor Wolfgang Dietrich, PhD, UNESCO Chairholder for Peace Studies, University of Innsbruck**

"A must-read for anyone interested in policing, politics or history. The stories contained within simultaneously transport the reader to far-off places and speak to the familiar values of Canadians here at home. The collection of works will make you proud of our officers who put on the uniform to teach, serve, and protect both at home and internationally." – **Dr. Veronica S.E. Fox, Advisory NCO (Sgt), E Division RCMP**

"Few individuals are better equipped to research and write about Canadian police peacekeeping missions than those that have served in the field and experienced peacekeeping ... The book is a welcome addition to literature surrounding Canadian policing and peacekeeping, and is highly recommended for students and practitioners."
– **Rick Parent, PhD, Associate Professor, School of Criminology, Simon Fraser University**

"Ben Maure is not only a student of history, but an active participant on the front line of peacekeeping at home and abroad. I highly recommend reading *Leading at the Edge*." – **Chief Jean-Michel Blais, Halifax Regional Police, Former Deputy Police Commissioner, MINUSTAH (Haiti) 2008-2009**

"This is an important addition to the body of knowledge on peacekeeping, capturing several civilian police missions and explaining them in layman's terms ... A must-read for anyone interested in another facet of the complex world of peace support operations."
– Wayne Mac Culloch, CD, Immediate Past National President, Canadian Association of Veterans in United Nations Peacekeeping (CAVUNP)

"Informative, enlightening, courageous, and inspiring. Ben J.S. Maure has produced an insightful and important work that offers an in-depth account of peacekeeping missions from a collection of experiences ... A recommended read for the layperson."
– Deborah L. Delaronde-Falk, Winnipegosis Library, Manitoba

"This book is a source of inspiration for all those who recognize the value of freedom and our fundamental rights of peace ... In addition to doing a remarkable police job and being internationally respected, these police officers are fully committed to their mission by trying to make a difference, if only for one person." - **Robert Pigeon, Director, Service de Police de la Ville de Quebec**

"*Leading at the Edge* provides rare insight into the important contribution the RCMP provides with respect to promoting and advancing peace, freedom, and democracy around the globe." – **Kelly W. Sundberg, PhD, Associate Professor, Mount Royal University**

"Based on memoirs and other original sources, with heartfelt anecdotes and details, the book is excellent and its stories deserve to be heard by general readers interested in peace missions and scholars in criminology and other social sciences."
– Professor Hongming Cheng, LLM, PhD, University of Saskatchewan

❧

"This book makes an original and valuable contribution to our understanding of international peace-keeping efforts by police. I would recommend it to anyone interested in this topic and consider it essential reading for police organizing or participating in international peacekeeping activities." – **Ron Stansfield, PhD, Associate Professor, University of Guelph**

❧

"The reader will not at any stage lose sight of the fact that policing is a dirty-hands business ... Ben Maure clearly understands the many pitfalls associated with policing at a local, national, and international level, and he displays the intellect of a seasoned practitioner and the skills of an accomplished writer. More power to the caretakers of the mess that is created by society." – **Professor Michael Kennedy, PhD, Western Sydney University**

❧

"Maure's well-researched book on the role of police in peacekeeping is not only timely but is likely to prove to be a timeless contribution to how law enforcers contribute to restoring justice in countries suffering from political turmoil." – **Dr. Henry Prunckun, Research Criminologist Australian Graduate School of Policing and Security, Charles Sturt University**

❧

"This is an important book for Canadians, bridging generations and eras ... [its] carefully recounted operational details are a primary source for students of international police operations—past and future." – **David Last, CD, PhD, Royal Military College of Canada**

❧

"*[Leading at the Edge]* is a thorough, comprehensive, and accessible account of practical contemporary police peacekeeping and nation building." – **Garth den Hayer, Ph.D, School of Criminology and Criminal Justice, Arizona State University**

I would like to dedicate this book to two fallen Comrades: Royal Canadian Mounted Police (RCMP) Chief Superintendent Doug Coates and Sergeant Mark Gallagher. I met and befriended Doug and Mark during my numerous trips to Haiti in 2009, when I was the RCMP Foreign Liaison Officer for the region. Doug and Mark were incredibly devoted police peacekeepers who made the ultimate sacrifice to uphold their convictions to serve and protect. Several years have now passed since they departed us, and they have been sorely missed—both by their families and by friends like me, whom they helped and inspired. May Peace be with you, Doug and Mark!

Ben

LEADING AT THE EDGE

TABLE OF CONTENTS

FOREWORD i

PREFACE iii

1. Birth of a Nation: UNTAG (United Nations Transition Assistance Group), Namibia 1989-1990 1

2. The Unity Highway: UNPROFOR (United Nations Protection Force), Former Yugoslavia 1992-1995 31

3. Guatemala—Never Again: MINUGUA (United Nations Verification Mission in Guatemala), 1994-2004 57

4. The Land of the Kosovo Harley: UNMIK (United Nations Interim Administration Mission in Kosovo), 1999-Present 85

5. Independence Day: UNTAET (United Nations Transitional Authority for East Timor), 1999-2002 107

6. Blood Diamonds No More: Special Court for Sierra Leone, 2002-2013 133

7. After the Sandstorm: UNMIS (United Nations Mission in Sudan), 2005-2011 153

8. Of Biblical Proportion: EUPOL COPPS (European Police Coordinating Office for Palestinian Police Support), Palestine 2006- Present 189

9. Defying the Taliban: ISAF (International Security Assistance Force), Afghanistan 2001-2013 215

10. The Ultimate Sacrifice: MINUSTAH (United Nations Stabilization Mission in Haiti), 2004-2017 253

11. Epilogue 285

APPENDIX A
The Selection Process 287

APPENDIX B
Peacebuilding, Peacekeeping, and Peacemaking 293

APPENDIX C
Abbreviations & Acronyms 297

APPENDIX D
Acknowledgements 301

APPENDIX E
About the Author 307

WORKS CITED 309

ENDNOTES 329

FOREWORD

BECOMING A POLICE officer is the result of a special calling, one that is generally driven by a desire to serve one's community in order to make it a safer and better place for all. Across Canada, the United States, and the globe, there are literally millions who have enthusiastically accepted this undertaking on behalf of a drive to enhance civility and improve quality of life. But there are only a select few in law enforcement who have opted to take this challenge to a higher level and travel to unstable and undeveloped regions of the world, often during or shortly after devastating conflicts or natural disasters, and bring their commitment to improve humanity to a highly-demanding stage. Ben Maure has taken the opportunity to outline in detail his personal experiences and those of his Canadian police colleagues who have volunteered for peace-building and peacekeeping missions across the world.

This enlightening book will take the reader from one end of the globe to the other, across a number of post-conflict zones to the scenes of devastating natural disasters, and put the reader through the demanding preparation, deployment, and engagement stages that every international police officer can attest to. In many of the described cases, the deployment of international police officers to these areas was viewed by the local population as the first glimpse of public security and hope for a stable environment that they may have experienced in years. And in those mobilizations following violent armed conflict or overwhelming natural disaster, arriving international peacekeepers have been viewed by the oppressed in a fashion that one can say is truly reminiscent of the arriving 'cavalry.'

The book covers three decades of effective law enforcement and rule of law development that examines international criminal justice/peacekeeping missions in Namibia, Croatia, Guatemala, Kosovo, East Timor, Sierra Leone, Sudan, Palestine, Afghanistan, and Haiti. This plethora of perspectives and experiences will continue to entice, inform, and impress the reader. It will be made clear that Ben Maure has proficiently and thoroughly highlighted the challenges, rewards, and sacrifices that only those that have accepted this admirable vocation can effectively describe.

Whether you are a government official, policy maker, researcher, student, criminal justice professional, law enforcement officer considering assignment to an international policing mission, or just a concerned human being, you will find the portrayals and anecdotes outlined in this book enlightening, fascinating, and awe-inspiring. And these accounts will clearly elevate the appreciation that society holds for law enforcement officers, peacekeepers, and those who have opted to travel abroad to make the world a better place. The desire to help fellow human beings has been acknowledged as being honourable and noteworthy for centuries. The most inspiring quote comes directly from the Bible: *"Blessed are the peacemakers, for they shall be called the children of God."*

James F. Albrecht is a retired NYPD Captain, former United Nations and European Union/United States Department of State Rule of Law Mission Police Chief (in Kosovo) and former United States Department of Justice ICITAP Senior Police Advisor (in Ukraine). Jimmy is presently a Professor of Criminal Justice and Homeland Security at Pace University in New York City and is the author of numerous books and journal articles that examine criminal justice and policing accomplishments and challenges from a global perspective.

PREFACE

THIS BOOK IS a reference for police officers, people interested in foreign diplomacy, international affairs, military affairs, criminal justice reforms or anyone who has an interest in peacekeeping. In this book, you will learn about the work of police peacekeepers in international operations. I have collected ten true stories to serve as a source of inspiration and provide a unique perspective on police peacebuilding, peacekeeping, and personal achievements. Although this book has a specific Canadian flavor, I submit that the fundamental principles raised therein are applicable to most, if not other jurisdictions. Therefore, the narratives presented herein could have been about the brave duties of other police peacebuilders and peacekeepers from nations around the world.

The officers depicted in the following pages, myself included, were often supported by a military component that was crucial to a conclusive outcome. The role of the various armies, whether they were Canadian, American, Australian, Brazilian, Chilean, or others, highly contributed to the overall success of the missions and to the work of the police officers. In fact, without the military component, moving forward to bring peace and stability to those neophyte democracies would not have been possible.

Through these pages, the reader will be transported to Namibia, Croatia, Guatemala, Kosovo, East Timor, Sierra Leone, Sudan, Jerusalem, Afghanistan, and Haiti. Although the narrative involves a large amount of historical data, this book is not intended to be a historical reference. Instead, I invite you, the reader, to join me in the exciting, fulfilling, and at times dangerous experience of being an international peacekeeper. From the Namibian Independence Day assignment in 1989, to the simultaneous National Police Reformation and Earthquake Response Mission in Haiti, to my own operation overseeing the end of a 36-year civil war in Guatemala, I present to you ten inspiring tales of courage, astuteness, and professionalism. I have also chosen to expose the challenges, frustrations, and, at times, the sentiments of helplessness that some police officers experienced during their respective tours of duty to provide as much of a true picture of a mission as possible.

Canadian Police Officers are renowned throughout the world for their expertise, impartiality, and their fairness. Thanks to their efforts, democratic policing is gaining roots in areas that were once noted for repression and abuse of human rights. These are the stories of these amazing officers!

1.

Birth of a Nation: UNTAG (United Nations Transition Assistance Group), Namibia 1989-1990

The birth of a nation! Who can actually boast participation in such a formidable event? A country that has been subjected to nothing but colonial power for the past hundred years finally obtains its own sovereignty and experiences its first democratic vote.

The year is 1989, and for the first time, the United Nations has invited Canada to supply its own civilian police contingent to act as international peacekeepers. 100 police officers from the Royal Canadian Mounted Police (RCMP) set off for a faraway land that will soon become Namibia. The contingent of 96 men and 4 women will become the pioneers of Canadian police peacekeeping. They will join forces with thousands of other international police officers, military personnel, and civilians who have arrived to the country. Their mission is of utmost importance: to ensure a smooth electoral process for the first election to be held in this new country.

Chief Superintendent Larry Proke will lead these first Canadian police peacekeepers to the country formerly known as South West Africa, to witness its first steps as its own nation: Namibia. Larry's story in this distant land is an inspiring tale of adventure and devotion. Its success paved the road for a new tradition, which would see Canadian police officers travel throughout the world for decades to come.

NAMIBIA IS LOCATED on the south-western coast of Africa. The country is bordered by South Africa to the south, Botswana to the east, Zambia to the northeast, and Angola to the north.[1]

BEN J.S. MAURE, M.S.C.

On March 21, 1990, Namibia gained its independence from South Africa, following the Namibian War of Independence.[2] Before 1989, Namibia was known as South West Africa.

Originally, the drylands of South West Africa were inhabited by indigenous people known as the San, the Damara, and the Nama. Other tribes, such as the Herero and the Ovambo, moved to the region on or about the 14th century.[3]

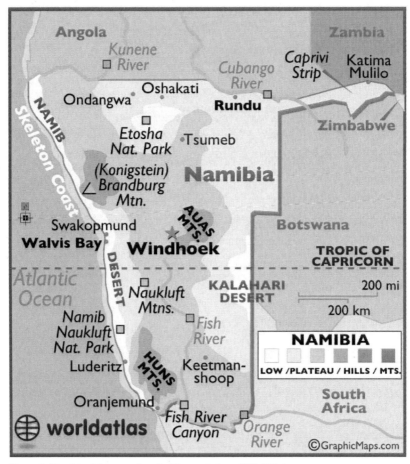

Figure 1: Namibia. Map reproduced with permission of WorldAtlas.com

In 1884, Namibia became a German colony, with little resistance given from British-controlled South Africa. With further German settlers arriving at the turn of the century, South West Africa saw an economic boost, primarily through recently-discovered copper and diamond mines. To accommodate them, a major railway was initiated between the towns of Swakopmund and Luderitz.[4]

Although relations between the tribes and the German settlers were initially peaceful, a war of resistance soon broke out in 1904. Unfortunately, the escalation that ensued led to large numbers of indigenous men, women, and children being driven into the arid Kalahari Desert and prevented from returning. Those who did not succumb to the desert were later rounded up and sent to local concentration camps, where some were subjected to field research on racial qualities.[5] Although clear numbers are not available, it is believed that as many as 90,000 indigenous people may have perished. Many historians consider this period to be the first attempt at genocide in the 20th century, and a precursor for medical experiments on Jewish people during the Nazi Holocaust.[6]

German colonial rule in Namibia came to an end during WWI, as a result of South African troops invading the area.[7] The newly-formed League of Nations placed South West Africa under a British mandate, to be administered by the Government of South Africa.[8] This initiated a gradual process by which the country became closely integrated to South Africa.

As a result of a fledgling market for diamonds and livestock after World War II, the area saw its prosperity increased. Alas, the new wealth was almost exclusively reserved for European settlers in the south. Distress further increased among the indigenous population as a result of the introduction of segregation laws by South Africa.[9]

The breakup of the League of Nations in the late 40s saw the newly created United Nations try to promote the interests of South West Africa's indigenous peoples. However, opposition from South Africa impeded success along those lines.[10] For the next decade and a half, growing sentiments for a liberation struggle saw more and more popularity amongst the black majority, and gave rise to the South West Africa People's Organization (SWAPO).[11]

Starting in the mid-sixties, SWAPO became a primary political force and national liberation movement, despite heavy resistance from South Africa.[12] By 1988, South Africa's own internal troubles were getting in the way of its suppression efforts against SWAPO, and eventually, it had to abandon the idea of controlling South West Africa.[13]

South West Africa remained a concern for the UN. Back in 1966, the General Assembly ended the mandate of South Africa over South West Africa, and placed it solely under UN responsibility. In 1968, the UN General Assembly formally recognized the territory of South West Africa as Namibia through its Resolution 2372 (XXII).[14] However, the UN was unable to enforce this policy, and South Africa continued to illegally occupy the territory for another two decades.[15]

In February 1989, South Africa finally agreed to the cease-fire that the UN had been trying to implement.[16] The agreement, Resolution 435, put forward a multitude of conditions in addition to the cease-fire between South Africa and SWAPO; among them was the earlier-proposed idea of UN-supervised elections in South West Africa. Further, the resolution established the United Nations Transition Assistance Group (UNTAG) to oversee both the electoral process and the subsequent withdrawal of South African forces.

In essence, UNTAG was a political operation, mandated to ensure the first free and fair elections in Namibia after more than a hundred years of colonialism. In order to establish the right conditions for such a process, UNTAG had to carry out a variety of tasks and duties. Included in them would be the overseeing of the disarmament of SWAPO combatants and the monitoring of the phased withdrawal of South African security forces, including the South West Africa Police.[17]

To achieve its objectives, UNTAG would count on a deployment of nearly 8,000 peacekeepers during its peak in November 1989. The personnel deployment consisted of 2,000 civilians, 1,500 police officers, and roughly 4,500 military personnel. Just prior to the November 1989 elections, UNTAG had 49 civilian police officers scattered throughout the territory.[18]

Within the mission, the role of the Civilian Police (CIVPOL) Monitors was to ensure that the South West Africa Police carried out its duty of maintaining law and order in a fair, professional, and impartial manner. This involved observing police investigations by accompanying police officers on patrols. CIVPOL Monitors travelled separately in their clearly-marked UN vehicles.

Some South West Africa Police officers resented the presence of the UN Monitors and, during patrols, would at times try to lose the UN vehicles. However, most CIVPOL stations established throughout the country had developed good working relationships with the South West Africa Police, and did not encounter much resentment. Still, a few South West Africa Police stations remained "unapproachable".

CIVPOL Monitors were also required to maintain a presence at political meetings, rallies, demonstrations, and all other aspects of the electoral process. Needless to say, CIVPOL presence during some political rallies and demonstrations was not entirely welcomed by all participants; however, tolerance grew as time went on.

The RCMP candidate selection for the Namibian mission took place towards the end of the summer of 1989. It started with an internal advertisement within the RCMP to identify interested volunteers. It didn't take long for 2000 applications to pour in; however, only 100 candidates would get selected from the ranks.

Chief Superintendent Larry Proke, the officer-in-charge of the RCMP Protective Policing Branch in Toronto, Ontario, also saw the advertisement call. After he conducted some research on the country and the mandate of the mission, Larry applied for a position, which promised adventure and a chance for him to contribute to something unique.

Within a few days, Larry received a call from the RCMP Commissioner, the highest-ranking officer in the RCMP, who informed him that he had been selected as Contingent Commander. Armed with a solid operational background coupled with outstanding leadership skills, Larry was the ideal candidate for this important mission.

Because this was the first time Canada provided police peacekeepers, Larry and two other police officers flew for a one-week reconnaissance mission to Namibia in September 1989. This was to acquire an understanding of the role the Canadian police contingent would play. It is important to note that the Namibian mission had already started by the time Larry and his colleagues traveled on their reconnaissance trip. Therefore, time was of the essence in identifying Canada's role and continuing with the RCMP's internal selection process for the other officers required for the mission.

At the time, Canada was the last country asked to provide police peacekeepers to the newly set up UN CIVPOL division. In past missions, police officers attending peacekeeping missions were always aligned with the military rather than the UN.

The civilian police component of the Namibian mission called for a total of 1,500 police officers coming from 23 countries, including Australia, New Zealand, West Germany, East Germany, and Nigeria. Of those, Nigeria supplied the most numbers to the cause; however, with the strength of 100 officers, the Canadian contingent would be the second largest, despite being the last one to arrive to the mission.

Larry's upcoming role in Namibia would be that of Canadian

Contingent Commander, as well as Chief of Staff for the entire CIVPOL component. In simple terms, this meant Larry would be the third-in-charge of 1,500 UN police officers.

Larry's mission management team in Ottawa had already been identified, including his Deputy Contingent Commander, Superintendent Mike O'Reilly. Back to Canada after his reconnaissance trip, Larry and his management team, along with the RCMP Staffing Section, began the daunting task of identifying and selecting suitable candidates. All of this had to be done in a record time, as the Canadian troops had to be in Namibia before the elections, now less than two months away.

Candidates with experience ranging from general duty first responders to latent fingerprint specialists were sought for this first mission. These officers, who came from a variety of ranks across Canada, would be, along with Larry, the pioneers of Canadian police peacekeeping.

Pre-deployment training for this mission was held in Ottawa and lasted one week. Resource personnel from the Department of Foreign Affairs and International Trade (DFAIT), the Canadian military, the Canadian Security Intelligence Service (CSIS), and the RCMP International Operations Branch came one by one to lecture the peacekeepers on security, the United Nations, and the basics of the Namibian conflict. Since the event was expected to draw media interest both at home and abroad, drill sessions were also a part of the curriculum to ensure sufficient discipline in the ranks.

Other parts of pre-deployment included: immunizations to tropical diseases, in-depth medical exams, and attempts to dress everyone with uniforms that met the requirement of an equatorial mission. With uniforms mainly suitable for personnel working "North of the 60th parallel", the RCMP was unable to provide tropical gear to its members. Outfitting the new contingent with wool pants and long sleeve shirts would not have been ideal in a hot desert climate such as that of Namibia. Consequently, khakis, short pants, and shirts were obtained from the Canadian military, while desert boots were purchased by the RCMP. This uniform was supplied to the peacekeepers, along with a brassard that displayed the RCMP shoulder flash and both the Canadian and UN flags. The UN blue beret and badge was the mandatory headdress.

On October 17, 1989, Larry and his troop of 99 officers departed Ottawa on chartered buses, which would take the peacekeepers to the Montréal airport. From there, the troop initiated a 22-hour journey to Namibia. If only they knew then how exciting that would prove to be!

The first leg of the trip, Montréal to London, was uneventful in the comfort of a British Airways Boeing 747. The troop then flew from London to Lagos, Nigeria, where it overnighted and got ready for the last leg of the journey.

The next morning, as scheduled, the troop mustered on the tarmac shortly before 08:00, ready to board the Trans Arabian Air Transport Boeing 707 that had been chartered by the UN to fly to Namibia. Apparently, due to a misunderstanding, the plane had not been fuelled in time for take-off. After a two-hour wait, Larry and his team finally got ready to board the refuelled Boeing 707 that would take them to their final destination.

Revolutionizing passenger air transports in the 60s and 70s, the Boeing 707 was a true harbinger of the jet age. However, by 1989, many of these majestic planes were getting a little old. One may suspect that the 707 that Larry and his colleagues were about to board fell into this category.

As the first wave of adventurous peacekeepers began boarding the old plane, one of them noticed something not quite up to the aviation safety standards he had been used to in North America. In a flash, he was out the plane, down the ramp, and on the tarmac, huffing and puffing to report his findings to Larry.

Hardly believing what he was hearing from his out-of-breath officer, Larry went up to see for himself. And what a sight it was! The two emergency exit doors at the rear had been sealed off with metal rails welded onto the fuselage. In the event of an emergency, those exits would be unavailable! Safety concerns quickly arose among Larry's officers. Who knew what else had been altered on the aircraft?

After another hour spent sweating under the hot Nigerian sun, and following much reassurances from a UN official that the plane was airworthy, the peacekeepers hesitantly boarded and prepared themselves for take-off. As the plane taxied to the runway, the atmosphere on board became more relaxed. An incredible experience lay ahead of them; this was but a brief stop on the way.

Properly lined up, the pilot applied full throttle and the old jet thundered down the runway, bouncing up and down as it went. Suddenly, a peacekeeper in a window seat yelled for Larry's attention in a trembling voice. Larry, who was seated nearby, looked over to investigate. He could only stare in disbelief at the wing on his side of the aircraft, flapping almost like that of a bird; some rivets holding it together were so loose that they were spinning.

Before Larry could say anything, half of the overhead bins abruptly burst open. Carry-on luggage tumbled out onto the horrified peacekeepers. While everyone gasped for air as if it were their last breath on earth, a resounding roar announced that the jet was now airborne. The plane banked left, and quickly soared. Though far from graceful, it eventually reached its cruising speed and altitude. Calm returned to the cabin, and Larry would later admit that the rest of the journey was a "piece of cake" compared to the emotionally charged take-off.

After roughly a four-and-a-half-hour flight, Larry and his team landed safely in Windhoek, the capital city of Namibia. There, all deplaned and formed rank so that the contingent could be welcomed by the CIVPOL Administration and Personnel Officer, Swedish Contingent Commander Chief Superintendent Jan Gustafson. Without a doubt, this was a historic and memorable moment for every contingent member: they were about to become the first troop of Canadian Police Peacekeepers to serve with the UN.

Figure 2: Deplaning in Namibia. Photo of the Trans Arabian Air Transport Boeing 707, which took our intrepid peacekeepers from Lagos, Nigeria to their final destination of Windhoek, Namibia. Larry and Superintendent Mike O'Reilly are in Red Serge. Photo courtesy of Larry Proke.

As the Commander of the Canadian contingent, Larry wore the traditional RCMP red tunic, which is made of wool, and is also known as the Red Serge. Although Larry made no mention of it, I imagine he and Superintendent O'Reilly, who was also wearing the red tunic for the occasion, must have been in some discomfort; temperatures on the tarmac reached well beyond 40 degrees Celsius under the mid-afternoon sun.

Following their landmark arrival, the Canadian contingent members were bussed to Windhoek. There, they spent the first few nights at the Safari Hotel: a fairly modern and comfortable facility, albeit still under construction at the time. Regardless, it was a relatively luxurious accommodation, and it would be the last night spent in comfort for most of the contingent members, who would soon be posted in rural areas throughout Namibia.

Figure 3: Swedish Commander Gustafson welcoming the newly arrived Canadian contingent. Larry is the officer wearing the Red Serge. Photo courtesy of Larry Proke.

October 20th, 1989 was the Canadian contingent's first day in-theatre. Larry received the troop's assignments from UN CIVPOL headquarters, and he and his fellow officers divided up the contingent and designated the members to eighteen different areas of the country.

As the Officer-in-Charge of the second largest troop, Larry remained posted in Windhoek. He was assigned the UN position of Chief of Staff, the 3rd in importance within the CIVPOL organization after the positions of Deputy Commissioner and Police Commissioner.

As Chief of Staff, Larry worked within the UN Headquarters building and oversaw the functioning of the 1,500 police officers that composed CIVPOL. Larry reported directly to the head of CIVPOL, Commissioner Steven Fanning, while contingent commanders from other countries, who fulfilled various other functions, reported to Larry.

Right from the start, challenges were daunting. For one, a strong feeling of apprehension existed amongst the Canadian CIVPOL peacekeepers, who arrived in-theatre less than three weeks away from the elections. By that time, acts of violence were being perpetrated throughout the country by groups opposed to the Independence, thus increasing the danger level for the newly arrived Canadians and their international counterparts.

On Larry's very first day as Chief of Staff, he got a true taste of the challenges related to his functions, along with the high level of diplomacy it required. Following an overnight gunfight incident in one of the regions, the Police Commissioner directed Larry to assign an investigator to look thoroughly into the matter.

As per the CIVPOL organizational chart, Larry approached a police Superintendent from New Zealand, who was in charge of directing all investigations. Larry then passed along the known details of the incident, and tasked the officer to have whomever he assigned the matter to report on their findings as soon as possible. The New Zealand officer acknowledged and left.

Five minutes had barely gone by when Larry heard hurried footsteps coming down the hall towards his office. In a matter of seconds, Larry found himself facing the imposing figure of the Deputy Commissioner. As the second in command, the Deputy Commissioner bluntly demanded an answer as to the reason Larry had not asked a black CIVPOL officer to carry out the investigation mandated by the Police Commissioner. He continued by questioning Larry's decision and his reluctance to put faith into the investigative capabilities of coloured CIVPOL investigators.

Calmly, Larry replied that he had assigned the matter to the New Zealand Superintendent because all investigations fell under the officer's purview according to the UN organogram. The Deputy Commissioner, a man of colour, then reminded Larry that this was the United Nations...and without saying much more, disappeared from Larry's office.

This unexpected visit from the Deputy Commissioner within his first hour-and-a-half into his Namibian duties exposed Larry to the harsh reality that even though officers from all nations were working together as equals, racial tensions were ever present, even among the ranks of the United Nations.

Going forward, he ensured that all tasks were equally divided amongst all police contingents, albeit still under the direct supervision of the New Zealand Superintendent. This turned out to be an excellent strategy, but one not without its challenges.

As a former peacekeeper and Canadian diplomat, I can truly appreciate how difficult and sensitive Larry's situation was. Rightfully and to avoid favouritism, Larry opted to equally share the tasks. However, the reality was that, even though he had police officers that were equal in status, not all had the same investigative capabilities. In my experience, not all police officers coming from developing countries possess the training needed for certain duties. Assigning investigations then becomes a true balancing act of tact and diplomacy as to not offend "less capable" contingents by assigning them mundane investigations while assigning the most important and serious crimes to the "more capable" ones.

Despite his initial predicament, Larry quickly fell into a UN routine. His day would start at 07:00 with a morning CIVPOL briefing with the contingent commanders. Another briefing would follow the first, this one in the presence of the Police Commissioner, the Deputy Commissioner, the various militaries, and other UN managers. All would discuss the major events of the last twenty-four hours.

A specific duty that Larry performed as the Canadian Contingent Commander was the completion of a weekly Situational Report that he sent to Ottawa. This report was based on the latest political events and other occurrences that took place in the many regions, as well as reporting on the well-being of all members and conveying any member requests.

As Election Day neared, attempts to destabilize the country and prevent the elections were on the rise. Polling stations were being burned and ballots stolen. In one particular incident, a UN vehicle was intercepted by armed rebels, who took all the ballots in the vehicle and quickly disappeared with their loot. Some of the undermining efforts came from neighbouring Angola, a communist regime whose leaders did not see much good in having a bordering country win democratic elections.

Other destabilizing attempts came from South Africa, which was losing its grip on its racial segregation policies. Neither neighbouring country wanted to see their control of Namibia vanish as a result of the country gaining its independence. Therefore, Larry's duties were to report on the many conflicting trends, and coordinate with all civilians and army personnel towards a safe unfolding of the upcoming elections.

Two days before the elections, armed with election manuals, election return forms, camping kits, and lots of insect repellent, peacekeepers from around the world moved into their assigned regions as part of the electoral deployment. One hundred polling stations, some of them mere huts made of mats, poles, and tanned skins, had been set up around the country and were now ready to receive voters.

Election Day, November 7, 1989, finally arrived. The voting for Namibia's first elections would actually run from November 7th-11th. For Larry and the UN, it meant that their primary role would be to ensure safety at the polling stations so that ordinary people could cast their votes.

Larry's first day started at around 05:00, to prepare for the long journey ahead and to be on time for the opening of the country's voting stations at 07:00.

In the early morning hours, something amazing had taken place in many regions: eager voters, even some very old men and women with young babies, had arrived at the polling stations and started to line up. The result was that by the scheduled opening time of the voting centres, many of them already had queues of voters more than half a mile long!

For Larry and the other peacekeepers, the day would bring a great sense of responsibility; it was, after all, an unequalled moment of significance for the people of Namibia. Larry's role from his headquarters' perspective was to receive intelligence and updates from the country's polling stations. Already on the first day, some incredible stories were coming in from the regions.

Take the example of a gravely ill woman out of Damaraland, roughly an hour away by air from Windhoek. She had not wanted to miss her chance to vote. Her son had helped her to make it to the polling station. After it was confirmed that her fingerprints matched those on record, she was given a ballot paper to select her party. The poor lady was so weak and ill that her son had to actually cast her vote in the box. Her desire to vote being fulfilled, she later passed away.[19]

Then, there was the story of an illiterate man. He had been given clear indications and explanations on how to vote and how to mark the ballot. When he replied positively as to whether he had understood the procedure, he was given a ballot and he hurried to the booth.

Minutes went by, and the election officer started to wonder what was taking the man so long to cast his vote. The man then called out in his native tongue that he could not find his party. An interpreter was quickly called in, who realized that the poor man had not been able to identify his party due to his illiteracy. To the laughter of many of his countrymen, he was provided further guidance by the interpreter and eventually cast his vote.

Even prisoners in police detention were given opportunity to vote. This obviously presented some security challenges, since they had to physically attend polling stations. Ensuring they would not escape and/or hurt other voters would be of utmost importance. Thus, along with UN election staff attached to the polling stations, CIVPOL teams would monitor the situation with the relevant police station commanders. Prisoners who were given the opportunity to vote were ever grateful.

At the end of the first day, it was apparent that more ballot papers would be needed at some of the polling stations. Voter turnout had been overwhelming. Although the role of CIVPOL did not require them to replenish polling stations with ballots, CIVPOL Headquarters was nonetheless made aware of the situation. Frustrated and disenchanted voters, who had queued at empty polling stations for hours, could present security concerns. However, all went well, and ballots were eventually transported by land or airlifted to those polling stations that had run out of ballots.[20]

Despite some mishaps, in the end the five-day elections were considered a success. Once all votes were counted, it became clear that the Namibian people had made up their minds: they wished for independence!

Once the elections were over, Larry's role changed: now, his duties would encompass the additional task of monitoring the creation and recruitment of a new Namibian police service. This was a daunting task, since a new police body had to be formed and structured, with its officers recruited and trained, all within four months; March 21, 1990 was the date set for Namibian Independence.

Taking over to aid in the transition were UK police force representatives. Since Namibia's Independence placed it within the Commonwealth organization, a political decision was made to have Scotland Yard and other UK law enforcement institutions involved in setting up training and curriculum. As Chief of Staff,

Larry would chair a committee on behalf of CIVPOL to oversee the above recruiting and training process, as well as set the new police infrastructure.

A training facility was identified, a location for the headquarters of the new police force was found, highly educated senior police management was appointed, and recruits from all walks of life were identified. The goal was to have 1,200 new Namibian police officers ready to serve and protect the country's 1.4 million inhabitants by Independence Day.

But selecting the right police recruits was no easy endeavour. Some candidates, coming from larger towns, were generally well-educated, while others, some coming from far-away villages, not so. There was a particular apprehension for those who came from afar. Imagine! Some recruits had never seen a toothbrush, or slept in a bed. Even though they had mentors to help them acclimatize, for the first few nights, those recruits unaccustomed with beds simply decided to sleep on the floor. Though bunk beds had been set up in the barracks for the recruits, not everyone had realized what they were for!

Although there was an obvious disparity between those recruits with more education and those coming from remote villages, nobody was illiterate. Eventually, recruit training started, with every candidate doing their 100% to succeed at the "police academy".

Of course, being the Chief of Staff, Larry was heavily involved in the security preparation for Independence Day. However, his role, and that of CIVPOL, was strictly in an advisory capacity; the CIVPOL Monitors themselves did not carry weapons. It was the in-theatre military component who would be responsible for providing "on the ground" security for Independence Day. In addition, there would also be the security personnel who travelled with the heads of government and other VIPs present to witness the birth of a nation.

What kind of conditions could these visiting dignitaries expect? When considering southern Africa, North Americans may think of stifling heat, rare reptiles, and large insects. For someone not accustomed to such things, the sight of a dung beetle working arduously at rolling its meal can be both spectacular and disgusting.

Forming large pieces of elephant manure into "apple size" and rolling them across Namibian highways, these giant bugs (some species can reach up to six centimetres) waste no time in burying their treasure to keep it "fresh" for a later feast. Would the sight of one of these bugs pushing its treasure trove be a presage of the cleanliness one was to expect in Namibia? In Larry's experience, thankfully not!

In Windhoek, Larry was relatively well taken care of. Staying at the modern Safari Hotel, he enjoyed most amenities a large city could offer. Food and water cleanliness was not much of an issue. However, the situation was quite different for those Canadian peacekeepers working on the outside of the city. Some lived in makeshift trailers, while others lived in tents where food and water had to be brought in.

ATCO trailers[21] were a common living arrangement. Officers would sleep on bunk beds with cheap, four-inch mattresses, a few sheets, no air conditioning, and experiencing heat of 40-plus degrees Celsius—all the while besieged by snakes and other undesirable creatures. Larry proudly states that his Canadian subordinates thrived under these challenges. Most amazing was that none of them complained. From the time they had volunteered for the mission, most officers expected difficult living conditions. Only one police officer, among the troop of 100, had to be sent home as a result of an injury.

In terms of living conditions, the Canadian military was indispensable to Larry and his troops. Since the RCMP's involvement in Namibia was its first assignment with the UN, it relied heavily on the assistance of the Canadian Forces (CF), who had plenty of overseas experience. In Namibia, the CF were in charge of the logistics for the entire mission. It was the CF that brought in clean water to UN staff in remote areas, trucking it in and storing it in large tanks.

This service was necessary for many CIVPOL officers, because the country's main water supply was a six-foot wide flume, best described as a large, open-air cement pipe, cut in half horizontally. Fresh water coming from the north had many opportunities to get contaminated during its long journey south. At certain strategic points throughout the country, the flume would come to rest in a basin, perhaps 15 feet wide. Women from nearby villages would use the basin to wash their clothing and bring its water home.

However, they were not the only ones to use the water. Cows and goats would often be seen standing in the basin, leading one to believe that they were not only using it to drink, but wash and do their dirty business as well!

In addition to providing water, the military also dispensed food to some Canadian CIVPOL. That food, known as "military rations", was great to have when one feared that local cuisine was not "on par" with the hygiene standards one might be used to in North America.[22] Though some officers ate solely from the half-dozen menu options these handy meals provided (some food could even be warmed up on the hot hood of a Jeep), Larry felt he would have missed out on some of the cultural experience had he only eaten army rations during his mission. However, Larry will admit that these came in handy when he travelled to more remote areas.

From time to time, Larry and some of his colleagues would venture for a traditional local meal. Having travelled so far to contribute to the birth of a nation deserved an opportunity to taste some of the local delicacies that Namibia had to offer.

Even though Windhoek had grocery stores and fresh meat available, many areas outside of the city did not. Since some Canadian peacekeepers lived in Windhoek and commuted to their worksites outside of town, they would, at times, stop at local meat markets where once or twice a week, Namibian farmers would bring cattle for the animals to be slaughtered and the meat to be sold.

Meat markets were rather rudimentary areas where animals were hung up from trees and their flesh sold in an assortment of lined-up shacks with tin roofs. The tools of the trade of those farmers were as basic as they came: a nearby tree to hang the carcass and a good, old axe to carve the meat. Customers would then line up in front of their favourite shack to buy the best cuts.

Figure 4: Meat vendor at the Windhoek meat market. Photo courtesy of Larry Proke.

One of these stands particularly attracted a dauntless peacekeeper one hot and muggy afternoon as he wished to buy meat for a "Namibian style" beef dinner. Perhaps it was the nice, red, glossy look of the meat that caught his attention, suggesting that the vendor knew the proper curing and hanging process that ensured freshness. Or perhaps it was that the meat displayed by this particular merchant harboured less flies than his nearby competition. Whatever the reason he elected this particular vendor, I can only guess!

However, what I learned was that as soon as the temerarious peacekeeper placed his order, out came a large spray can of strong household insecticide. The vendor then dosed off the hanging meat, creating a toxic cloud around it and nearly emptying the can. After the cloud dissipated, not one fly could be seen near that meat! Well, I should add that the merchant not only succeeded in getting rid of the flies, but also in scaring the living daylight out of the poor peacekeeper, who hastily changed his dinner plans!

Despite what one may assume from this account, food and water consumption was not the primary health concern for Larry and his comrades. Perhaps one of the most serious illnesses that struck a few Canadian officers was malaria. Despite religiously taking anti-malaria pills, some were unlucky enough to contract the tropical disease. The good news, if we dare say, was that the illness was kept under control thanks to appropriate medical treatments the officers received from the CF doctor.

For those not acquainted with the illness, malaria is a tropical disease transmitted by a mosquito named "Anopheles". The mosquito normally bites between dusk and dawn. Typically, it takes 10-28 days before victims experience the symptoms of the illness, which may include a combination of chills, fever, headaches, muscle aches, vomiting, diarrhea, and cramps. The disease can be fatal if untreated.[23]

The risks of contracting malaria can be minimized by using protective clothing over the arms and legs, mosquito repellent, and by sleeping under a bed net.[24] Though the taking of antimalarial drugs as a preventative measure does not keep someone from being bitten by the mosquito or restrain an individual from coming down with the illness, the medication is important to take, since it will help fight the disease if contracted.[25]

The threat of serious injuries or death for peacekeepers was ever present during this mission. In all, nineteen international peacekeepers, including military, police, and civilians, made the ultimate sacrifice and perished, serving as a reminder that though the war was over, peril still remained.[26]

Hundreds of thousands of landmines were believed to have been planted during the height of the civil war. Ammunitions and undetonated explosives, such as hand grenades, lay abandoned in the different parts of the country. These posed a serious concern to the safety of both peacekeepers and Namibians. Although no reliable statistics existed on the number of landmine casualties, over 100 civilians were believed to have been killed in landmine-related incidents between 1989 and 1998.[27]

When Larry and his colleagues travelled, they had to make special efforts to ensure they remained on a beaten path, or use heavily-armoured vehicles if they journeyed to an unknown area. The northern border regions with Angola were particularly dangerous, due to SWAPO and UNITA fighters' incursions into Namibia and the many minefields in those areas.[28]

In comparison to grenades and minefields, who would assume that local Namibian residents could pose much of a threat? Add some traditional Namibian homebrew to the mix, however, and you may have to reconsider that assumption! In some remote areas of the country, liquor could be hard to come by, so locals made homebrew with fruits that they fermented. Firearms, on the other hand, were not so rare a commodity. As such, many would get severely intoxicated and cavalcade with their weapons.

Although the countrymen had no animosity towards peacekeepers, the fact that they walked around armed and highly intoxicated represented a real danger for CIVPOL Monitors, who were often called to those areas. As far as Larry is aware of, no CIVPOL ended up a casualty as a result of a call to one of those regions…but it is believed that many inebriated civilians died.

For this first mission, the Canadian contingent members had received permission to bring their own service firearm, the now retired .38 calibre Smith & Wesson revolver. Interestingly, all the weapons were kept locked up throughout the mission, as the UN management did not want its CIVPOL Monitors to carry them. It is supposed that the idea of having weapons around was that they could be accessed and used in case of extreme necessity.

Figure 5: Larry, other Canadian peacekeepers, visiting Deputy Commissioner Roy Moffatt and Corps Sergeant Major Eric Young are taken on a tour of the northern border in an armoured UN transport vehicle. Photo courtesy of Larry Proke.

For unarmed UN police peacekeepers, Angolan militia incursions into Namibia were major security risks for those who, at times, had to meet in remote areas with Angolan leadership in order to advance peace negotiations. Larry recalled an instance where two Canadian CIVPOL Monitors and an interpreter were on a mission to meet Angolan Army leaders at a specific location on the Angolan border. On the way, their UN-marked vehicle was ambushed by a platoon of Angolan Army fighters (even though still in Namibian territory). The two CIVPOL Monitors and the interpreter soon found several machine guns being pointed at them.

Thanks to the interpreter, who was able to explain that the team was on its way to meet a waiting Angolan Army commander, the team was allowed to proceed unharmed, albeit under tight escort from the Angolans.

These situations, although not frequent, were always a nightmare for the UN CIVPOL. For many of the militiamen living and fighting in the jungle, the presence of a uniformed UN police peacekeeper, even driving a UN-marked vehicle, meant nothing. Some did not even know what the UN was! Wearing a blue beret and a uniform could mean to them that you were the enemy.

As we will discuss in subsequent chapters, peacekeepers are not out of danger simply because they wear a blue beret, a UN armband, and have peaceful intentions. In some countries afflicted with the aftermath of civil war, a number of individuals may be opposed to the UN presence, not know what it represents, or even mistake a peacekeeper for a government soldier. All of these could lead to a situation where the peacekeepers could be seriously hurt, or even killed.

Considering all of these risks, communication with loved ones back home also served as a means of reassuring them that one was safe and sound. In Namibia at the time, communications through regular phone lines were not all that great. If one was lucky enough to have access to a phone (many rural villages did not have any), dialling overseas could become a frustrating endeavour. This was because the few phone circuits working would be busy most of the time.

Despite this dilemma, Larry managed to entertain weekly communication with his family, who would call directly from Canada. Interestingly and for unknown reasons, it was much easier to receive calls from overseas than try to call out.

Therefore, for Christmas that year, the plan was for Larry's family to phone in from Canada. However, Christmas Eve went by and no call was received. Puzzled, Larry repeatedly tried to call out, but was unable to do so successfully; he could only wait as the 25th and 26th went by without any word from his family. His repeated query to reception if there had been any calls for him always evoked the same response—none, Sir!

On December 27, he received a surprise call through the UN HQ from the RCMP Commissioner, who wanted to verify that Larry was safe and sound. It seemed Larry's family had called the hotel where he was staying, and had been told by reception that he was no longer there. Perplexed and worried, the family had contacted the RCMP Headquarters in Canada and asked for assistance in finding out what was happening.

As it turned out, an administrative mistake had been made by the hotel staff, who had placed Larry as checked out. When his family called from Canada during the Christmas holiday, the unaware clerk answering the phone wrongfully informed the family that Larry was no longer there. On December 27, Larry's distraught family finally reached him…after he convinced the hotel reception that he was still their guest.

Though normally a time of happiness and reunion, for Larry, Christmas 1989 would be remembered as being somewhat stressful. Not being able to call out and talk to his spouse was a frustrating experience; however, Larry understood the realities he was facing living in a technologically underdeveloped country. Thankfully, better means of communication exist today, and peacekeepers can now enjoy a wide range of methods to keep in touch with loved ones. E-mails, telephones, Skype, FaceTime, and satellite phones, only to name a few, are means by which the modern peacekeeper can correspond with family and friends at home.[29] But don't be fooled: there still exist many places around the world where communications are not at par.

Between fierce anti-liberation sentiments, violent remnants of the civil war, and even uncertain living conditions, Larry had more than his fair share of challenging moments to deal with during his Namibian mission. However, Larry will admit that the incidents involving criminal activities committed by certain UN peacekeepers were the most challenging, and required considerable diplomacy to handle.

For example, there was one UN CIVPOL Monitor who had been suspected of sexually abusing village women. Prior to the elections, the officer had been assigned to a small rural community, where the UN had established a post to oversee the voting process. At the same time, the officers provided security for the village's water supply. When some of the village women came to get water to bring back home, the officer would only allow them access to water in return for sexual favours. The officer was able to carry on his depravity for some time, until one victim finally spoke out.

However, trying to get the officer's contingent commander to take disciplinary or criminal action against his subordinate became a nearly impossible endeavour. The commander, who came from a country that tended to consider women inferior, thought nothing of the actions of his subordinate. Of course, the commander's unwillingness to act infuriated other peacekeepers as well as the victimized villagers.

Outraged by the inactions of the contingent commander, Larry appealed to the mission's Commissioner, explaining why the oppressor had to be removed. In the meantime, villagers and other UN peacekeepers were getting angry. Larry had to find a solution and act on it quickly.

As a former peacekeeper, I understand exactly how delicate the situation was for Larry. Though the actions of the officer and his abuse of authority should be punished, even criminalized, one of the general rules for providing UN assistance to a country is that UN workers and peacekeepers will be granted some form of diplomatic immunity. This immunity is necessary in order for a peacekeeper to perform their duty without fear of being arrested for an action (or inaction) that may not be criminal in the peacekeeper's home country. Thus, when a peacekeeper is caught in misconduct, under normal circumstances he would be expulsed from the mission and subjected to some sort of disciplinary action or criminal charges by his own country, if warranted.

In the above case, the contingent commander of the abusing officer did not see any fault in his subordinate's actions; it may have been considered common practice in his own home country. Forcing that officer out of the mission for an act condoned in his native country would have upset leaders of that country. And let us not forget, the vast majority of fellow officers from that country were great contributors to the mission and to the betterment of Namibia. Thus, finding a way to expulse the officer from the mission without embarrassing any of his countrymen would require serious tact and diplomacy.

Larry's solution was to have the officer redeployed to another area until he was scheduled to leave the mission. Although Larry would have liked to have had the officer disciplined and removed from the mission immediately, having him transferred was truly the best he could do under the circumstances.

Larry's actions were also prompted by the fact that many villagers went around armed, and, if angered to the point of violence, could have started shooting at any peacekeepers, regardless of their national identity. Once the officer was removed, the situation returned to normal, and the village's trust in the UN remained unaffected.

Not all internal challenges are criminal in nature, either. One such episode proves just how devoted Larry was to his staff, as well as his duties. Towards the end of the mission, one of Larry's subordinates approached him with a rather unusual request.

The officer, a Staff Sergeant with pensionable service, who had devoted more than 30 years of his life to policing, asked if he could retire from the RCMP while he was overseas. His plans were to purchase a vehicle, and he and his spouse would travel within Africa for six months before returning home.

This was certainly an unorthodox request. RCMP Policy had nothing written about such a process. In 1989, the RCMP as a corporate culture operated in a regulatory environment, which did not necessarily welcome rapid changes, or promote new perspectives.

Larry advised the officer that he would inquire with RCMP Headquarters in Ottawa. Because he worked so closely with the Canadian Forces, Larry learned that CF rules prohibited a soldier from retiring in-theatre; however, he wanted to confirm if the same would be true for civilian officers.

As promised, Larry inquired with Ottawa, and soon found out the endeavour would not be possible. RCMP administrative rules were such that it seemed less problematic to emulate CF policy rather than taking an accommodating approach. But Larry persisted. He questioned RCMP management as to why the organization couldn't accommodate the retiring officer. After more than a week of back-and-forth communication between Larry and RCMP senior management, the RCMP finally obliged and allowed the officer to retire in-theatre.

At last the big day came: Independence Day, March 21, 1990. At midnight that day, all of the South African Police and military troops still in Namibia departed. The sole exception was a few South African law enforcement officers, who supported Namibia Independence and had agreed to stay to help with the police transition. All other South African Police officers and military personnel operating in Namibia had to return to South Africa.

In Windhoek, hundreds of thousands of people had gathered on the streets to witness the take-down of the South African flag and the raising of the new, Namibian flag. All were rejoicing to finally have a country of their own! Representatives and dignitaries from all of the Commonwealth countries were also present; their security details all fell within Larry's purview. Thanks to the military and months of preparation, all went well.

The moment the Namibian flag went up, Larry witnessed Namibian indigenous embrace their Caucasian countrymen, celebrating that, after all these decades of fighting, forgiveness was in order. Black, white, young, old: all were rejoicing with tears in their eyes.

And just like that, a new country came to be! Being part of the birth of Namibia and witnessing the atmosphere of celebration is something Larry will never forget, and can be proud to have contributed to.

Larry was a devoted leader, with strong ethics and a belief that police organizations have to adapt to changing circumstances in order to experience the most success. Humorously, Larry compared many large police forces of the time to ballroom dance studios, where learners would follow a set of predetermined steps without deviation. Policies and rules are made to be followed; however, there are always exceptions that should be accommodated or adapted to when circumstances dictate.

One of the positive aspects of Larry's mission was that, from a cross-cultural perspective, the experience he gained in dealing with others was second to none. Larry felt that he, and the entire Canadian contingent, came out of the mission better persons as a result of working in Namibia. Perhaps working in a multi-cultural environment made them realize how fortunate they had been to live in Canada.

Interestingly, the learning experience turned out to be more than just a one-way street. Some international colleagues, whose countries may have had little knowledge or respect for Human Rights policies, learned a great deal on high ethics in policing. Being able to pass that on to police officers from other countries was something very dignifying for Larry and his colleagues.

Having contributed to the birth of a nation was also something that none of the Canadian peacekeepers will ever forget. The pride they felt in serving Canada for the betterment of another nation was simply overwhelming.

Figure 6: Canadian Troop Medal Ceremony towards the end of the Mission. Supt. Mike O'Reilly, in the Red Serge in the foreground, receives a medal from the mission Deputy Commissioner, while Larry receives his from Commissioner Fanning. Each contingent member received a UN Peacekeeping medal during this ceremony. Photo courtesy of Larry Proke.

Chief Superintendent Larry Proke and his colleagues were true pioneers of RCMP and Canadian Civilian Police missions abroad. Their successes and accomplishments remain highly inspirational to this date.

Larry retired from the RCMP in 1998, having achieved the much-regarded rank of Deputy Commissioner: the second highest distinction in the RCMP. His successful career lasted 40 years, and took him to many provinces in Canada. Larry's approachable demeanour and pioneering leadership skills were essential contributing factors in making the Namibian mission a true success: a model for missions to come.

2.

The Unity Highway: UNPROFOR (United Nations Protection Force), Former Yugoslavia 1992-1995

Mission overview: 167 UN personnel killed[30]; mass hostage situations; corrupt UN representatives; a country still harbouring hostilities towards UN troop involvement. Every one of the families of the 44 Canadian Peacekeepers who were getting ready to leave for the former Yugoslavia had reasons to be worried. In that part of the world, UN peacemakers were being shot and killed. Wearing a uniform and providing humanitarian service would not necessarily protect them from harm. No one knew this more than 18-year police veteran Corporal John Buis.

As the story of John Buis unfolds, many of the challenges and adversities early peacekeepers had to face will come to light. John's story is that of personal devotion to the people of a war-torn nation he learned to love. His tale in Ilok, Croatia, from June until December of 1994, encompasses deep sorrow, offset by a profuse hope and genuine empathy for the civilian victims of the conflict.

THE FORMER YUGOSLAVIA was created as a result of the Balkan Wars of 1912–1913, after the defeat of Austria-Hungary in World War I.[31] The Balkans, which in Turkish means "chain of wooden mountains", is an area of south-eastern Europe delimited by the Adriatic Sea to the west, the Mediterranean Sea to the south, and the Black Sea to the east. This vast area was under the control of the Ottoman Empire until 1913.[32]

Figure 7: Croatia. Map reproduced with permission of WorldAtlas.com

After WWI, the Paris Peace Convention established new patterns of state boundaries in the Balkans. As such, a new Kingdom of Serbs, Croats, and Slovenes was created.[33]

At first, great difficulties were experienced in crafting the multinational state. Its inception had been based mainly on geography and the commonality of one language. The distinct history and religious backgrounds of the different ethnicities living in the region had been ignored when the new kingdom was formed. As a result, tensions among the various groups were high.[34]

In 1929, King Alexander I,[35] who had been leading the nation since its inception, declared a royal dictatorship and named the kingdom Yugoslavia.[36] As part of a continued effort to unify all the ethnicities, he outlawed all political parties based on ethnicity, religion, or regional distinction. In the process, a police state was created, which required the army to ensure its survival.[37] However, this all changed with the onset of WWII and the German invasion, which dissolved the kingdom.

Yugoslavia saw a rebirth in 1946, this time under the socialist regime of General Josip Tito, whose communist-led group had helped liberate the country from the Germans.[38] As a result of the war, Yugoslavia now consisted of six provinces. The included the neighbours Croatia, Serbia, and Bosnia-Herzegovina in addition to Macedonia, Slovenia, and Montenegro.[39]

Following General Tito's death in 1980, the presidency of Yugoslavia was transferred to a difficult-to-manage assembly of regional representatives.[40] Political instability and rising nationalism amongst the various ethnic groups followed. This rising nationalism was also fuelled by the political elites of each distinct ethnicity, who wished to mobilize large audiences to support their struggle for power.[41]

In the summer of 1991, Croatia declared its secession from the central Yugoslav Federation. This independent move fuelled a military response from the Federation, who moved in to support rebel Serbian forces in Croatia. This ignited the Croatian War of Independence.

Violence erupted in Serbian areas of Croatia, where Serb entities, self-proclaimed as the Republic of Serbian Krajina, wished to become a part of Serbia. This set the stage for further outbreaks between the Serbs and Croats.

By 1992, the war had significantly intensified. When the United States and the European Community recognized Croatia as an independent state in April 1992, Serbian forces moved to

Bosnia-Herzegovina and started to shell the city of Sarajevo, a cosmopolitan city where many Muslims lived.

During that time, many of the towns in eastern Bosnia-Herzegovina[42] which had large Bosniak populations, became targets of the Yugoslav Army.[43] Entire populations of Bosniaks were expelled from these areas or murdered en masse in a process described as "ethnic cleansing."[44]

The United Nations became involved in the Yugoslavian war as of September 1991, when the Security Council adopted Resolution 713 (1991). The resolution communicated deep concerns to member states about the fighting in Yugoslavia.[45]

In January 1992, the UN Security Council adopted Resolution 727 (1992), which saw the dispatch of 50 military observers to Croatia. This was followed by the approval and deployment of a full peacekeeping force in Croatia, UNPROFOR, in February 1992.[46]

UNPROFOR was an interim arrangement to promote the conditions of peace and security that were desperately needed in order to mediate the Yugoslavian conflict.[47] Initially, the mission's mandate was to ensure that the "United Nations Protected Areas" (UNPAs) in Croatia [48] were demilitarized, and that the people residing within these areas were protected from armed assaults.[49]

Later, as the conflict escalated to reach Bosnia-Herzegovina, the mission's mandate was enlarged to deliver security to the Sarajevo Airport, and to provide humanitarian aid to civilians throughout Bosnia-Herzegovina. UNPROFOR's mandate was also broadened to include the protection of convoys of Internally Displaced Persons (IDPs) and assist, promote, implement, and monitor a cease-fire between the Serbian authorities and the Croatian government.[50]

John Buis, a police veteran with nearly 18 years of experience at the time, was part of a contingent of 44 Canadian police officers assigned to UNPROFOR's fifth mission to the former Yugoslavia.

His tour of duty started in June 1994, and ended in December of that same year.

Selection criteria for this mission required that applicants not only have many years of investigative experience as a police officer, but, and perhaps the most problematical requirement, be eligible for release from current policing duties. This was a difficult condition to meet, as potential candidates were not replaced in their home unit. Depending on the size and how busy a volunteer's home unit was, being released for a mission in those early years depended on perseverance, proven police experience, and, to some extent, luck.

On this mission and many others around the globe, the requirement for one to be able to drive a standard transmission would be paramount. Though in the early 1990s, most North American drivers were familiar with standard transmission vehicles, such was not always the case for many UN participants, who may not have had easy access to cars.

Take the example of one of John's UN police colleagues, whom he would meet later in Croatia. The man came from a technologically undeveloped country and had never learned how to drive a manual transmission vehicle. However, he found a practical way to remedy his shortcomings: he simply drove the vehicle in second gear, whether he operated the vehicle at speeds of 10 or 100 kilometres per hour. Needless to say, it provoked some laughter from his colleagues.

Pre-deployment training for this mission took place in Ottawa, and lasted approximately ten days. The training encompassed classroom work in addition to bringing in subject matter experts with previous UN mission experience. These people brought with them real-life accounts of what to expect on a UN Mission. Much of the pre-deployment training was generic, and thus most participants welcomed any related matter that could be taught to them.

John will admit that prior to his departure he obtained a book entitled *Peacekeeper: Road to Sarajevo*, authored by retired Canadian Armed Forces Major-General Lewis MacKenzie. MacKenzie had recently completed a tour of duty in Bosnia-Herzegovina, and John wished to add to his understanding of the conflict in the area he was heading to. John also browsed chapters of Michael Ignatieff's book, *Blood and Belonging*, which discussed nationalism, Serbia, and Croatia.

The experience of travelling to other countries, whether for work or leisure, can often be improved by first enhancing one's knowledge and perspective of the location. These books provided John with an additional insight into the conflict, which ultimately contributed to better prepare him for his upcoming mission.

Travel from Canada to Zagreb, Croatia was an interesting experience. In accordance with RCMP policy, all members of the contingent travelled in uniform, wearing combat pants, boots, shirts, and patrol jackets. Wearing uniform was not that significant for the first part of the voyage, and, as expected, the first leg of the trip from Montréal to London went relatively smoothly.

All that changed when the contingent members boarded the Croatian Airlines flight between London and Zagreb. For a group of officers who were on a mission to bring peace to a war-torn country, they did not get a very warm welcome from the flight crew of the Croatia Airlines jet. Perhaps this was due to the incorrect perception that the peacekeepers were a "whole bunch of internationals" going to protect the Serbs.

A reason for this apprehension may have been due to the fact that the United Nations had set up "refugee" areas within Croatia, which were designated as United Nations Protected Areas (UNPAs). These places held large segments of Serbs, and were controlled by Serbian self-proclaimed authorities.[51]

These were the areas of Croatia where the Canadian peacekeepers were heading to. John will later admit that the flight with Croatia Airlines gave him and his comrades a foretaste of the deep ethnic divisions that reigned in the former Yugoslavia.

Anticlimactic would best describe the mood during John's first two days in the former Yugoslavia. Upon landing in Zagreb, the Canadian contingent was taken by bus to a local hotel, where everyone waited to be assigned to their respective districts.

The next day, the Canadian contingent was split, and each member was assigned to a specific area. To everyone's surprise, the selection process to send a candidate to an area was random rather than based on the candidate's personal police expertise.

John boarded a UN vehicle that would take him to the town of Ilok, Croatia, in Sector East, his final destination. As the vehicle roamed through the countryside, John imagined how life might have been before the war. The route he was on, once a beautiful motorway named "The Brotherhood and Unity Highway", had been built on General Tito's own initiative and united all of Yugoslavia. It stretched across a country that boasted historic and picturesque towns, mountains, sunny beaches, and antique monasteries.

As the landscape unfolded in front of him, John experienced a sensation of déjà vu: this was the same highway that had been depicted by Michael Ignatieff's book *Blood and Belonging*. The landscape had not changed much, but the destruction all around was more and more evident as he neared the Serbian border. Sections of the highway were noticeably damaged by the war.

Figure 8: June 1994 rotation of Canadian contingent members deployed to Sector East. From left to right: Cpl. John A. Buis, Sgt. Bruce Kineshanko, Cpl. Darrel Aucoin, Cst. Dennis Doyle, Cpl. Jim Nadon, Insp. Jim Newman, Cpl. Jerome Aylward, and Cpl. Blair Taker. Photo courtesy of John Buis.

As John approached his final destination, a reminder of the atrocities that had taken place not so long ago appeared before him. To his right on the horizon, he could see a house with a blown-off roof sitting just beside a gigantic water tower that had been heavily damaged by artillery fire.

John was entering the city of Vukovar, the site of one of Yugoslavia's most notorious massacres. Less than 40 kilometres away from Ilok, Vukovar's image of destruction would be forever imprinted in John's memory.[52]

Unlike Vukovar, Ilok had been left untouched by the war. It was a beautiful town near the banks of the Danube River, with many vineyards and historic buildings. There, John found himself as part of a small United Nations contingent of fourteen International Police officers coming from Nepal, Portugal, Jordan, Sweden, Denmark, and Kenya. Their work over the next six months would be as challenging as it would be frustrating.

Figure 9: The Vukovar water tower has been preserved as symbol of the city's agony. Photo courtesy of John Buis.

In Ilok, John began in the role of Motor Transport Officer for the detachment, but soon became the School Liaison and Humanitarian Officer. His shift schedule would be that of 30 days' work and six days off. His shifts lasted an average of nine hours; sometimes they started in the morning, other times in the afternoon, and, on occasions, he started in late afternoon and went round the clock.

When he started early in the morning, one of his first tasks would be to review the Daily Occurrence Report of the past twenty-four hours, and forward the report to the local UN Headquarters. Back in those days, the Daily Occurrence Report had to be physically taken to the Headquarters in Erdut, which stood an hour's drive away from Ilok. One of the reasons to physically take the report to HQ was that, while there, the peacekeeper could perform other tasks that could only be completed at HQ, such as picking up mail and parcels, completing vehicle maintenance, and so forth.

Figure 10: Destroyed buildings on a main artery in Vukovar. Photo courtesy of John Buis

As part of his duties, John also had to assist in monitoring the activities of the local police. To help him with the language barrier, he and his colleagues could count on the assistance of three UN translators. John admitted that the task of monitoring the local Croatian police officers required considerable diplomacy even at the best of times, because it often involved investigating human rights complaints against the same police they were trying to build good relations with.

The second of John's assigned duties was that of a School Liaison Officer. That role required him to frequently visit local elementary schools and ensure that they had the basics to function. Interestingly, even though John was assigned as a UN School Liaison Officer, the UN did not have any program in place to provide for school necessities. Therefore, his role was almost solely that of reporting, which brought on many frustrations.

One of the biggest issues faced by schools was the lack of heating fuel, which would become a critical issue during Croatia's bone-freezing winters. The shortage of fuel was the result of an oil embargo that had been imposed on the area by the United

Nations in order to prevent the fighting factions from bringing in heavy artillery.

Unfortunately, one of the consequences of the embargo was that it also affected the most destitute, among them schools, which were left on their own to find fuel for heating or face closure in the winter. John and his colleagues were very attentive to the evident lacunae in the UN's administration, and found some ingenious ways to provide much-needed assistance to a few of the local schools.

For instance, John learned that one of the schools he had been visiting had a furnace that could burn wood. But how could he gather enough firewood to heat an entire school during winter? Put an obstacle in the way of a Canadian policeman, and he will find a way around it. This is exactly what John did!

Because wood was in abundance in the region and not facing any type of embargo, John gathered a small army of local volunteers and started to cut wood for the school. It was not long before the team amassed an incredible 20 tonnes of cut wood. Believe it or not, this was only the minimum amount required to allow the school to heat up all its classes during the long winter months.

Transporting 20 tonnes of wood from the cutting area to the school, although located only 5 kilometres away, would be the next obstacle. However, John did not allow this to pose a barrier to him. He first sought authority from UN Headquarters to transport the wood from point "A" to point "B". Then, he approached local UN commanders with access to 5-tonne trucks.

Although the intentions to transport the wood were honourable, finding a vehicle available and a commander willing to assist was not as simple as it seemed. The first UN contingent commander that John approached was not favourable to the idea. It was later learned that this specific commander had some of his men being investigated for corruption by the UN CIVPOL, which may have overshadowed his desire to assist. In the end, a group of Belgian peacekeepers overheard John's efforts to find a 5-tonne truck such as theirs and volunteered for the task.

No need to say that school officials were thrilled to see all that firewood, and were very grateful to John and his colleagues. Their contribution would provide the school with enough heating wood for the entire winter.

Figure 11: From left to right on the grass, Master Corporal Schrijvers, John Buis, an unknown parent, and Superintendent Limbitu. Photo courtesy of John Buis.

Bringing humanitarian assistance to refugees as a Humanitarian Officer was another duty John and some of his colleagues performed on a regular basis. Their task consisted of monitoring the essential needs of the refugees, which were often in short supply.

Take medication, for example. Many refugees needed prescription drugs to treat ailments that had developed as a result of the conflict, or simply due to old age. Obtaining a prescription from a doctor was one thing, but filling it was another. With no health care and little to no money, most refugees or elderly citizens could only wait and watch as their health condition deteriorated. John would later admit that witnessing their suffering and not being able to immediately help them was disheartening.

In Ilok, through United Nations contacts, John found accommodation in a very large and beautiful home that belonged to the widow of a wealthy local businessman. Can you believe it! Her husband had passed away early in the Yugoslavian conflict only because he had not been able to obtain the medication he needed as a diabetic! Despite the tragedy and following the death of her husband, the widow started to rent rooms to peacekeepers. This turned out to be greatly advantageous for both her and her international tenants. For a price of $300 US dollars (USD) per month, John had it all: rent, food, housecleaning, and the washing and pressing of his uniforms. Food was prepared by the landlady, who, as John attests, was an outstanding cook.

In all, four to five rooms were rented at all times to United Nations staff, which provided more than enough income to supplement the landlady's meagre widow's pension of $35 USD per month.

At home in Ilok, John's water came from a well, which supplied water that was clean and safe to drink. Unfortunately, water cleanliness in the former Yugoslavia was hit and miss in certain towns and villages John traveled through.

On one occasion, after he had been living in Croatia for some time, John visited a nearby village as part of his school liaison duty. Perhaps feeling a little bit more adventurous than he should have, he accepted a glass of freshly-made lemonade that was given to him in good faith by a local woman. It was not long after John had taken the refreshment that he felt the rumbling growl of his stomach, a warning sign of an impending hazard to come. John returned home just in time to deal with a severe headache, vomiting, and diarrhea, which, thankfully, only lasted 24 hours.

As mentioned at the beginning of this chapter, the Yugoslavian assignment carried real dangers for peacekeepers, as reflected by the 167 human casualties the mission suffered. During the assignment, restriction of movements imposed by Serbian authorities on UNPROFOR (Army and CIVPOL) would severely affect the peacekeepers' abilities to monitor rural areas and properly distribute food and medicine. This was especially true in the North and South Sectors.[53] In addition, daily manifestation of hostility towards UNPROFOR's presence was sometimes accompanied by the pointing and cocking of firearms at troops near checkpoints.[54]

The pointing of firearms at UNPROFOR members was not always voluntary, but rather sometimes the result of pure carelessness. On one occasion, John went for a jog around town and came across a wedding celebration in the street. Although all participants appeared to be in a jovial state, many guests were intoxicated and carrying automatic rifles.

As John ran past the procession, he was stopped by a group of men that were a part of the celebration. Suddenly, at a distance of less than a metre from John's face, one of them began to fire his AK-47 in the air in carousal. Another man presented John with a Rakia, a liquor made from distilling plums, and grumbled in poor English for him to drink.

Although drinking alcoholic beverages and jogging was not John's favourite mix, he thought he should better acquiesce to the invitation, so as to not offend any of the intoxicated men.

Even though John will later admit that none of the men ever threatened him, he nonetheless could have been seriously injured by bullets falling back down to earth.

I will sheepishly admit that as a driver, I ended up lost a few times around the towns I lived! Have you ever? Not a great feeling, was it? Thankfully, it never turned into a potential life-and-death situation. Poor John! It is with reluctance and a little bit of embarrassment that he admitted to getting lost once in

Croatia after taking a wrong turn.

John had only been at post for a few days when he was required to bring the mail to the local UN Headquarters and fill up his fleet vehicle with fuel on his way back. As he returned from UN Headquarters, John thought he might be able to save some time getting to the airport where he was to refuel. He then took a shortcut through a road that looked familiar...or so he thought!

It was not long before he found himself in the middle of a field of tall sunflowers that stretched for kilometres in all directions. John had neither a detailed area map nor a GPS, and all he could make out in the field were a few odd, beaten paths crisscrossing the tall sunflowers in different directions. John stopped his vehicle, looked around, and uttered a few words that reflected his discontent with the hasty decision he had made to take a shortcut. Here he was, in the middle of nowhere Croatia, low on fuel, with no one around, no mountains or any other identifying landmarks to guide him... nothing. Just plain sunflower fields as far as the eye could see.

To add a little bit of discomfort, John suspected that he was next to the zone of separation between Croatia and Serbia: a no-man's-land allegedly dotted with landmines, snipers, and other great surprises.

After more than half an hour trying to figure out from which way he had come, John was able to backtrack himself to safety... but he will laughingly admit that this experience gave him the scare of his life!

Figure 12: Forefront from left to right, John Buis, an unknown Belgian soldier, and Neils Lydefeldt, Danish CIVPOL officer. Photo taken in Sector East, near the town of Darda, in the separation zone between the self-proclaimed Republic of Serbia Krijina (Croatia) and Croatian military forces. Photo courtesy of John Buis.

Although he is very humble about what he accomplished during his tour of duty, there is no doubt that John's interactions with the local people changed their lives for the better. Shortly after he arrived at his post in Ilok, John had an idea that would get many local youths thrilled.

The idea originally occurred to him before he left for the former Yugoslavia. Being an avid basketball fan and a major high school tournament organizer, John approached Spalding Canada and told its administration he was heading off to the former Yugoslavia as a peacekeeper. John explained that he was seeking the company's assistance to provide him with a few basketballs so that he could get closer to the community through the game.

Perhaps contrary to popular belief, Yugoslavs were not foreign to basketball, having won two silver medals (in both the men's and women's teams) at the 1988 Seoul Summer Olympic Games.

After some convincing on John's part, Spalding Canada, through a local representative named Mr. Bill Field, donated 24 basketballs. These were then deflated by John to facilitate transport.

In Ilok, on a warm June evening, John wandered down to a nearby park, where children and youths were playing with old and patched-up basketballs. Quietly, John, a former high school basketball favourite for the North Delta Huskies, started to shoot his new basketball at a dilapidated hoop opposite to the one where most of the kids were playing.

Five minutes had barely passed before one of the more audacious youths approached him and challenged him to a one-on-one match—with John's new basketball, of course! Soon John had a cheering audience of 25 youths, who thought it was pretty cool to see this "old guy" beat the energetic teen 11-6.[55]

Figure 13: John with teachers, children, and other UN staff at a school in Opatovac, Croatia. This is the school that benefitted from the 20 tonnes of firewood that John and his Belgian colleagues brought. Photo courtesy of John Buis.

With time, John got to know many of the village youths, who would come to the UN base to borrow new basketballs for their games and return them after their match. In addition to helping him stay fit, John conceded that playing basketball with the kids enabled him to develop better relations with the adults in the community. Indeed, as once quoted by former United Nations Secretary-General Kofi Annan: "Sport is a universal language that can bring people together, no matter their origins, background, religious beliefs, or economic status."⁵⁶

One evening, as John and his other colleagues were at a local pub, John observed a Croatian man painstakingly wheel himself in. His name was Jovan, a 21-year-old former Serbian soldier. Like many Serbian males, he had been shot during the conflict, and his legs had been amputated. Now with two stumps, he was confined to move around in a dilapidated wheelchair from the 1950s.

Seeing an opportunity to strike a conversation with Jovan, John walked over and introduced himself. You see, John had a secret he was about to share with the young man! Allow me to take you back in time for a brief moment!

It was on a cool, Sunday night in April 1979, in the City of Burnaby, British Columbia. John was on police patrol with a colleague when they stopped a speeding vehicle bearing Texas license plates. There were seven people onboard.

Upon being stopped, the driver got out and approached the officers with his vehicle registrations. While this was taking place, John noticed that a front passenger was getting very anxious, and John asked him to get out of the vehicle. The man exited, and admitted that he had just been released from prison and was on mandatory supervision.

By then, another officer had arrived at the scene to act as additional backup. John walked back to his cruiser to complete background checks, while the other two officers searched the vehicle. Little did they know that the front passenger had taken the opportunity to reach back into his seat to grab a sawed-off shotgun, which he momentarily hid in the back of his pants, under his jacket.

Completion of the search uncovered a second illegal weapon, a short-barrelled rifle, in the trunk. At the same time, John got a radio confirmation that the vehicle was stolen. He barely had time to inform his colleagues of his findings when the front seat passenger pulled out his shotgun, aimed at John, and fired!

John was hit in the thigh and fell down to the ground. In the staccato gust of bullets that ensued, John's partner, Constable Jack Robinson, whom had also been wounded, managed to hit the passenger in the right knee and left ankle. It did not stop him. The passenger limped his way towards John, who was face down on the pavement, heavily bleeding and in agony. The passenger then grabbed John's service revolver, cranked the hammer back, and pressed the gun to John's head.

Other police officers had now arrived at the scene, and after a short negotiation, convinced the passenger not to kill John and give himself up.

John was rushed to a hospital where medical staff attended to his potentially life-threatening injuries. That night, in addition to being nearly killed, he also came very close to losing the use of both legs. Thanks to his strong will, determination, and the excellent reconstructive vascular surgery he received from Dr. Kimit Rai, he was able to recover and return to work.[57]

But Jovan would not have the same fortune! With no reconstructive surgeon available and no means to frequently travel to the hospital for follow-up care, this young man was literally left on his own to deal with his misery.

Throughout their conversations, John learned that Jovan's wooden prosthetic legs were really hurting him and had caused many sores on his stumps. For this, he also required frequent trips to the hospital. Having empathy for Jovan, John offered to take him to the hospital on days he required treatments. This little gesture may have seemed insignificant, but meant the world to Jovan, who felt blessed to have met John.

Medical assistance was a common humanitarian need for the people in Ilok. In the 5 to 6 villages that came under his purview,

John's visits became highly expected events. Everyone knew that John went out of his way to attend the local doctor's office to determine who was the neediest or in urgent requirement of medicine.

In one instance, John was informed by the local doctor that a woman was in dire need of medication to alleviate complications with her pregnancy. One has to understand that, for many villagers, prescribed medications were often unavailable due to travel restrictions or for simply being unaffordable.

In the case of the pregnant woman, John was able to obtain the sought-after medication from a Japanese Non-Governmental Organization (NGO) that was dispensing medication for those unable to afford it. The result was that, with a proper diet and the help of the medication, the woman was able to have a normal delivery. All thanks to John's assistance.

There was also an elderly Croatian couple living in the occupied Serb area that John and his colleagues became closely involved with. Because they were Croatians, they had little status in town and lived in extreme poverty behind a barn. They did not have decent clothing or any proper food. No family members were available to help them. They had been left behind because they were old; anyone young enough to leave town had done so when the Serbs had moved in.

In their misfortune, the couple fell within the radar of John and his colleagues, who took it upon themselves to ensure the couple would receive better food and clothing. One may not think that this was very much, but for this unfairly outcast couple, these simple actions meant everything.

Being in the middle of an armed conflict was not the only challenge CIVPOL officers faced. Sadly, and unbeknownst to United Nations Missions management, some of the police and military personnel that came along with a country's contingent were sometimes of dubious backgrounds or of poor ethics.

Situations where internal crime or questionable ethics occurred fell under the purview of a distinguished kind of CIVPOL officers: those of the Special Investigation Unit. Though John and the Ilok office were not directly involved with that team, it nonetheless impacted their work in Croatia. Members of the Special Investigation Unit were tasked with investigating internal United Nations offences such as theft and corruption.

For instance, it came to CIVPOL attention that some officers and military personnel were bringing prostitutes into their compound. Others would breach the oil embargo by selling United Nations fuel to Serbs for personal profit.

Investigation into these kinds of actions required a profuse amount of tact and diplomacy, because certain offences were sometimes committed by members of a specific contingent. Having Canadians or officers from other developed countries investigate dishonest officers from other, sometimes politically opposing countries always risked creating friction amongst nations participating in the mission. Therefore, in all instances, it was of paramount importance that a prima facie case be made, so that the peacekeepers investigated could be removed from the mission.

As a result, internal investigations were often led by the Special Investigation Unit of CIVPOL. On one occasion, enough evidence was amassed to support the repatriation of a high-ranking military General on allegations of corruption and connivance with Serbian forces.[58] However, as one could imagine, the incident instigated tension between CIVPOL and the military peacekeepers from that country, which made it all the more difficult for both to carry on their duties.

Figure 14: The elderly Croatian couple living in the Serb-occupied area near Ilok. Photo courtesy of John Buis.

When I asked John about his most challenging experience, he had no hesitation in answering that the real challenge had been for his family. His spouse Kellie, thousands of miles away, was raising three children on her own, then aged 7, 9, and 11.

The decision for John to go on a mission had been a family one, and had been thoroughly discussed. Although she was fully supportive, now that John was thousands of miles away, Kellie was the one who had to deal with the day-to-day house chores and the growing demands of the family. This was not an easy task, and being far away from his family proved to be one of John's most stressful experiences.

John's most critical circumstance in Croatia took place a week prior to his scheduled departure from the mission. Although he downplayed the dangers of the situation, it was the event itself that led to John's premature withdrawal from the mission.

At 07:00 hours on a sunny Sunday morning, the UN Deputy Station Commander showed up at John's residence, frantically pounding on his door.

Still holding a freshly brewed cup of coffee, John opened the door and was astonished to be ordered to grab his stuff immediately and report to the Ilok office within fifteen minutes. As he complied, John had to wonder what was going on. The only answer he could get from the Deputy Station Commander was that they had to leave—now.

As it turned out, all peacekeepers had to be evacuated: there was no time to explain the reason why. John showed up as ordered at the Ilok UN office, and without much information, he and his colleagues got into a small convoy of UN CIVPOL vehicles and hastily departed. John later learned that they were heading for safety at the nearest UN Armed Forces base, which was manned by Russian officers.

Arriving at the Russian base, John and his fellow officers learned that the city of Sarajevo, in neighbouring Bosnia-Herzegovina, had just been hit by a NATO (North Atlantic Treaty Organization) airstrike. A Serbian police officer had been killed in the event. Word was that Serbian forces were out to kidnap and/or kill UN peacemakers as a means of retaliation. This was no rumour! Less fortunate peacekeepers working in Serbian areas of Bosnia-Herzegovina soon found themselves trapped and held against their will.[59]

This Bosnian Serb response of massive "kidnappings" of UN troops was meant as insurance to guard against further NATO airstrikes. By the first days of December 1994, the international press was already reporting that over 300 peacekeepers from more than 12 nations, among them 55 Canadians, were being held against their will by Bosnian Serb forces.[60]

In the Serbian-controlled territories of Croatia, John and nine other colleagues had managed to find some safety at the Russian base. However, they were incommunicado and under the constant threat of attack by the surrounding Serbian forces.[61]

At home in British Columbia, John's family could not have been more worried. Many days had now passed without any news from John, who used to call every two days or so. The family's distress was suddenly acerbated when a government official contacted Kellie and informed her that her husband and other peacekeepers had been taken hostage.

At the Russian camp, things were not necessarily rosy. Although John and his colleagues had been provided with makeshift living quarters, they were only the basic necessities. No showers were to be had. Communication with UN Headquarters was extremely limited, and news about what was happening outside the base came in scattered messages heard on BBC Radio.

After four days of being confined to the UN Russian base, restrictions on movements were lifted, and John and his colleagues were finally allowed to move out of the area. However, with limited communication, nine days would go by before John could talk to his family and reassure them that he was safe and sound.

John will later candidly admit that the real ordeal had been for his family rather than for him. Other than being confined to the UN Base and having had only one shower in five days, John and his colleagues were completely unscathed.

Thankfully, the 300-plus peacekeepers that had been held hostage by the Bosnian Serbs were also eventually released and allowed to return home.[62]

After that, John and his Canadian colleagues were evacuated, flying out of Zagreb and back to Canada. It is with sadness that John recounted his hasty departure from Ilok days prior. It had really troubled him to have "abandoned" friends and acquaintances, like Jovan, without even having the time to say a proper goodbye. Leaving in such a hurry also made him feel like his mission had been unsuccessful.

Sometime after John had returned from his Yugoslav mission,

he was approached by the City of White Rock seniors group. They wanted John to speak about his mission at one of their meetings, and learn more about what they could do for the people of Yugoslavia. They had raised $850.00 Canadian dollars (CAD) to help the cause.

John accepted their offer to speak, and brought with him some ideas for ways they could help the impoverished in Yugoslavia. He recalled a makeshift senior citizens' complex in one of the villages where he had worked, which was in dire need of a washer and dryer. What better way for this senior citizens' group in Canada to contribute than to have them aid another seniors' centre in Croatia? However, John's next challenge would be to funnel the funds to Croatia, and from there ensure the funds were applied to the intended purpose.

Though a complex task, once again John made it happen. A United Nations contact who was still in Croatia accepted the idea to help, and funds were sent directly to him in US dollars via a money order. The gentleman then facilitated the purchase of the washer and dryer for the Croatian seniors' complex, to the great delight of its residents.

Although I will admit that what was accomplished above was simply remarkable, an element of risk was present in that the funds could have been lost or misused. For this reason, anyone wanting to do a similar good deed should carefully weigh the pros and the cons before involving themselves in comparable efforts. Having said that, I applaud John, who, once more, contributed to making a difference in the lives of some of the most destitute.

For a long time after his mission ended, John continued to harbour feelings of incompleteness; he wanted to go back and carry on the mission. He could not help but hold a deep conviction that he had abandoned the people he served and protected. But John had not been forgotten!

John's landlady in Croatia had two grandsons, Sava and Mischa. One day in 2010, sixteen years after his mission, John received an e-mail that contained a photo of himself…beside Sava and Mischa. The photo had been taken in Croatia and Mischa, now an adult, had managed to find an email address for John and wished to re-initiate contact. John was quite moved by this evidence that people had not forgotten about his sincerity and devotion to the people of the former Yugoslavia; despite his worries, many did not feel as if they had been abandoned after all.

At the time of this writing, John was off to China to help with another great cause: that of bringing smiles to impoverished children, as a volunteer administrator for the non-profit organization "Operation Rainbow Canada".

Throughout his story-telling, John Buis remained very humble about his exploits in Croatia. He said that every peace officer in his team would, and had, done the same. I believe it! But between you and me, it takes a special kind of person to go to the same kind of lengths that John went (and is still going) to give humanitarian aid. Here's to his actions serving as an inspiration for many others to come!

3.

Guatemala—Never Again: MINUGUA (United Nations Verification Mission in Guatemala), 1994-2004

Hidden high in the mountains of Guatemala exist numerous small communities displaced by the Guatemalan civil war. Many are just trying to escape the conflict; all are doing everything they can just to survive. Little do they know, they are about to turn a new chapter in their lives.

The year is 1994, and a Cease-Fire Agreement is in the works between the government of Guatemala and the Guatemalan National Revolutionary Unit (URNG). Thirty-six years of civil war are about to end. The hope for a better life is in the air! [63]

Unfortunately, the woes of the native Mayan villagers, many of whom are young adults and children, are not quite over. Deprived of education, land, and other basic needs, their fight for justice and re-integration into civil society will largely depend on the goodwill of the government and the influence of the United Nations; both will be necessary to ensure that the signed Peace Accords will be respected.

This chapter is Ben Maure's story: my story. It took place nearly 20 years ago, when I was a 10-year police Constable with the RCMP. At the time, I was among a small contingent of five Canadian police officers who traveled to Guatemala to monitor the newly-signed Peace Accords. My assignment began in December of 1998 and ended two weeks before the new millennium. In a country deeply entrenched with racism and institutional corruption, my tale is fraught with difficult and complex challenges. Operating in a country as intricate, multi-ethnic, and multi-cultural as Guatemala would prove to be the undertaking of a lifetime.

GUATEMALA IS ONE of seven nations that form Central America. It is bordered by Mexico to the north and west, the Pacific Ocean on the south, and by Belize, Honduras, and El Salvador to the east.[64]

Figure 15: Guatemala. Map reproduced with permission of WorldAtlas.com

Guatemala is among the earliest Spanish acquisitions of the American continent. In 1523, Spanish adventurer Pedro de Alvares, a member of Ferdinand Cortes' party in the Conquest of Mexico (1519-1521), was sent south to defeat the indigenous Mayans. He and his forces turned the area known as Guatemala into a Spanish colony.[65]

Nearly three hundred years later, in 1821, Guatemala gained its independence from Spain, and in 1823, from the Mexican Empire. However, the move to statehood was somewhat tumultuous; liberal and conservative factions fought relentlessly for power, leaving the country in an almost permanent state of civil war and chaos.[66]

Early 20th Century Guatemala saw the arrival of the United Fruit Company to the country. The simple company developed into a powerful enterprise with the support of General Jorge Ubico's dictatorship in the 1930s. Ubico's open policy on foreign investment proved profitable for both Guatemala and the United Fruit Company. The company later responded by pouring investment capital back into the country, buying controlling shares of the railroad, electric, and telegraph utilities, as well as almost 42% of the country's agricultural land.[67]

In 1951, Jacobo Arbenz, a former minister of war in a previous government, became President.[68] During his tenure, Arbenz made land reforms the central project of his administration, often expropriating (for minimal compensation) any land left uncultivated in order to re-allocate it to landless peasants.[69]

While Arbenz's reforms may have meant well, his left-wing approach antagonized the United Fruit Company, who by that point owned large parcels of land.[70] The treatment that the United Fruit Company endured at the hands of Arbenz's land policies in turn outraged lawmakers in Washington. This combined with the growing unease during Eisenhower's Cold War era administration, led to the assumption that communists were being allowed to participate in Arbenz's government. A plot was engineered by the CIA (Central Intelligence Agency) to oust Arbenz.[71]

On June 16, 1954, Colonel Carlos Castillo Armas, an exiled former Guatemalan military officer, invaded Guatemala with a CIA-supported force of exiles. The Guatemalan military, which was already disenchanted with Arbenz's radical policies, offered no resistance, and Arbenz was forced to resign from the presidency on June 27, 1954. He later claimed asylum in Mexico.[72]

As soon as Armas took over the presidency of Guatemala, he reversed almost all of the reforms that had been introduced since 1944, which prompted a return to violence and turmoil.[73] After Armas was assassinated in 1957, a succession of rulers, mainly military, kept the country repressed through the use of death squads.

Mounting discontent and human rights abuses of the indigenous population from 1960 onward contributed to the birth of indigenous guerrilla groups, supported by Marxist revolutionaries, which then formed a rebel group called the URNG. This initiated the civil war that would cost approximately 200,000 lives and last until 1996.[74]

On December 29, 1996, the 36-year civil war between the URNG and the Guatemalan government formally came to an end with the signing of an agreement for a firm and lasting peace.[75] The agreement brought into effect a number of accords that had been negotiated with support from the United Nations over a period of six years.[76]

Although the United Nations Verification Mission in Guatemala (MINUGUA) started in September 1994 with an advanced group of civilian human rights monitors, it was not until 1997, when military observers were added to the mission, that the disarmament and demobilization of URNG fighters started in earnest.[77] At that time, 132 military troops, 13 medical personnel, and 43 civilian police officers from 18 different countries joined the United Nations personnel already on the ground. Included were legal and human rights experts, as well as indigenous affairs professionals.[78]

Canada contributed to the mission by deploying 15 Spanish-speaking military officers, who arrived in Guatemala in February 1997. They would be followed by five members of the RCMP, who arrived a few months later.[79]

As a result of MINUGUA's personnel efforts, 2,928 URNG combatants were demobilized, 535,000 weapons and rounds of ammunition were turned over to military observers, and more than 378 landmines were cleared.[80] It should be noted that once the URNG combatants were demobilized, MINUGUA focused on integrating URNG fighters into civil society. The monitoring of human rights, assisting the return of refugees, and a myriad of other institution-building activities in support of the peace process were also an integral part of the mission.[81]

Candidate selection criteria for the Guatemalan mission were no different than other UN CIVPOL recruitments, with one exception: understanding the Spanish language was mandatory. The candidate needed to have a minimum of 5 years of police experience, preferably operational; have good interpersonal skills; and have demonstrated investigative capacities. Familiarity with driving standard transmission vehicles was a great asset; Guatemala has a rough landscape, with many gravel roads off-the-beaten-path.

What made potential participation to this mission more difficult than others was the language requirement. In order to be considered for the Guatemalan mission, the candidates had to demonstrate that they possessed a working knowledge of the Spanish language, meaning that they could speak, read, and write in Spanish. In 1998, RCMP officers who could meet this language requirement were few and far between. Therefore, those who could meet this criterion had a definite advantage over many other officers who may have wished to participate in this mission.

A good command of the Spanish language was necessary because, in addition to being the official language of Guatemala, Spanish was the official language of the mission. All reports and correspondence were to be in Spanish.

In 1998, at the time the posting for this mission became available for its second rotation, I was attached to a federal Drug Section in the Greater Vancouver area. Little did I know that my Spanish-speaking skills would eventually place me at the forefront of a very small Canadian contingent of five Spanish-speaking police officers to go to Guatemala.

A French-Canadian born in Montréal, I joined the RCMP in 1989 at the age of 24. Armed with only a Grade 12 education, and barely able to speak English, I had one quality that would be decisive in helping me reach my set goals: determination.

Shortly after I started as a patrolman in the City of Surrey, British Columbia, I had a vision. In the early 1990s there was much talk about the Free-Trade Agreement between Canada and the United States, and specifically about the possibility of extending it to Mexico as a result of a proposed North American Free-Trade Agreement (NAFTA).[82] I believed that as a police officer, economic exchanges with Mexico could open the doors to new opportunities within the RCMP.

This prompted me to enrol in Spanish language classes at a local high school. Later, with the meagre savings I had accumulated, I traveled to Mexico and signed up for two months of intensive studies in the local language.

Despite my determination, I have to admit that I required a dosage of good fortune on my side in order to be released from my functions within the Federal Section, and be allowed to participate in the Guatemalan mission in 1998.

Pre-deployment training was held in Ottawa at the Canadian Police College and lasted approximately three days. As the Canadian mandate for the mission was still being developed at the time, pre-deployment training was minimal. I did, however, receive pre-mission briefings on general topics such as administrative responsibilities, in addition to compensation, insurance, and health matters.

An overview of the general geo-political situation in Central America was provided by a Canadian Armed Forces officer who had recently served in El Salvador. Even though the session was deficient in material specific to the Peace Accords that had been signed in Guatemala, it nonetheless proved quite helpful.

Unlike other UN missions that were going on at that time, the Guatemalan mission only had a small number of Canadian police officers involved. This meant that only one or two officers would rotate out at a time. When my rotation took place at the end of November 1998, I was the only Canadian police officer to head to that part of the world.

The problem with being the only member of a small contingent was that I missed out on some of the training provided to larger groups, albeit some of the material taught to those larger detachments would have most likely been irrelevant to my mission.

Keeping the right attitude, even in the face of adversity, will determine one's chances of success.[83] A few days before I was scheduled to attend the pre-deployment session, and after having traveled from Vancouver to Ottawa, I learned that my candidacy to the mission was in danger. This was because Canadian Government officials were considering downsizing the Canadian contingent from five to four members. This was not good news, especially after I had gone through so much physical and mental preparation.

After a few days of uncertainty that I would now describe as a balancing act between the assuring news that I was going to Guatemala versus the disappointment that I was not, I finally learned that my Guatemalan rotation would go ahead. One thing is certain: although I had no control over any outcome, the positive attitude I kept enabled me to carry on throughout this stressful period.

Since my mission to Guatemala, much improvement has been made to the formation of peacekeepers. For one, training now draws upon the experience from a wider pool of officers who have participated in previous missions and are willing to share their thoughts and advice. Second, rollercoaster situations like the one I went through have been minimized by better planning and communications between all parties involved.

I landed in Guatemala City at night in early December 1998, after a 9-hour journey from Ottawa. Although my arrival was uneventful, things would have been different had I travelled a few days earlier: a major volcano had just erupted near Guatemala City, which had left the city covered in a blanket of several inches of ash. The airport had closed to air traffic. Thankfully, I did not end up having to wait in transit. After I landed in Guatemala, I was welcomed by the Canadian contingent commander, Inspector Len Babin, who offered me hospitality for the first few days before I got assigned to my post.

My first day in Guatemala was somewhat a bit of an eye-opener, to say the least. The day after I arrived, Len took me for a ride in a United Nations vehicle in order to acquaint me with Guatemala City.

For those readers who love travel and history, Guatemala is a place to visit. It offers beautiful architecture and many Mayan ruins. Unfortunately, 36 years of civil war had left the city a rather dangerous place to be for the unaware visitor. In December 1998, the murder rate in the country was 34 per 100,000 inhabitants.[84] With a population estimated at 12 million people, this roughly represented 10 homicides per day, the majority of which were taking place in urban areas like Guatemala City. As a contrast, the murder rate in Canada for the same period, a country of nearly 30 million people, was 1.8 per 100,000 inhabitants. This represented an average of 1.4 homicides per day.[85]

Thanks to Len, my city tour was educative, very safe, and uneventful. That is, until he drove past an overcrowded and dilapidated city bus that stood on my right side. As we slowly passed the bus, I realized with horror that one of its passengers, a young male perhaps in his twenties, had decided not to wait until the next stop in order to relieve himself. He simply pushed down one of the bus windows, whipped out his pride, and started urinating. In a reflex, I rolled up my window just in time to avoid a golden shower!

The next day, I attended the UN Mission headquarters in Guatemala City in preparation for deployment. Most of the day was spent getting to know the UN international and local staff, and obtaining my UN identifications. It was also during this first 48 hours that I met with the Guatemalan Canadian Embassy staff. In addition to the warm welcome I received from our diplomats, I was briefed on Guatemala's current political situation: a somewhat animated affair as a result of the death of a prominent bishop a few months before.

In April 1998, before I arrived in Guatemala, the ongoing peace process suffered a heavy setback when Monsignor Juan Gerardi, a member of the Episcopal Conference and an Auxiliary Bishop of the Archdiocese of Guatemala, was assassinated. Monsignor Gerardi was the principal force behind a Catholic Church human rights report entitled "Guatemala, Never Again". The report elaborated on the atrocities of the war and proposed the creation of a government commission to investigate disappearances that occurred during Guatemala's 36 years of civil war.

Monsignor Gerardi's murder, which occurred only 48 hours after the report was published, brought a wave of protests throughout the country. Among other themes, the report had brought to light some of the cruellest acts of violence in the country's history, and assigned blame to the army in 79% of the violations committed.

The UN exerted its political pressure towards the Guatemalan government so that the perpetrators of the crimes could be brought to justice.

It was against this fragile political climate that I completed my basic orientation and found out I would be posted to ORQUE (Regional Office Quetzaltenango), the UN office in the city of Quetzaltenango. The office was the second in importance in the country, with its city's population reaching 250,000 inhabitants.

On a beautiful Wednesday morning in early December, I set out to the Guatemala City airport to board the UN helicopter that would take me to Quetzaltenango. Located 8,000 feet above sea level and sitting in a small valley surrounded by volcanoes (the Santa Maria and the Santiaguito), Quetzaltenango, also known as Xelajú by the native Mayan people, is a truly picturesque city.

After a 30-minute flight, I landed in Quetzaltenango and was welcomed by my new colleagues: a small team of three international civilian police officers and a military attaché from Brazil. The first day at my new post would be spent getting acquainted with the office staff and finding a temporary place to stay. The principal duty of the police officers, who were from El Salvador, Italy, and Spain, was to liaise with the local police units in the region and support local civilian staff in monitoring the twelve peace accords.[86]

Figure 16: Getting ready to leave for Quetzaltenango. From left to right: Canadian helicopter pilot Mike, Norwegian Police Inspector Renate Melbye and RCMP Inspector Len Babin. Photo courtesy of Ben Maure.

The duty of monitoring the peace accords could be particularly tasking, and encompassed many different assignments. For example, if I were to monitor the accord on the *Resettlement of Population Groups Uprooted by the Armed Conflict*, it meant that I had to travel to remote and sometimes difficult-to-access areas of the country. This was in order to report on the welfare and living conditions of the resettled individuals, often ex-guerrilla members and their families.

Monitoring the *Comprehensive Agreement on Human Rights* or the *Agreement on the Strengthening of Civilian Power and on the Role of the Armed Forces in a Democratic Society* could mean that I had to attend the local police office and report on suspected cases of corruption or torture committed by the police.

The development, training and re-organization of the new Guatemalan police force, called *The Policia Nacional Civil*, was spearheaded by Spain. This meant that a number of officers from Spain's *Guardia Civil* had been attached to the Guatemalan police academy and did not report to MINUGUA.

Figure 17: Monitoring URNG combatants' resettlement near Retalhuleu. This area had no sanitation and was infested with malaria. Photo courtesy of Ben Maure.

From time to time, I was called upon to supervise entry examinations for applicants to the newly reformed Guatemalan

Police. Because there were few applicants with high school diplomas, many were allowed to write the exam despite having only a Grade 6 education.

Responding to general public complaints regarding the non-compliance of the Peace Accords was also a duty I had to perform. Admittedly, the challenges related to this task were impressive, and often frustrating. For instance, a complaint could be received that the living conditions on a certain tract of land given to refugees did not meet with the basic infrastructure (clean water, electricity, etc.). However, reporting the matter through the UN did not mean that the government would act upon it immediately. Months could go by without any improvement while refugees suffered.

Responding to general public complaints had another interesting aspect that required patience, tact, and understanding. Many individuals living in the vicinity of the city of Quetzaltenango belonged to one of the many Mayan groups whose native tongues were not Spanish. Illiteracy being relatively high in rural areas of Quetzaltenango, a number of individuals who came to the ORQUE to denounce matters did not really understand the parameters of the Peace Accords. As such, it was not uncommon to receive complaints that were outside the purview of the mission and had nothing to do with the Peace Accords.

For instance, I once received a complaint from a Mayan father who wanted to stop the wedding of his 21-year-old daughter. I had to spend several hours with the man before he calmed down. He was eventually referred to a local Mayan authority, and he left.

Report writing on the monitoring of the different peace accords was another duty that I undertook. Most of the reports I wrote had to be sent to our mission political officer, who would review the content and add it to a regional report sent to UN Headquarters in Guatemala City. A monthly police report on the situation in the district also had to be prepared and forwarded to the Canadian contingent commander, Inspector Babin, to be included in his monthly report to Canada. Report writing turned out to be an important, but also fairly time-consuming, aspect of my mission.

Figure 18: Some of the ORQUE civilian staff, police, and Army attaché. From left to right top row: Myself, Ben Maure (RCMP); Wellinton Filgueiras (Brazilian Army San Marco office); Marilu Orozco (civilian staff); Paolo Belligi (Italian Carabinieri); and Paula Berrutti (civilian staff). Bottom left: Juan Jose Hernandez (El Salvador Police), Severino Paixao (Brazilian Army), and Luis Jurado (civilian staff). Photo courtesy of Ben Maure.

In Quetzaltenango, and as a matter of fact, throughout Guatemala, drinking tap water was highly discouraged. The water came from freshwater streams and ponds whose waters were not fully treated, if they were treated at all. Although bottled water was readily available in most developed areas of the country, foreigners like me had to be extremely conscious of what we ate and drank; gastro-intestinal parasites, like the amoeba, were found even in some prepared foods or water.

One universal thing about UN missions is the camaraderie that soon develops amongst peers. When I first arrived in Quetzaltenango, no living quarters were immediately available. Thankfully, the Italian Carabinieri officer in post at the mission, Giuseppe Constantini, offered for me to stay at his place of residence until such time as I could make other arrangements to find my own place.[87]

The first night at Giuseppe's apartment was memorable in many ways. Giuseppe was a great Italian cook. The welcome dinner he served might have been simple, but it was absolutely delicious: Spaghetti à la Bolognese! I have a fond memory of that dinner, with the aroma of his cuisine filling up the small apartment. The Italian red wine he served with the meal was a perfect match.

I went to bed early that night, looking forward to a good night's sleep. Suddenly, I was awakened in the middle of the night by a boisterous sound. What I had failed to realize was that my bedroom in Giuseppe's apartment directly faced a yard, which I soon learned was roamed by the neighbour's rooster. That bird seemed to love to exalt his loud cock-a-doodle-doo every morning at 03:00. I will admit that I often felt like strangling the thing!

Through the review of local newspapers ads, within a month of my arrival I was able to identify a small, one-bedroom apartment near the ORQUE for the bargain price of $300.00 USD per month. The apartment was being rented by a local entrepreneur named Francisco.

I was very fortunate to have met Francisco. At the time, I was in search of a place to live, and Francisco just happened to be the person with an available place. Francisco and his family, including his in-laws, were instrumental in making my Guatemalan experience a memorable one. Through his friendship, I was able to better understand how Guatemalans perceived their government, the United Nations, and where they saw themselves heading as a country. This provided me with a local perspective that few international colleagues had a chance to acquire during their stay.

It was Francisco and his family who introduced me to Guatemalan cuisine. Nothing could beat the taste of fresh chicken (caught live one hour before dinner) and home-grown vegetables and fruits at his in-laws Papá Tim and Mamá Reina's farm.

In addition, Francisco was an accomplished Karate Shito-Ryu teacher. Upon moving into his rental apartment, I started taking Karate lessons with him during my off-duty time. Francisco's Karate teachings and philosophy would be instrumental in helping me maintain my composure in many stressful situations.

Having met Francisco was a truly rewarding experience; I made a long, lasting friendship and learned much about Guatemalan culture.

Figure 19: Francisco's in-laws "Papá Tim" and "Mamá Reina" at their ranch in Rethalhuleu. Photo courtesy of Ben Maure.

Like the old saying, "Who finds a faithful friend, finds a treasure", making good friends while abroad on a mission or, for that matter, anywhere one lives in the world, will enhance one's life to new levels.

I can speak happily of my time in Guatemala, but the mission nevertheless counted many perils. There is a particular situation that I am not about to forget!

It took place in the mountainous Mayan village of Pologua on February 1, 1999. Four suspects, who were allegedly involved in a vehicle theft that had taken place two weeks' prior, were captured by an angry mob as they entered the village of Pologua. The alleged suspects were soon beaten up by the angry crowd, and subsequently tied up. The crowd turned the gang leader over to the police with the condition that they would accompany the leader to the place where the stolen vehicle was. This was in an attempt to have the vehicle returned to the lawful owner.

However, the crowd refused to turn over the other suspects to the police, and threatened to immolate them on the spot. By virtue of the intervention of the local auxiliary mayor, who calmed the crowd, the three suspects were instead taken to the mayor's office where someone stood vigil.

It was only the next day that our ORQUE office learned that the people of Pologua had captured three thieves and threatened to burn them alive. Consequently, the ORQUE was in touch with the local police and the justice department. Arrangements were made for a team composed of civilian lawyer David Bahamondes and myself to travel to the entrance of the village and meet the authorities. As usual, I wore my police uniform and a blue beret.

When David and I arrived at the meeting point, we found no one there. We learned that the police and justice department had already entered the village. Since there were no signs of imminent danger, we drove into the village and met with our police counterparts. There, a justice department's representative was addressing a crowd of a few hundred.

At this point, everyone in the village was calm, and appeared to agree with the proposition made by the justice department representative to give the police enough time to recover the stolen car. Shortly after, the police and the justice department representative departed the village, and the crowd dispersed.

From a personal security point-of-view, we made three grave mistakes. The first one was to misunderstand the lack of trust that some native Mayans held towards the United Nations. Because of this, David and I remained in the village to monitor the situation. After all, the ambiance was calm, and we were representatives of the United Nations, generally well perceived by native Mayans… or so we thought!

We spoke with the Auxiliary Mayor, who confirmed that the three suspects would be safe and sound so long as they remained in his office, out of sight of the village population. However, the Auxiliary Mayor confessed that he feared that he might not be capable of ensuring the security of the suspects if the police did not return with the stolen car. Since little could be done, David and I headed back towards our parked vehicle. As we crossed the central park, a citizen on a loudspeaker approached us and asked that we explain the presence of the United Nations.

The second mistake was to acquiesce to the request. Frankly, we should have exited the village as soon as the police and the justice department representatives left. But, in a genuine attempt to explain to the few curious still left in the central park that the United Nations wanted a peaceful resolution to the matter and the return of the stolen property, David took the microphone.

Alas, this action would keep us there for the next three hours. In no time, approximately five hundred people surrounded us to listen to what we had to say. This feeling of being encircled by so many people did not go well with either of us. However, at first the crowd was not hostile, and seemed to appreciate our presence.

The third mistake sealed our fate! We failed to recognize that there was still time to leave as more people were coming. Within ten minutes, the crowd of five hundred grew to more than a thousand, with many intoxicated individuals joining in.

Then, out of the blue, one of the drunken men shouted that the United Nations should remain in the village until such time as the police and the department of justice brought back the stolen vehicle. Alas, the crowd cheered at the remark, and we suddenly found ourselves with no escape. More intoxicated men showed up, some of whom were enticing the crowd to take the law into their own hands.

The euphoria that ensued is hard to describe. An individual suddenly shouted that the United Nations' role was to protect the criminals, and that it should not be trusted.

Noticing that David and I were in imminent danger, the auxiliary mayor tried to come to our rescue. In an attempt to calm the crowd, he was told by members of his own community that if he tried to get the United Nations out, he would be executed. Calmly and discretely, he advised that he would return to his office and seek help.

As time went by, more inebriated men arrived in vehicles from nearby villages, joining the ever-growing crowd. In less than an hour, the crowd had reached an estimated 5,000 people. At that point, David and I heard the crowd cheer at the sight of a vehicle that brought tires and canisters of gasoline.

The sight of this chilled my spine. You see, in many rural areas of Guatemala, people do not understand the Western justice system, and simply do not trust authorities. Thus, there had been reported instances where people from an entire village would take it upon themselves to execute a suspect, more or less on the spot. First, a mob would grab the accused and place tires around his waist until he could no longer move. Then the suspect would be doused with gasoline, and set on fire for everyone to watch.

With that in mind, a smirking drunken man approached David and I. He suddenly pulled out his machete and waved it near our necks, threatening to chop us up!

Fortunately, other citizens in the crowd who were closely watching the drunken man eventually grabbed him and pulled him away from us. Their action was a reassuring sign that not everyone in attendance wanted to see us either hacked to death or burned alive. I will admit, however, that the general atmosphere around us was rather dire.

Perhaps the most frustrating part of the ordeal was that we could do little to improve our situation. At one point, we noticed a small breach in the crowd, where David and I could have sprinted to our vehicle, parked only 200 metres away. However, attempting to dash away would have only enticed an already agitated crowd. We could imagine that with hundreds of people running behind us, the odds of making it to the vehicle, unlocking the doors, starting the engine, and racing away to safety were rather slim. Frankly, the only thing we could do was to remain calm. Admittedly, I practiced some of the breathing techniques that Francisco had taught me during our Karate lessons. They certainly came in handy and helped me lower my anxiety in addition to keeping me focused.

Throughout the ordeal, we had been in radio contact with Quetzaltenango ORQUE to apprise the UN of the situation. Although the police and the army had been made aware of what had happened, no one was in sight. David and I would later learn that plainclothes members of the Guatemalan Army had been closely monitoring the event, and might have intervened if things had taken a turn for the worse.

After approximately two hours, it was still impossible for us to go anywhere, even though the atmosphere around us had calmed down. Thousands of angry people still encircled us.

Suddenly, we heard the crowd roar, and noticed two women walking towards us. One wore local Mayan Indian garments, and the other jeans and t-shirt. David and I recognized the familiar faces of our ORQUE colleagues Francesca, the Guatemalan Quiché translator, and Soledad, the office's Mayan Ethnic Liaison appointee.

Figure 20: Centre Square in the village of Pologua moments before a crowd of thousands gathered around David and me. Photo courtesy of Ben Maure.

Needless to say, I had mixed emotions about seeing my colleagues. For one, I truly admired the courage these two women displayed by putting themselves at risk for us. I should explain that as Mayan Ethnic Liaison, Francesca and Soledad had privileged connections with that particular community. Nonetheless, there were so many intoxicated individuals in the crowd with whom dialogue seemed futile, that David and I feared they might also become hostages.

Alas, that is what happened. Francesca and Soledad's presence agitated the crowd, who insulted them and pushed them close to us. Now there were four of us who risked being burned alive!

What Soledad and Francesca did not know, and later learned, was that out of the thousands of people present, only a few hundred were from the village of Pologua. The rest of the people present, many of whom had been drinking, came from surrounding villages.

As the crowd became more agitated with the arrival of the two ladies, the auxiliary mayor and a handful of people from Pologua pushed their way through the crowd, and joined us in the middle of the village square. The auxiliary mayor had observed the situation deteriorating, and in a genuine attempt to save us, came up with a plot to get the four of us out of sight of the main crowd.

To achieve this without causing a riot, he informed the crowd that we needed a telephone to contact the justice department representative and obtain an update. Since there was only one telephone in the entire community, the auxiliary mayor and his assistants led us to the small building a hundred metres away where it was kept. There, we were out of sight from the crowd.

The four of us were then taken through a back alley that led to our United Nations vehicles. In a flash, we jumped into our respective cars and barrelled out of Pologua. In the rear-view, I could see in the distance that the crowd had realized what had happened, and was now pouring into the area where our vehicles had been.

I will never be thankful enough to Auxiliary Mayor Bonifacio Cutz, who risked his own life to save ours. I should add that in the end no one was hurt, and the culprits were turned over to the police after a few more hours of captivity and intense negotiations with the crowd.

There are several elements that need to be commented on about the event. The whole situation could have been avoided if we had been educated on the near-total distrust some villages had towards authorities, and the misperceptions they had of the UN. Knowing that some villages in rural areas had, in the past, taken the law into their own hands and immolated suspects, we would not have stayed around, even when the atmosphere looked quiet. We had been under the wrong assumption that everyone in Guatemala understood the role of the UN.

This was not always the case in parts of rural Guatemala, where villagers often mistakenly associated the UN as a defender of criminals. Had this been clearly explained upon arrival in the country, David and I would not have placed ourselves in the vulnerable position we did.

The decision to send Francesca and Soledad to our rescue was well-intended, but in my view as police officer, was quite imprudent given the few details available that our office, the ORQUE, had on the situation. As it turned out, there were too many intoxicated individuals within the crowd, who made negotiations almost impossible. From a safety perspective, Francesca and Soledad should never have been allowed to enter Pologua.

One important comment remains. Although the crowd counted many drunks, it also encompassed many active onlookers, such as women and children. This made it much harder for an armed rescue intervention, by either police or Armed Forces, because of the risk to bystanders. It would have been a public relations disaster and a political nightmare for the UN to have its members saved while women and children lost their lives.

Fortunately, none of that happened. My advice to anyone: be on your guard, and do not take anything for granted. Like David and me, one may end up in an area of the world where the role of the UN is not understood, or simply not well perceived by the public.

Thankfully, interviews with peacekeepers who have gone to more recent missions have shown that the UN has much evolved. In-depth local custom awareness is an integral part of training now provided to mission newcomers.

Perhaps the most unique experience in Guatemala that my mission granted me was an opportunity to meet with my World Vision sponsored child, Jorge Borrayo Cubule, and his family. They lived in the village of Cerro Alto, near Guatemala City.

My story with Jorge debuted in 1996, when I began sponsoring him through World Vision Canada. Jorge was then a seven-year-old boy living with his family in an impoverished village. Although I had wanted to visit Jorge for some time during my mission, the opportunity only presented itself in September 1999, after I already had been in Guatemala for nine months.

Earlier, I had contacted the Guatemala World Vision office and explained to an employee that I would be working in Guatemala for a period of time, and would be interested in meeting my sponsored child. World Vision had strict guidelines for visiting sponsored children (and even more so nowadays); nevertheless, in late August of that year, I received an e-mail from the Cerro Alto World Vision project coordinator informing that a visit to the project site had been organized.

On a warm and sunny September day, I obtained a special permission from the UN to take one of its vehicles for this endeavour. I drove to Guatemala City in order to meet and pick up the local World Vision worker with whom I would travel to Cerro Alto, located two hours away.

When we arrived at the village, we met with a local health care worker who debriefed us on the work being done in the village. I was warned that some villagers would possibly approach me for cash donations, and I was strongly advised not to give money. Once the meeting was over, we walked to Jorge's home to meet him and his family.

As I had anticipated, Jorge's family was extremely poor. Jorge, his four siblings, and parents all lived in a brick-and-mud wall house that had no floor, no electricity, and no running water. There was no stove, and only two dirty beds to accommodate a family of seven. Jorge's father made firecrackers for a living. His meagre $5.00 USD per day wage obviously could not provide enough to support his five children and wife.

During this visit, I learned that Jorge and his two brothers also made firecrackers on a part-time basis to bring more money to the family. Although having Jorge work part-time was not an ideal situation, World Vision had played a paramount role in convincing his parents to let him attend school rather than work all day making firecrackers.

On that subject, Jorge's parents were too ashamed to tell me exactly how much money Jorge and his brothers earned, but a villager later informed me that on average, for an eight-hour day's labour, a child who handled hazardous gun powder earned around $0.75 USD.

Figure 21: Jorge's family. From bottom left to right, Jorge, myself, and Jorge's little sister. Photo courtesy of Ben Maure.

Since I had been informed by the World Vision worker that bringing some food for the family would be welcomed, I came prepared! On my way to the village through Guatemala City, I stopped at a local restaurant, where I purchased two large buckets of fried chicken, two pounds of French fries, and several large bottles of soft drinks. Not surprisingly, when they saw the treasure I carried, word spread like wildfire amongst Jorge's extended family that fried chicken (obviously a treat) was on today's menu. Aunts, uncles, and many cousins soon joined in for a get-together with me that turned out to be memorable for all present.

During the visit to Cerro Alto, I learned that Jorge's mother was expecting another child. Under normal circumstances, I would have thought this to be very happy news. However, when someone cannot earn enough money to feed one child, having a sixth one will no doubt become an added burden.

The local health care worker later explained that family planning was not a topic well received within the community, and for that matter, within Jorge's family. Many in the community, including Jorge's parents, were illiterate, and either did not understand or did not approve of contraceptives. This created a serious problem, and made it almost impossible for families like Jorge's to improve their socio-economic situation.

Sadly, Jorge did not talk very much during my brief stay; he revealed himself to be a shy and timid young boy. This was in contrast to his younger sister, who displayed a huge smile and followed me everywhere I went in the village.

The visit to Cerro Alto had a profound effect on me. For one, it made me realize how blessed I had been in this world. Second, it reinforced the conviction that my sponsorship through World Vision was definitely making a positive difference in the life of Jorge and his family.

Obviously, one does not need to sponsor a child to make a difference in someone's life. As former US Secretary of State, Condoleezza Rice, once said: "We who flourish in freedom have a moral responsibility to help others who have the desire to succeed, but just need an opportunity".[88]

As a note, Jorge's community became self-sufficient in 2001, and no longer required the financial assistance of World Vision.[89]

My most interesting, challenging, and perhaps most frustrating experience was related to a Human Rights complaint I investigated after I had been in Guatemala for approximately six months. The allegations were quite serious, and encompassed an individual being unlawfully arrested, beaten, tortured, and thrown in jail by the local police. Furthermore, the man accused the police of planting evidence on him.

I first met the complainant at the Quetzaltenango detention centre on a warm afternoon. According to the man, three police officers had arrested him a week prior for possession of cannabis. He alleged that following his arrest, one of the officers hit him on the leg with the butt pad of a rifle. Then, the officer wrapped a bicycle tire inner tube around his head and mouth and pulled on each side. This caused great pain but left no marks.

Not admitting to anything else, he alleged that cannabis was planted on him and charges of drug possession were unlawfully laid. Upon completing a very superficial examination of the complainant's arms and legs, I was unable to observe any signs of physical abuse, and thus unable to confirm whether or not he had been tortured. Nevertheless, I had a look at the police report regarding his arrest, and realized something was not quite right.

The report indicated that only two agents had arrested him after they observed him smoking what they believed was marijuana. The officers then moved in and apprehended their suspect, who was concealing a bag of marijuana in his pockets.

The report sounded too simple. After all, the arrest had taken place in a small village, where the police seldom go. Furthermore, the agents making the arrest were from a special property crime unit, and not from a drug section, although this did not prevent them from arresting people for other offences. Nonetheless, I had a feeling some crucial facts had been omitted from the report.

As part of my Human Rights investigation, I conducted basic neighbourhood inquiries in the village where the man had been arrested, and soon found out from witnesses that a pick-up truck with three individuals had stopped by a house under renovation and had taken the complainant away. The witnesses believed the three men to be plainclothes officers.

I also learned that the complainant had previously renovated another residence, which had later been broken into and a digital

VCR (Video Cassette Recorder) stolen.

Further investigation revealed that the complainant was a prime suspect in the theft of the VCR. As it turned out, the complainant was a local break-in artist that the police suspected was behind a rash of other thefts of electronics in that neighbourhood.

The picture was now clearer, and I suspected that since the police had not been able to gather sufficient evidence to arrest him on the break-ins, they had resorted to planting drug evidence. It was a theory I would never be able to substantiate, but that was highly plausible. One could argue that the end goal of the police was to stop the break-ins and make the village safer. Though a just cause, as a leading government agency in a fledgling democracy, the Civilian National Police could not afford to breach human rights in the process.

In the end, I was never able to prove without a doubt that the man had been tortured, as he had no obvious signs of beatings. However, I felt confident that he had been set up, and was innocent of the possession of the cannabis. My report was forwarded to the UN chain of command. I learned later that disciplinary actions had been taken against one of the Guatemalan officers involved in the break-in investigation. I never saw him again.

My year-long mission in Quetzaltenango showed me that tact and diplomacy were two important attributes to possess in order to be a successful peacekeeper. Developing local friendships was also an important part of the mission, which made it unique and that much more of an unforgettable experience. To this date, my mission in Guatemala remains as one of the most rewarding experiences of my policing career.

4.

The Land of the Kosovo Harley: UNMIK (United Nations Interim Administration Mission in Kosovo), 1999-Present

Imagine finding yourself driving on a countryside road, surrounded by trees and ditches that stretch as far as the eye can see. Suddenly, you need to answer a "quick call of nature"! Since there are no public facilities anywhere near, you stop your vehicle. You jump to cross a small roadside trench, and take a few steps to a nearby tree. As you look down between both feet, you notice that there are three prods sticking out of the ground. A cold chill suddenly engulfs you as you realize that you have just entered a minefield!

Welcome to Kosovo, the land of many landmines and last territory to break away from the former Yugoslavia! In this chapter, we will meet Lorin Lopetinsky, a 10-year police veteran at the time of the mission. Lorin's tale in Kosovo is an inspiring lesson on how to use good judgment to overcome dangers, and how to push one's abilities to tackle demanding tasks. Lorin's peacekeeping mission, which lasted for nine months between August 2001 and May 2002, was a key engagement that paved the way for Kosovars to develop and enjoy a substantial autonomy.[90]

BEFORE IT DECLARED itself the Republic of Kosovo in 2008, Kosovo was a province of Serbia, one of the six states that once constituted Yugoslavia. From a geographical perspective, Kosovo is landlocked between Serbia to the north and east, Macedonia to the southeast, Albania to the southwest, and by Montenegro to the northwest (see Figure 22).

The narrative account of Kosovo has its roots in long-term ethnic tensions between the Albanians and Serbs.[91] For hundreds of years, the people of Serbia have considered Kosovo to be the homeland of their history and culture.

A turning point in Serb history was the 1389 Battle of Kosovo, which saw the Ottoman Empire invade the Serb Kingdom and take control. Serbia reacquired it during the First Balkan War of 1912.[92] Over the course of the Turkish Ottoman rule, many Serbs either left Kosovo or converted from Christianity to Islam. Also, the Albanian Muslim population of the area grew, until the majority of Kosovo inhabitants were no longer Serb Christians, but Albanians.[93]

Figure 22: Kosovo. Map reproduced with permission of WorldAtlas.com

The disintegration of Yugoslavia, which started after Marshal Tito's death in 1980, continued throughout the 90s. Demands for independence and auto-determination eventually reached the heart of Serbia: Kosovo.

During Slobodan Milosevic's mandate as President of Serbia (1989-1997), he pursued policies that would rouse ethnic hatred and build a Serbian nationalistic mass movement.[94] One of the nationalistic approaches he took in 1989 was to abolish Kosovar autonomy, which had been granted under Marshal Tito's ruling.

Milosevic re-asserted direct Serbian rule over Kosovo and purged Kosovars (mainly Albanian ethnics) from employment in government and education. He even passed a law preventing Albanian Kosovars from purchasing land owned by Serbians.[95]

This infuriated the Kosovars, who responded with a boycott of Serbian institutions in a non-violent campaign. The result was the creation of school, healthcare, and municipal government systems that paralleled that of, but remained separate from, Serbia. Serbian riposte was to stem the Kosovar movement with arrests, detentions, and harassments.[96]

By the mid-90s, when the non-violent struggle failed to attract Western support, a small ethnic Albanian paramilitary group calling itself the Kosovo Liberation Army (KLA) began to gather arms and plan for an uprising directed at the Serbian Police and military installations in Kosovo.[97] Operating from bases inside the neighbouring country of Albania, the KLA started with disruption attacks, and endeavoured to kill Serb policemen and other Serb government officials.

Retaliation was swift from Serb authorities, who raided civilian villages and killed ethnic Albanians that gave shelter to the KLA guerrillas. Soon, more villages were rocketed and ethnic Albanians murdered by Serb authorities in an effort to root out KLA guerrillas.

It is unclear whether or not the excessive and indiscriminate use of force against KLA guerrillas amounted to ethnic cleansing. However, a fact remained: over 200,000 Kosovars of Albanian origins were driven from their homes into the mountains and into neighbouring countries. Indiscriminate use of force against ethnic Albanians soon started a refugee crisis, which would eventually threaten the stability and security of the whole area.[98]

However, it was not the United Nations that first got involved in the Kosovar conflict, but the North Atlantic Treaty Organization (NATO). Providing a clear understanding as to the reasons NATO first intervened in the conflict without the UN Security Council's approval is somewhat intricate, and beyond the scope of this book.[99] Simply put, with the influx of ethnic Albanian refugees, and evidence of indiscriminate killings of ethnic Albanians, NATO feared a full-scale genocide. A bombing campaign against Serbian military installations in Kosovo began.

Later, the military campaign moved to the heart of Serbia: its capital city, Belgrade. The offensive was taken in a bid to stop the killings and bring Milosevic back to negotiations.[100] Coined by many journalists covering the story as "an exercise in coercive diplomacy aimed at bringing Milosevic back to the bargaining table", the NATO operation was somewhat controversial.

Essentially, while the assault lasted only eleven weeks (from March 24 to June 10, 1999), and although it did compel Milosevic to agree to a number of concessions, it failed to stop the continuing systematic deportation and killings of Kosovars. As a result, nearly half a million Kosovars were driven to neighbouring countries like Albania, Macedonia, and others.[101] Furthermore, the conflict also left behind a severe problem of unexploded remnants of war.[102]

On June 10, 1999, the UN Security Council introduced Resolution 1244. This resolution called for the resolve of the humanitarian crisis in Kosovo, and stood for the rights of all refugees and displaced persons to be able to return to their home in safety. It would be accomplished through an agreement with the Milosevic Regime (the Federal Republic of Yugoslavia), which promoted a complete withdrawal of all Serb military, police, and paramilitary forces from Kosovo within a set timeline.

Under the agreement, NATO, with a 50,000 multinational Kosovo Force (KFOR), would be responsible for the security and the demilitarization of the KLA and other armed Kosovo Albanian groups. Furthermore, a UN peacekeeping presence (UNMIK) of more than 4,700 civilian police personnel, 1,178 international civilian staff, 38 military attachés, and over 3,300 local staff would contribute to promoting the establishment of a substantial autonomy and self-government for the people of Kosovo.[103]

Amongst the numerous mandates falling under UNMIK were a few of paramount importance. These were: the protection and promotion of human rights, the maintaining of civil law and order, and the establishment of a local police force.[104] It is by way of these mandates that Lorin would have an opportunity to travel to Kosovo and contribute to the rebuilding of that nation.

Completing a UN mission had been one of Lorin's career ambitions from the time he joined the RCMP in 1991. An opportunity for Lorin to realize his dream came along in 2001 during an RCMP Staffing interview. At that time, Lorin had been working at the RCMP Burnaby detachment for 10 years and was due for a transfer.[105]

Having kept excellent yearly performance assessments throughout his service, and having acquired a range of police experience from General Duty, Traffic, School Liaison, and Serious Crimes, Lorin was asked if he would be interested in going on a United Nations mission. The RCMP was seeking mature and capable members to go on a nine-month tour-of-duty in Kosovo.

Lorin eagerly agreed.

From that point, all Lorin had to do was to pass the medical and physical fitness tests that were required in order for him to join the mission. Later, having successfully completed all the requirements, Lorin was on his way to Ottawa, where he would meet twenty other police officers from different Canadian law enforcement agencies. They would be part of the Canadian CIVPOL mission in Kosovo.

Pre-deployment training took place in Ottawa, in July 2001, and lasted two weeks. This included a brief overview and history of the conflict in Kosovo, a review of police arrests, and hand-to-hand combat techniques. A First Aid refresher course, cultural sensitivity interviews with Serbs and Albanians, a landmine awareness session, and a firearm requalification were also part of the curriculum. This was an armed mission, in contrast to other missions at that time. Lorin and his colleagues would have full powers of arrest while in Kosovo.

Lorin's journey to Kosovo started with an uneventful six-hour flight from Montréal to Zurich in a comfortable Swissair Airbus 340. Once in Zurich, he and his comrades had a four-hour layover before they boarded the next plane, which would take them to Pristina, the capital of Kosovo. From the window seat of the taxiing commuter plane, Lorin and other peacekeepers admired the airport landscape, which boasted a modern control tower and rows of Swissair planes, all displaying the familiar white crosses painted over red on their tails.

On the tarmac, glancing back at the terminal where the plane had been, Lorin caught a familiar sight: blue hockey bags containing the troops' police equipment. Obviously, they had not made it to the plane! Despite words of alarm from some of the peacekeepers, the plane continued on its course to the runway and took off as scheduled.

After a relatively uneventful two-hour flight, the plane landed in Pristina, the heart of Kosovo. When the door of the aircraft opened, Lorin found himself overwhelmed by a pungent smell that engulfed the entire cabin. What was it, he wondered? It would get worse before he got the answer…and by the time he stepped out of the plane, his throat and eyes were burning like never before!

What he soon realized was that a thick haze floated in the air near the airport. That thick haze turned out to be the by-product of coal-burning electrical power plants. With a number of negative health effects on humans resulting from prolonged exposure to coal, such as chronic bronchitis, asthma, loss of intellectual capacity, and even a reduction of life expectancy, the mission suddenly no longer appeared exciting…

Eventually, Lorin and his colleagues managed to get away from the smell, and met up with the Canadian contingent commander, RCMP Inspector Gerry Locke. Inspector Locke had come to the airport with other Canadian CIVPOL officers to greet and pick up the newcomers.

Gerry's presence was much appreciated by the newly arrived. It was also with a sigh of relief that the peacekeepers learned from a Swissair official that the blue bags containing their police equipment would arrive the next day. Lorin was one of the few lucky ones whose equipment had made the trip.

The troop headed up to the Pristina Grand Hotel for a well-deserved rest: the next day promised to be busy. Thanks to Inspector Locke, transport of the troops from the airport to the hotel had already been arranged, and everyone travelled in UN Toyota 4Runners.

The Pristina Grand Hotel, located on Mother Theresa Street in Pristina, Kosovo, was once described as a five-star hotel. It had been built in the late 70s during the Tito era to accommodate traveling Yugoslav government officials. The simple thought of staying in a five-star hotel after a long journey from Canada made some of Lorin's colleagues grin with satisfaction.

Regrettably, a decade of neglect, worsened by economic crisis and war, had plucked the Grand Hotel of a few of its stars! Arriving at the site they found an unwelcoming brown and grey, 13-storey block of concrete. Judging from the outside, the short stay at the hotel wouldn't be as exotic as first thought!

Lorin's adventure at the Grand Hotel started soon after check-in, when he was informed that he would be sharing a small room with a colleague. Lorin took this in stride, although under normal circumstances, individual rooms were afforded, allowing a peacekeeper some privacy after a long travel day. However, the Pristina Grand Hotel was nearly fully booked, so our peacekeepers had to sleep two per room.

Lorin and his roommate ended up with a room on the 7th floor. Since there was no concierge service, he and his buddy carried their suitcases and heavy blue duty bags (some weighing more than 50 lbs.) to the hotel's only elevator. At the elevator's doors, both were greeted by a sign that read "Out of Service"! Tired and looking at each other in disbelief, Lorin and his comrade had no option but to grab their heavy luggage, head to the stairs, and start their way up to the 7th floor.

Standing by and chuckling at the whole situation were the CIVPOL members who had picked Lorin and his colleagues at the airport. But as camaraderie would dictate, they were quick to help our intrepid peacekeepers with taking their equipment up to their room.

The door to their 7th floor room opened up to a rather abrupt reality: filthy windows, threadbare green carpet, old-fashioned red drapes, and lots of bed bugs!

But Lorin had come prepared. Stupefying those present, he calmly opened one of his bags, picked up a can of insecticide, and sprayed the entire contents of the can onto the twin beds. Soon, all had to run out to the hallway to escape the cloud of heavy toxic fumes that filled the compact room.

Lorin would later laughingly admit that a member of the current mission, with whom he had been in touch prior to his deployment, had forewarned him to bring the insecticide for his "first night in town". We learned one thing: the little invertebrates would not have an easy feast on Lorin while he stayed at "The Grand". [106]

The next morning, Lorin woke up refreshed, despite his night being "enriched" by the continuous barks of what sounded like hundreds of stray dogs roaming near the hotel. Lorin put on his uniform and headed to UN headquarters to be issued identifications and be debriefed on the general terms of the mission. Since this was an armed mission, with the peacekeepers possessing powers of arrest, Lorin was issued a 9mm pistol.

However, it was not long before Lorin realized that some serious gun cleaning and lubricating needed to be done; many of the guns had received poor maintenance, and plenty of rust was present.

UN introduction training continued the next day with a UN firearm qualification. This consisted of having the peacekeeper use his pistol and hit a two-by-two-foot paper target at close range. Shooters were given ten bullets for that purpose and had to hit the target with eight of them in order to qualify. This test was not really difficult for Lorin, who was already a qualified shooter under Canadian laws.

Figure 23: Grand Hotel Prishtina, in Prishtina, Kosovo. Attribution: Kristoferb at English Wikipedia.

The rest of the training was broken into learning segments on the operation of the UN radio communication systems, the history and overview of the conflict, and the mission's administrative processes. In the end, a quick test of one's ability to drive a standard vehicle was administered, to which Lorin passed with flying colours.

On the last day, Lorin received his position: Executive Officer to the Chief of Human Resources. Not a bad job for a first-timer, and a great one to have listed on one's Curriculum Vitae! This position meant that Lorin would have more than 145 UN police officers reporting to him for the purpose of writing policies, overviewing Kosovo police training needs, and the set-up for a promotional process for the Kosovo police. Wow!

What was Lorin's secret to landing such a coveted and important job right at the start of the mission? Let me start by saying that Lorin, as well as the other Canadian CIVPOL attending the mission, were quite sought-after by mission section heads in order to fill key positions. This may have been due to the excellent international reputation that Canadian police officers hold for being professional, knowledgeable, and humanitarian.

Although Lorin was a capable police officer, he had an additional weapon in his arsenal: he understood the importance of creating and maintaining strong social networks in order to succeed in both business and personal life.

Lorin's fascinating journey as the mission's Executive Officer to the Chief of Human Resources actually started in Canada. A longtime hobby of his was motorcycle riding. Through his affiliation with a motorcycle fraternity, Lorin met an American police leader.

As fate would have it, this police leader took a leave of absence to work for the UN, and sought a position as the Chief of Staff to the Deputy Commissioner of the Kosovo police. Once in-theatre, he learned that Lorin would also be joining the mission and arranged for him to have a job interview—something that none of the other Canadian peacekeepers had landed.

Capitalizing on Lorin's operational background, demonstrated investigative capabilities, and pleasant personality, the Chief of Staff determined that Lorin would be the most suitable candidate for the challenging but rewarding position of Executive Officer to the Chief of Human Resources.

Despite being a competent police officer, it is uncertain that Lorin would have been able to secure that specific assignment had it not been for his networking abilities. Furthermore, the fact that he held the rank of Constable at the time, a rank often unfairly judged as low-status by other countries that send high-ranking police officers, Lorin's chances of being appointed to that respected position would have been highly unlikely.

Judging by Lorin's success in seeking a coveted position, it is not farfetched for me to claim that networking can greatly enrich someone's life.[107] Many may frown at the metaphor that positive networking is "kissing as many frogs as possible in order to find a prince". In reality, it is much more than that. Positive networking endorses the concept of discovering what one can do for someone else.¹⁰⁸ Ultimately, this can lead to a win-win situation for all sides.¹⁰⁹

Lorin's functions as the Executive Officer to the Chief of Human Resources meant that he would be developing and writing policies for the Kosovo police. This challenging and exciting position, however, did come with some measure of stress. Expectation was high within UN ranks to develop a professional set of police procedures. These would become paramount in guiding and governing this new force of 4,000 members (created in 1999), made up of both Serbs and Albanians (including some ex-KLA combatants).

On a typical day, the Human Resources Department would receive news from the five UN regions within Kosovo. These would address topics such as police training needs, recruiting, and others. Lorin's duty would be to analyze all of the information received, identify the most relevant items, and prepare a comprehensive report for the Chief of Human Resources. This daily report would then be used by the latter to make decisions that directly affected police developments in each of the regions.

Lorin's duty also called for him to frequently travel throughout the five regions and meet UN sub-office training coordinators. These coordinators were UN CIVPOL members, who directly oversaw the training needs and development of the Kosovo police officers in each of their respective districts. Some of Lorin's travels to these areas were significant, not only for the beauty of the landscape and the cultural richness of its people, but also for the unexpected dangers that lurked around.

Dangers such as landmines! They were all over the countryside. In order to avoid catastrophe, the UN had cautiously advised its entire staff to remain on paved roads when travelling, and for good reason. Lorin was the man described in the introduction to this chapter, coming close to being maimed or killed that day.

He was very lucky to have been able to backtrack and get out of there unhurt!

In Kosovo, unexploded landmines and other lethal remnants of war represented a constant threat. However, there was another danger that threatened the safety of the peacekeepers. That was the Kosovar themselves—when behind the wheel of a vehicle! "They are absolutely the worst drivers in the world," Lorin would humorously exclaim.

For many Kosovars, holding a valid driver's licence was a luxury; this applied even to some police officers. Although those without a driver's license would swear they could drive safely, the truth of the matter was that they could not.

Take, for example, the manoeuvre Kosovars would take to avoid the numerous potholes littering the road. When a driver came up to a pothole, he would simply swerve around it, even if it meant driving into the path of an oncoming vehicle. The consequences were at times totally disastrous! Lorin recalled an incident when one of those drivers unexpectedly veered directly onto the path of an oncoming multi-ton UN Armoured Personnel Carrier (APC). Only metres away and unable to avoid a collision, the UN crew could only watch in horror as their APC hit the other vehicle head-on, crushing its occupants to death.

Then, there were the so-called "Kosovo Harleys". Getting their nickname from the famed motorcycle chopper with its long handlebars, the Kosovo version was a far cry from the safety and aesthetic of the Harley Davidson!

With its long shaft that split into two handlebars, the homemade Kosovo Harley resembled a cross between a rototiller and a hay wagon. Poorly manoeuvrable, without any lights, reflectors, horn, turning signals, or mirrors, these rigs were a true danger on the roads. To make matters worse, they would often be carrying stacks of hay or other goods, making them even more difficult to see, especially at night.

Dreaded by many, including Lorin and his colleagues, these machines were believed to be responsible for a number of accidents. It came as no surprise to the author that Kosovo's scrap metal exports business is said to have thrived during that time.[110]

Towards the middle of his mission, Lorin participated in the creation of a promotional examination for the police. Although the rank structure of the organization had been put in place by the United States, and key leadership positions had already been granted by appointment, the police force still needed a structure to provide for individual promotion within its ranks.

Figure 24: Photo of a "Kosovo Harley": a cross between a rototiller and a hay wagon. Photo courtesy of Lorin Lopetinsky.

With this in mind, Lorin was tasked with developing the first promotional examination that would enable police officers (the lowest rank) to be promoted to Sergeant (the next level in a scale of ten ranks). With a small team of both UN CIVPOL and civilians, including a computer programmer, Lorin developed a forty-question examination that would test a candidate's policing skills and leadership abilities in order to advance to the rank of Sergeant.

To create the exam, Lorin first researched past promotional material data available to him. He sought the expertise of former colleagues, and drafted the forty-question test with his team in three languages: Albanian, Serbian, and English.

Administrating the test would be the next challenge. In a country where corruption was prominent, ensuring that none of the 3,000 copies of the test were sold off before exam day was paramount. To succeed, Lorin and his team sought the support of other peacekeepers, who would literally be in attendance "around the clock" at the printing facility to account for every copy.

Delivering the exams simultaneously to all eligible candidates within Kosovo's five regions was accomplished by having dedicated teams traveling to each region at the same time. In the end, the multiple-choice promotional exam, written by all eligible candidates, was a success.

Figure 25: Lorin beside a painting (Kosova means Kosovo in Albanian) on a wall in the Serbian village of Gracanica, located 10 kilometres away from the capital city of Pristina. The village of Gracanica became a Serbian enclave after the war. Photo courtesy of Lorin Lopetinsky.

Poisonous to drink! These were the words uttered by many peacekeepers when they talked about the quality of the tap water in Kosovo. Water analysis studies conducted in 2001 by the United Nations Environment Program (UNEP) showed that the water in Kosovo and Bosnia contained higher levels of natural uranium compared to that of other European countries.[111] These higher levels of uranium were believed to have some type of correlation with the usage of ammunition containing depleted uranium in the area.[112]

In the end, even though the study concluded that the higher level of natural uranium found in tap water was deemed non-hazardous to humans, the sole mention of "tap water" was, at the time of Lorin's mission, enough to discourage the bravest of the peacekeepers from drinking it. Luckily, bottled water was readily available and quite affordable in Kosovo: approximately $0.50 USD for a week's supply.

Conversely, eating out in Kosovo was a "supreme culinary experience", and quite safe. Both Serb and Albanian restaurants served meals many consider to be gourmet food. There were choices for all tastes. Influenced by centuries of Austrian and Austro-Hungarian rules, Serbian cuisine was exquisite. Whether it was coleslaw, pickled tomatoes, pork, or other meats and vegetables cooked to different flavours, Lorin found Serbian dishes to be delicious. Serbian desserts, like cherry pie and other sweets, were all titillating to the palate.

While the Albanian Muslims stayed away from pork, their cuisine was just as mouth-watering. Influenced by Italian, Turkish, and ancient Greek cuisine, the Kosovar Albanian menu was characterized by the use of various Mediterranean herbs, including oregano, mint, basil, black pepper, and rosemary. Olive oil and butter were also frequently used. Two of Lorin's favourite Albanian dishes were chicken with walnuts, or its variant, veal with walnuts. These were slow-cooked meat dishes in a walnut sauce…Yummy!

In Kosovo, Lorin and a colleague took over the living quarters of a departing UN officer in the village of Badovac. The village was part of a Serbian zone enclave that lay some 15 km away from Pristina.

Living outside the capital had its pros and cons. On the positive, the prices of rental units were much more affordable. For example, in Badovac, Lorin and his colleague rented a whole house for a few hundred dollars. This was half the price that someone in Pristina would pay for a similar size apartment.

On the negative side, living on the outskirts, and for that matter, in a Serbian zone enclave, meant that water shortages and electrical blackouts were frequent. On some days, Lorin would be lucky to have five minutes' worth of uninterrupted electricity. This was barely enough time for him to rush and have a hot shower.

With the landlord, his wife, and three sons living downstairs in a basement suite, one might think that Lorin's accommodation deal would have many restrictions to conform with. Well, maybe not! Other than the common courtesy for him and his colleague to make as little noise as possible late at night, Lorin and his roommate had a great arrangement.

For one, this was farmland. Pretty much all vegetables grown on the property were canned by the landlady. Chicken and pigs were also raised on the farm. These were slaughtered every now and then to provide meat to the family. Tenants would often be the invited guests to delicious Serbian homemade cooking. Who could refuse a meal served with garden vegetables and roasted meat from a pig killed the same morning? It could not get any fresher than that!

For a small additional fee, Lorin would have his landlady take care of his laundry and the ironing of all his uniforms. With the exception of the frequent electrical blackouts, and the fact that the old television set in his room would only work to catch pixelated, out-of-focus BBC News broadcasts, life in Badovac was a great adventure!

There were many moments during Lorin's mission that were memorable and unique in their own ways. Take, for example, the day Lorin drove through the town of Mitrovica, a Serbo-Albanian town in an area once rich with diamonds and oil reserves that the war had destroyed.

As Lorin and his CIVPOL colleagues were passing through on their way to the UN regional office, a soccer ball rebounded in front of their vehicle. Anticipating that a child might come running after the ball, Lorin came to an abrupt stop.

However, no one came out. Around them stood the lonely, desolate sight of bombed-out homes and buildings. Puzzled, Lorin parked his vehicle and everyone got out. As they walked towards the shell of a building where the soccer ball had appeared to have originated...a scene unfolded!

Hiding in a dark corner of the building were 8 to10 young Albanian children, all aged between five and eleven years old. They had been playing soccer inside the ruins of the building, but had been too afraid to run after the soccer ball when it inadvertently bounced out. What made this moment unique was to see all these children playing and having fun despite the sheer devastation and unwelcoming hazard of the environment they were in. It was with a grin on his face that Lorin brought back the soccer ball to the children so that they would keep playing. All waved goodbye as Lorin and the other officers drove away.

Figure 26: Children playing with a soccer ball inside the ruins of a bombed-out home in Mitrovica. Photo courtesy of Lorin Lopetinsky.

Of course, the novelty of a mission or living in a new country is likely to bring about many new opportunities. One such opportunity is to set aside savings. In most missions around the world, UN employees are entitled to receive what is known as a Mission Subsistence Allowance or MSA.

An MSA is a daily financial allowance paid by the UN to the staff member in order for them to cover living expenses in connection with their assignment. Depending on the location of the mission and conditions such as the cost of accommodation or food, in 2001 an allowance could range anywhere between $50.00 – 100.00 USD per day. Throughout his mission, Lorin saved up his funds for an anticipated return to school and the realization of a life-long dream: to earn a pilot's licence.

Being away from family and loved ones was the most challenging experience for many peacekeepers, including Lorin. He dearly missed his parents and brothers. At age 31, this was his first time traveling overseas.

Being in a country devastated by years of war, it was only normal that his family and relatives were constantly worried about his welfare. To reassure them, he relied on an intermittent Internet connection to get on MSN Chat every morning to share his latest adventures.

Then, one fateful morning, everything changed when a disaster took place half a world away. The date was September 11, 2001. It was early morning rush hour in New York, and news stations around the world were broadcasting word of the plane crashes that devastated the United States. Kosovo was no different, though news of the 9/11 attacks could only be partially heard from a snowy German satellite television screen that had been set up in the UN Police Commissioner's office.

With the Internet down, Lorin could only guess at what had taken place. All he knew was that whatever happened in New York was serious enough to justify the UN mission going into what is known as "Condition Black", the highest mission security level and a near lockdown.[113]

Up until then, the Kosovo UNMIK mission had been a relatively desirable one, meaning that European and American financial engagements were plentiful. The events of 9/11 changed all that. UN state builders in Kosovo were soon faced with some important constraints: a reduction of available human and financial resources.[114]

This was because the international community shifted its focus to other areas it deemed crucial to intervene, namely Iraq and Afghanistan.[115]

Figure 27: Lorin, second from the left, at a November 11th Remembrance Day commemoration at the UK military base in Kosovo. Lorin is joined by two Metropolitan Police Force officers and one Royal Ulster Constabulary member (now the Police Service of Northern Ireland). Photo courtesy of Lorin Lopetinsky.

Although the impact of 9/11 was felt in Kosovo in the sense of financial and manpower reduction of international aid, the war on terror was of minor importance to Kosovars; fundamentalist Islam members were not prominent amongst the Albanian Muslim population.[116]

In the end, Lorin's experiences in Kosovo taught him many life lessons. One of them was to be grateful and more appreciative of our privileged North American lifestyle. Second, Lorin came to understand the importance of setting goals for himself as a crucial step in accomplishing his objectives. Learning how to fly had been a childhood dream for him, which had seemed unattainable until he made that dream a goal. A year after he came back from his mission, he used his savings to enrol in a private pilot's licence course. He graduated less than twelve months later.

Perhaps an important lesson for us to learn from Lorin's mission is that it is never too late for someone to pursue their dreams. For Lorin, the Kosovo mission meant that he was able to work in a UN environment, travel, explore nearby countries, and, later, become a pilot. With effort, dedication, and goal setting, one dream led to another. Like Lorin, we can all accomplish our dreams and goals, provided that we are willing to discipline ourselves and make sacrifices.

5.

Independence Day: UNTAET (United Nations Transitional Authority for East Timor), 1999-2002

What if, for the first time in your life, you could freely cast a vote without fear of reprisal? A vote that could also rewrite history? For the people of East Timor, that time came in August 2001, after centuries of Portuguese colonialism and two military occupations. It was the birth of the new millennium's first nation.

Present in East Timor for the elections was RCMP Inspector Rick Taylor. He and a contingent of nineteen Canadian police peacekeepers travelled to East Timor to ensure a smooth electoral process, which would eventually clear the path for the independence of this island nation.

Rick's story is one that highlights the achievements of the mission, but also points out its weaknesses: a frustrating internal UN bureaucracy that, at times, was more of a barrier than an aid to the people it was meant to serve and protect. Rick's honest and candid account may leave some questioning the efficiency of the UN; but in the end, we cannot deny that what was accomplished in East Timor gave that nation the tools it needed to start building its future.

PART OF THE Indonesian archipelagos, East Timor occupies the eastern half of an island in the Timor Sea, just north of Australia. Two small islands, Atauro and Jaco, are also part of the country, as is a small enclave named Ambeno, located on the Indonesian half of the island.[117]

 The first European settlers to arrive to the region, the Portuguese, landed around 1515. Dutch traders were the next to arrive in

1556, settling on its western side. They went on to colonize the archipelago that was later to become Indonesia.[118] [119]

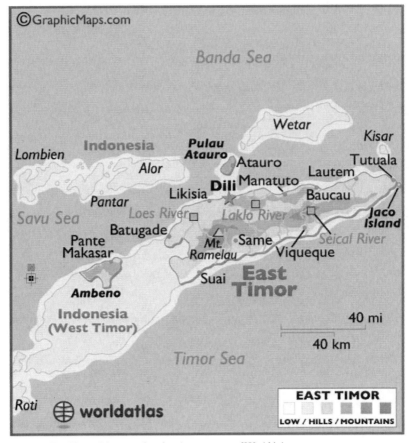

Figure 28: East Timor. Map reproduced with permission of WorldAtlas.com

In 1942, the Japanese Imperial Army invaded Timor. The civilian Timorese population helped the Australian and Dutch forces resist the invasion for a year. However, in 1943, the Allies evacuated the island. For assisting the Allied forces, the local population was severely punished by the Japanese invaders. Timorese villages were burnt, food supplies were seized, and many civilians were killed. It is believed that the Japanese occupation of both East and West

Timor resulted in the deaths of 40,000–70,000 inhabitants.[120]

After WWII, Portuguese Timor was handed back to Portugal, but the motherland continued to neglect her colony. Very little investment was made in infrastructure, education, or healthcare. In 1949, the Dutch recognized the western part of the island as Indonesia, while East Timor continued to be ruled by Portugal. The colony was officially declared an "Overseas Province" of the Portuguese Republic in 1955.[121]

In the mid-70s, Portugal's fascist regime collapsed. This opened the way to democracy, and impacted all of Portugal's overseas colonies.[122] For East Timor, this meant that its people would now have the freedom to form their own political parties.[123]

The Fretilin (the Revolutionary Front of an Independent East Timor) was one such party. In the summer of 1975, after a rival political party's failed coup d'état killed nearly 2,000 civilians, the Fretilin gained control of most of the territory of East Timor.[124] Later in November of that year, the Fretilin party declared the independence of East Timor from Portugal.

However, this newly gained freedom was short-lived. Ten days after independence was decreed, on December 7, 1975, Indonesian troops invaded East Timor. At the time, the western super-powers of the world sanctioned the invasion in fear of communists infiltrating the left-wing Fretilin party.[125] The area was then annexed as an integral part of Indonesia, and named Timor Timur (East Timor).[126]

It is believed that more than 60,000 Timorese lost their lives in the early years of the annexation, either by resisting the Indonesian occupation or as a result of famine and disease.[127]

Resentment of Indonesia grew stronger among a population who never accepted the annexation and were determined to keep their culture and national identity.[128] In October 1991, a confrontation ensued between the Indonesian Army and a group of independence activists. This resulted in a young East Timorese student being killed.[129]

The killing of the student angered the East Timorese who, in November 1991, organized a peaceful march in the cemetery where a memorial service for the young student was to be held. The unarmed protesters carried protest banners, East Timorese flags, and chanted East Timorese slogans in defiance of the Indonesian Army.

What ensued next made international news. The Indonesian Army, claiming the protesters had become violent, opened fire on the crowd, killing 250 East Timorese men, women and children.[130]

In 1998, the Indonesian president Suharto's government was shaken by a severe economic crisis, which led to widespread demands for political changes. President Suharto was eventually forced to resign, and was replaced by his vice-president, Dr. Habibie.[131]

By late 1998, responding to mounting international pressure, the Indonesian government of Dr. Habibie authorized a referendum to be held in order to determine the future of East Timor.[132] This prompted talks between Indonesia and Portugal; successful agreements were made in May 1999.[133]

The two Governments then entrusted the United Nations with organizing and conducting a referendum in order to ascertain whether the East Timorese people would accept or reject a special autonomy for East Timor within the unitary Republic of Indonesia.[134]

Even though there was no opposition to Habibie's proposal when it was introduced to the Indonesian cabinet, it did not mean that all were in favour. On the contrary: antagonism was especially high within the Indonesian Armed Forces, who, for right or for wrong, feared that a referendum would bring up the legality of the 1975 Indonesian take-over of East Timor. Worse yet, it believed a referendum would create a dangerous precedent for other Indonesian territories, like Aceh and West Papua, to seek independence.[135]

The Indonesian Armed Forces was still the most powerful political institution in the country. It devised a strategy whereby it would ensure that if a popular consultation was to take place in East Timor, it would produce an outcome favourable to integration to Indonesia.[136]

How? By promoting East Timorese Militia groups that favoured integration. Slowly but surely, these began a campaign of intimidation and violence that started well before the referendum, but which reached its apogee once the results of the popular consultation were known.[137] All told, it is estimated that Indonesia's administration of East Timor cost approximately 200,000 East Timorese lives, nearly one-third of the entire population.[138]

United Nations involvement in East Timor dates back to 1960, when its General Assembly placed the country on its list of Non-Self-Governing Territories.[139] When Indonesia invaded East Timor in 1975, the United Nations strongly objected and called for Indonesia's unconditional withdrawal.[140] Unfortunately, lacking political support from a number of its own Security Council member states, the United Nations was powerless in challenging the Indonesian take-over.[141]

On June 11, 1999, in order to carry out the referendum, the United Nations Security Council authorized the establishment of a United Nations Mission in East Timor, named UNAMET. UNAMET, with a staff of approximately 241 unarmed international observers, plus local volunteers, would oversee a transition period pending the decision of the referendum.[142]

On the day of the referendum, August 30, 1999, some 98% of East Timor registered voters (roughly 438,968 people) went to the polls. It soon became clear that the majority of voters wanted independence.

On September 4, 1999, the results of the referendum were announced: 78.5 % of East Timorese rejected the proposed autonomy package offered by Indonesia, and supported a transition towards complete independence.[143]

Enraged by the results of the referendum, pro-Indonesia integration militia gangs responded by brutally killing over a thousand people. Some victims were shot, others decapitated, disembowelled, or even hacked to death with machetes.[144]

The instant violence forced hundreds of thousands to flee and resettle in refugee camps in West Timor and other nearby islands.[145] As arsons, lootings, and shootings continued across the country, most of the unarmed United Nations personnel were forced to evacuate.[146]

In light of the sheer violence, and in an effort to prevent a full-scale genocide like the one in Rwanda in 1994, the UN Security Council authorized a multinational force: the International Force for East Timor (INTERFET). Under the unified command structure of a member state, Australia, INTERFET arrived in East Timor on September 20, 1999 as a non-UN Force. Their goal was twofold: to restore peace and security, and to protect and support UNAMET.[147] Despite INTERFET's relatively quick intervention, an estimated 70% of East Timor's infrastructure was burnt or destroyed.[148]

Inspector Rick Taylor's story with East Timor started in the fall of 2000. He was working as a non-commissioned officer in the city of Red Deer, Alberta, when a promotional opportunity came along. The UN was seeking a skilled leader with a strong background in serious crimes for the position of Canadian Contingent Commander to the United Nations mission in Sierra Leone.

Having years of major crime investigations, and being a qualified officer candidate (meaning he had passed all the promotional requirements to become a commissioned officer), Rick applied for the position. It was not long before he learned that he had been selected.

Scheduled to be deployed in January 2001, Rick's excitement was soon dulled when the RCMP Peacekeeping Branch cancelled the mission deployment due to continuous instability in the region.

The dream of this pioneer and explorer would be temporarily shattered. However, as fate would have it, Rick was re-approached by the RCMP Peacekeeping Branch a few months later, this time with an offer to travel to East Timor to serve as a replacement for the current Contingent Commander and United Nations Chief of National Investigations.

Wanting to add a UN mission to his Curriculum Vitae, Rick accepted the offer. On May 13, 2001, Rick bid farewell to his wife and two teenage sons and left for the first leg of a voyage that would take him to the other side of the world.

First stop: Ottawa, Ontario. Rick landed in Canada's capital, home of the RCMP's National Headquarters. There, he would receive his mandatory 10-day pre-deployment training.

In class, Rick was exposed to the general history of East Timor, its political climate, the 1999 Declaration of Independence, and the chaos that followed it. Perhaps the most fascinating part of the training was the life stories of some of the invited guests, who had witnessed and survived the 1999 massacre that followed the United Nations referendum.

For the remainder of the training, Rick reviewed RCMP internal policies, received his equipment and uniform, and got to know the nineteen other contingent members that would accompany him on the mission. These were police officers from the RCMP, the Ontario Provincial Police, and the Halifax Regional Police.

After Ottawa, Rick was on his way to East Timor. The plan was for him to arrive at post and shadow the departing Canadian Contingent Commander for a week. That way, Rick could be exposed to his duties as Canadian Contingent Commander and as the mission's Chief of National Investigations.

Getting to East Timor from Ottawa, Canada was a long journey—one that lasted almost two days. Rick's itinerary took him from Ottawa to Toronto, then to Los Angeles, and finally to Sidney, Australia, where he got a few hours' rest after nearly 24 hours in the air.

At daybreak, he flew to Darwin, the smallest and most northerly of Australia's capital cities. There, the United Nations had a base camp where peacekeepers on their way to East Timor received basic information on the mission, their UN Identification Card, and a taste of the extreme heat that awaited them on the island. The temperature in Darwin was nearly 40 degrees Celsius when Rick landed—a big difference from the cool 7 degrees Celsius he had left behind in Ottawa.

Tired and jetlagged from the long trip, Rick managed to get a few hours' sleep before embarking on a United Nations C-130 Hercules plane. The Hercules took him and other international peacekeepers over the Timor Sea directly to Dili, the capital of East Timor.

Upon landing in the capital after a one and a half-hour flight, Rick was greeted at the airport by the current Canadian Contingent Commander and other colleagues. From there, Rick was taken to UN Headquarters, where he was introduced to the UN Police Commissioner.

Figure 29: A United Nations Lockheed C-130 Hercules plane, similar to the one that transported Rick from Darwin, Australia to Dili, East Timor. Photo courtesy of Andrew J. Muller at www.airliners.net

Although Rick had been prepared to take over the functions of the Canadian Contingent Commander and that of Chief of National Investigations, he soon learned that the Police Commissioner had other plans in mind for him.

First off, Rick would not be assigned as Chief of National Investigations. This was a surprise, as he had been selected for that specific duty by the RCMP, with the support of the United Nations Department of Peacekeeping Operations in New York.

Second, despite his extensive background in serious crime investigations, he was now being relegated to the duty of District Commander in a remote, malaria-infested part of the island, several hours away by either helicopter or road.

Although Rick had always been aware that once in-theatre his expertise might be used to other ends, the unilateral decision taken by the Police Commissioner was questionable, at best! The new assignment neither called for Rick's realm of expertise in serious crime nor acknowledged that his other duty, that of Canadian Contingent Commander, required him to be centralized in Dili.

Being in a remote area with limited communications did not suit his role, and made no sense. The Police Commissioner's decision had the appearance of having everything to do with the strained relationship that was apparent between himself and the outgoing Canadian Contingent Commander, with Rick being the unwitting "beneficiary".

Figure 30: Inspector Rick Taylor outside UN Headquarters in Dili, East Timor. Photo courtesy of Rick Taylor.

It was also clear that the Police Commissioner had another candidate in mind for the job: a senior police officer from his own country. Rick stood his ground, asserting to the Police Commissioner that he would be informing his superiors in Canada of this development, who in turn would likely be engaging the UN department in New York.

Recognizing this as an opportunity to redefine the relationship with the Police Commissioner, Rick took a diplomatic route in convincing the Commissioner that, as the Canadian Contingent Commander, it was imperative that Rick be posted in Dili. From there, he could direct his full energy into supporting the Commissioner's Leadership Team, while ensuring a strong contribution to the mission from the Canadian Contingent.

The approach worked! Seeing an opportunity to improve relations and avoid a showdown with Canada, the Police Commissioner relented and assigned Rick to the newly created position of "Border Liaison Officer" at CIVPOL HQ in Dili.[149]

That day, Rick parted company with the Police Commissioner on good terms. Over the course of the next few months, he took every opportunity to prove to the Police Commissioner that he had made the right choice.

But Rick's colourful encounter with the Police Commissioner would only be a presage of what was yet to come. Rick's no-nonsense, regimented, and structured approach to operational policing soon made him identify many internal issues that negatively affected the delivery of services to the people of East Timor. The good news was that, for the people of the area, life was about to change for the better.

Rick's second day would signal the beginning of his 4-day induction training. The induction training focused on mission administrative requirements, mission safety, and further classes on local history, conflicts, and customs. Sessions about the mission structure and services were also provided.

Although some of the material presented had already been discussed during Rick's pre-deployment training in Canada, this in-the-field training turned out to be very informative. Rick later commented that the induction at the mission had been well presented, and provided him and the other arriving peacekeepers with the information they needed to complete a successful mission.

As briefly mentioned earlier, Rick's duties in East Timor were two-fold: Contingent Commander for the Canadian deployment, and UNTAET's Border Liaison officer. This latter duty meant that Rick liaised between the UN Civilian Police Headquarters in Dili and the Border Service Agency of the Timorese government.[150]

At the time of Rick's mission, the Border Service Agency was made up of Immigration, Passport, and Border Services agents from many countries, including Canada. Rick, as the conduit of information between the two agencies, was mainly concerned with ensuring that border integrity laws were not breached.

In the early days of Rick's appointment, many of the issues he had to deal with concerned UN peacekeepers who were themselves in contravention of Immigration and Passport policies. For example, peacekeepers who had spent their time off abroad and were coming back to the mission with over $5,000.00 USD had to declare it. Otherwise, they would be in violation of East Timor border regulations. A quota on the importation of cigarettes, liquor, coffee, and other items was also imposed.[151]

Therefore, depending on the seriousness of the breach of a regulation, a civilian police officer could receive a mere reprimand or could ultimately be expelled from the mission and repatriated to his/her home country.

At the time Rick arrived at the mission, approximately 41 countries were contributing to the UN effort. With a rough total of 7,700 military and civilian police officers combined, who were supported by nearly 2,500 international civilians and local staff, the mission was one of the world's largest of the time.[152]

One of Rick's main grievances with his duty was the bureaucracy surrounding internal UN administrative procedures. These were truly inefficient, and seemed to have only one purpose: to frustrate! Even UNAMIR (Rwanda) Force Commander Lieutenant-General Romeo Dallaire referred to this frustrating type of "UN policy" in his best-selling book *Shake Hands with the Devil: The Failure of Humanity in Rwanda*.[153]

These bureaucratic regulations ranged from the extreme to the mundane. One day, Rick needed paper in order to print several copies for a large report he had produced for the Police

Commissioner. Off he went to the logistics office, where the supplies were kept. In a room inside a protective cage stood a skinny UN police officer, who was in charge of monitoring the supplies.

Rick greeted the officer, and informed him that he needed printing paper for a report. Through the bars, Rick could see stacks and stacks of the necessary paper. As Rick's photocopy machine was almost empty, Rick thought one bundle of 500 sheets would be sufficient for him to print all his reports, and still leave paper in the printer for other future tasks.

Politely, Rick asked to take a bundle. The officer looked at the stack of paper behind him and asked in broken English how many sheets Rick required: only then would he receive that exact amount of paper.

Puzzled and slightly annoyed at such a restrictive cap, Rick looked over the officer's shoulders and pointed to approximately 200 sheets on top of an opened bundle. The officer once again shook his head, and said the maximum was 25.

Feeling his blood pressure rise quickly, Rick managed to calmly explain that he needed to print an important report for the Police Commissioner, and for that reason, he needed at least one hundred sheets and probably more. The officer shrugged his shoulders and told Rick that he could come back for several trips, but could not have more than 25 now.

Frankly, this was not the answer Rick was hoping for. Leaning forward, and resting both his cheekbones in between the cage's bars, Rick pointed to a bundle of paper and politely said that he needed that bundle of paper—or he was going to have to come through that cage.

Seeing Rick's imposing stature as compared to his own, and firmly believing that Rick would probably manage to get through the bars, the officer grinned and cordially obliged.

Rick and the skinny UN officer eventually became good friends. Thankfully, similar rules eventually slacked off within the mission, to allow for some good reasoning to take over. This was in part due to Rick's insistence, and to the arrival of a new Police Commissioner.

As the Canadian Contingent Commander, Rick's duties required him to ensure the welfare of his Canadian troops, and to prepare a monthly Situational Report on the mission and its challenges. Such reports contained information that was obtained from a variety of sources, including other Canadian contingent members. The Canadians were not the only ones to send Situational Reports back to their home countries: most of the other contingent commanders were doing the same.

For example, early in his mission, Rick recalled an occasion where some senior police officers were criticizing the Police Commissioner's leadership skills in their reports to their superiors back in their home countries. This in turn filtered back to the Department of Peacekeeping Operations in New York. Having been informed by the Department of the general discontent of his troops with his leadership, the Police Commissioner made some efforts to adapt his style to better cater to his international subordinates.

Working for the UN, one might think that there was little to no injustice within a mission. On the contrary: although the UN put forward its best effort to minimize harassment, sexual harassment, and other injustices within a mission, with so many different cultures working together, conflicts were, at times, unavoidable. Therefore, part of the Contingent Commander's role was to ensure his troops were treated equitably.

Figure 31: Visit to a neighbouring district in July 2001. From left to right: Timorese interpreter, Thai Army soldier, L/Col. Nick Keam from the Royal Australian Army, Rick Taylor, and RCMP Sgt. Pit Cyr. Photo courtesy of Rick Taylor.

For instance, peacekeepers often worked long hours, for stretches of days (sometimes up to a month), before time off is required. If there is ever a question of fairness in shifting these stretches, it is the Contingent Commander's duty to ensure that all peacekeepers are being treated equally.

Such was the duty of Rick as Canadian troop commander. On a few occasions, he did have to engage in order to bring back some balance in situations that were unfavourable to his subordinates. Thankfully, this didn't happen often. Despite some initial hiccups, Rick's forthrightness, pleasant demeanour, and extensive police experience garnered him respect within the mission.

Being posted in the capital had huge perks. One of those advantages was that reliable and clean restaurants were available throughout the city. This was unlike the outskirts, in the jungle, where living conditions for peacekeepers could be quite austere (malaria-infested areas, no electricity, marginal living quarters, cooking over fires, etc.). As for water, even though Rick's compound had clean water, he always made a point of only drinking bottled water, which was readily available everywhere.

Living conditions in Dili were very decent, and as a matter of fact, Rick was rather well taken care of. Shortly after his arrival at the mission, Rick came across an Australian Non-Governmental Organization (NGO) that owned a housing compound made of modified trailer units. Every unit was equipped with air-conditioning, clean running water, electricity, and in all, was considered quite comfortable. As an added bonus, the Australian NGO had hired maids to help with the cleaning of the units and other household tasks, like washing and ironing the tenant's clothing.

No need to say that Rick was only too happy when an opportunity arose for him to rent one of the units for the duration of his stay.[154]

Figure 32: Exterior and interior photos of a modified trailer unit similar to the one rented to Rick during his mission. Photo courtesy of Ben Maure.

Travelling to the different UN sub-offices around the country in old Russian MI-8 UN helicopters was always an adventure that did not inspire much confidence for Rick. It was not that the MI-8 was unreliable. Quite the opposite: the helicopter had been an impressive feat of Russian engineering since its introduction in 1961. With good visibility in the cabin, a versatile airframe, twin-engine gas turbines, a maximum payload of 4,000 kg, and a maximum cruising speed of 250 km/h, the helicopter was a workhorse. However, poor visibility, mountainous terrain, and a plethora of other circumstances, including, at times, the questionable state of sobriety of certain pilots, made for an interesting ride!

Rick recalls a particular incident early one morning where he and a few colleagues had to visit a UN sub-office away from town. That day, he had left his compound early and made his way to the airport, proudly wearing an impeccable uniform.

On the field was an older Russian MI-8 helicopter being readied for take-off. What caught Rick's attention when he entered the passenger cabin was the demeanour of one of the pilots, who looked like a "seasoned drinker". The pilot wore a soiled uniform, had unkempt hair, was unshaven, and appeared to have a flushed face. Although Rick did not smell any liquor coming from the man, his unprofessional appearance did nothing to inspire confidence.

Rick buckled his seatbelt and hoped for the best. The cabin shook and rattled in a loud roar as the helicopter took off and gained altitude. Although not impressed at the sight of the pilot, the air travel back and forth to the sub-office proved relatively uneventful.

Although there were no revealing signs of actual impairments, Rick's observation nonetheless brought an interesting polemic: that of the UN ascertaining whether or not it has the ability, especially in remote locations, to police itself and ensure officer sobriety. Pilots can be especially concerning, for many of them are normally employees of companies that have a service contract with the UN. Though the UN has staff (former pilots) who handle air movement and aviation safety, they may not be located at every mission around the world.

In-theatre, security officers may be relied upon to intervene if an issue with a suspected intoxicated pilot were to surface. But even with the best rules and regulations in place to ensure passenger safety, breaches can happen.

In the UN, air safety rules are governed by the country or state under which an Air Operation Certificate (AOC) for the contractor is issued. The rule goes even further, requiring that the AOC comply with a policy stipulating that no crew member shall undertake a flight within 12 hours of having consumed any alcoholic beverage or while having a blood-alcohol level in excess of 0.02 percent.[155] To the author's knowledge, there has not been a UN aviation crash that has been caused by one of its pilots being intoxicated by alcohol.

It comes as no surprise that many perils and dangers on the mission were not necessarily related to work. According to Rick, even spending a day off at the beach could become deadly if one was not aware of their surroundings.

Unlike Hawaii, where one can have a stroll on the beach and enjoy the sun or sheer beauty of the scenery, some of East Timor's beaches harboured a nasty guest: the saltwater crocodile. This ferocious animal, the largest of all living reptiles, reaches lengths of 18 feet, and can weigh nearly 2,000 pounds. They particularly enjoy silt, muddy waters near river mouths, and certain sandy beaches. Bathers who were not careful could end up being the animal's meal of the day. Fortunately, no peacekeeper was injured by a crocodile during Rick's mission, thanks to many warning signs that were put up near beaches.

Mosquito-borne illnesses such as malaria or dengue fever were a constant concern on the island. A long term anti-malarial drug was available to peacekeepers, but it would not prevent one from getting the disease. Adverse effects caused by prolonged use of anti-malarial medication could also be hard on the body, causing blurred vision, dizziness, and other unwanted effects.[156] Having mosquito repellent and sleeping under a net treated with repellent helped in dealing with this scourge.

As for dengue fever, the best treatment is prevention. Unlike malaria, which is seldom a threat in large cities, the mosquito that carries dengue fever will also be found in urban areas. To prevent being bitten, officers had to use plenty of insect repellent and leave as little exposed skin as possible. Steps were taken so that any sources of standing water (buckets, vases, etc.) where the mosquito could breed would be eliminated.[157]

Prior to the August 2001 parliamentary elections, Rick was seconded to yet another duty, this one as Chief of Strategic Planning. This third assignment placed Rick in charge of a team of a dozen individuals, whose duties were to support the country's first upcoming elections. In his role, Rick worked closely with the Australian military, with whom he set up a Joint National Operations Centre. District Operation Centres were also created, which would go "live" during the forthcoming elections.

Rick's duties would require him to travel to the various districts, attend security briefings, and "coach" the regions on: how to get ready for the election process; how to manage the election process; and how to contact the UN Joint National Operations Centre in Dili, should any incident take place on Election Day.

For example, if there were election violence in a district, then the region needed to be able to report it immediately, so that police or military resources could be deployed in a flash to the area.

The first parliamentary election was set on August 30, 2001, two years after the militia violence that ravaged the country. Even though the militia responsible for the 1999 massacre had been disarmed, and some of its leaders imprisoned for crimes against humanity, remnants of the groups were still roaming the country.

As Election Day drew closer, Rick could not help but think about all the violence that had marked the last vote. With his troops ready and backed up by more than 8,000 armed peacekeepers, Rick could only hope that the elections would take place without violence.

On August 30, 2001, 93% of eligible voters turned out to the polls. That day, Rick had started early, attending the Joint National Operations Centre for a security debriefing on the day's activities. One of his tasks was to monitor incoming security reports from the various districts. Other than logistical challenges at some of the voting stations (such as spoiled ballots and confirming voter eligibility), all went relatively smoothly.

Another task that Rick performed was foot and vehicle patrols in Dili at various times throughout the day. Rick remembers that there was a sense of excitement and euphoria in the streets among the Timorese people. Although he admitted that he felt somewhat nervous at the thought of the previous election's violence, this one, thankfully, turned out to be uneventful. Rick would later share that his experience on that day was an amazing and inspiring one, something he was proud to be a part of.

Results of a victory for the "Revolutionary Front for an Independent East Timor" (the modern Fretilin party) were later announced; the party had won 55 of the 88 seats. Although humble about his involvement, Rick's role was an important contributing factor in ensuring safe and successful elections.

Rick's role as Chief of Strategic Planning continued after the elections. This time, his duties would focus on ensuring the support and training of a new police force, the National Police of East Timor.

Rick's assignment would be pivotal in helping build the future nation. He would have oversight of firearms training, general police investigation techniques, and the formation of specialized police units, such as Border Patrol, Family Violence, and Professional Standards. He would also have to ensure that these units would be ready in time for the country's Independence Day, scheduled for May 20, 2002. [158]

Like many missions discussed in this book, UNTAET had its difficulties with certain nations not sending their best officers. To officers like Rick and others who had been selected based on competence and merits, having to work with those few incompetent, corrupt, or unethical officers was something truly frustrating.

A number of officers coming from emerging countries aspire to be sent on UN missions due to the pay and benefits.[159] Some officers return home after a mission with more money than they would have earned in a lifetime in their home countries. Rick heard many anecdotal stories of officers from some nations actually "paying a kickback" to get selected for the mission, although he never found anyone willing to corroborate the stories.

In one instance, Rick recalled the conduct of a particular officer in his unit, whose behaviour was both unacceptable and disgraceful. By the time Rick had been placed in charge of the officer, the latter had already spent close to two years in East Timor.

That officer's contribution to the mission was to prey on young Timorese girls, whom he reportedly paid to have sex with him. Why the activities of this individual were not discovered and dealt with earlier remained a puzzle. While off-duty, and on occasion while on-duty, the officer would wear ethnic garments that made him look like royalty in order to attract young women. Young and impoverished Timorese women were drawn by the officer's apparent high status. Although there was no hard evidence that he had sex with minors, the girls he had been seen with looked very young to Rick and other dismayed peacekeepers.

Rick reported the officer's unacceptable conduct to his superiors. Despite protests and accusations of harassment levelled back at Rick, he was eventually successful in having the officer held accountable for his behaviour and transferred to another unit.

Sadly, as I noted previously, efforts to promptly remove this type of individual from missions were not always met with strong support. Often, the officer's own police commanders supported the behaviour, which they viewed as an acceptable norm by their own country's standard. When denounced or targeted by other peacekeepers, they, in turn, would often complain to mission management that their officers were being targeted by racially motivated co-workers.

Unless a crime was such that it could be proven immediately, an internal investigation needed to be conducted. In many instances, it would take several months to amass the necessary evidence of wrongdoing. By that time, many culprits had completed their tour of duty, or were near the end of it. Still today, the issue of peacekeepers' accountability, ethics, and misconduct throughout UN missions around the world remains a hot topic.

For example, a study was published in 2012, sponsored by the Government Accountability Project (GAP): a non-profit organization that promotes corporate and government accountability. It identified serious issues within the United Nations system, whereby peacekeepers' misconduct often went unpunished.[160] The report underlined the many difficulties encountered to prosecute culprits, citing cases of: seeking sexual favours from applicants; sexual exploitation of civilians; storing pornography on UN computers; threats to kill a supervisor; beating a spouse who was also a UN volunteer; theft and sale of UN computers, cameras, radios, and other UN properties; and using forged UN airline vouchers for unauthorized persons and companies.

In a two-year period, the report identified a whopping 68% complaint dismissal rate; this even after a new reform process was implemented.[161] The reform was meant to bring a fair balance into the evidence gathering process against UN peacekeepers; therefore, the higher evidential and procedural standards the reform brought meant that many complaints could not be supported.[162]

In itself, a higher standard of proof is not a bad thing; it eliminates the many frivolous and unwarranted complaints the UN continuously receives against its peacekeepers. However, in my opinion as a former peacekeeper, accountability for UN workers should be at the highest standard, especially in cases where the evidence supports misconduct or criminality.

For the great majority of devoted and committed peacekeepers, it is very distressful to observe that a handful of unethical officers or civilians have the potential to tarnish the reputation of an entire UN contingent with their inappropriate behaviours.

On a more positive note, the UN is aware of the issue, and is continuously seeking to improve its system and strengthen managerial accountability. Cases of individuals whose self-conduct is shameful to the organization are taken seriously. Such persons are nowadays repatriated much faster than before. In some cases, depending on the circumstances, an individual might even be prosecuted in their own country for crimes or unethical behaviour committed abroad on a UN mission.

A case in point was demonstrated by Pakistan, when, in March 2012, three of its police peacekeepers working in Haiti under the MINUSTAH mission were found guilty of sexual exploitation of a 14-year-old Haitian male.[163] Following the accusations, the three officers were court-martialed by a Pakistani military tribunal, found guilty, repatriated to Pakistan, disgracefully dismissed from the police, and jailed.[164]

Figure 33: Inspector Rick Taylor receiving his UNTAET Medal in October 2001. Photo courtesy of R. Taylor.

Perhaps one of the most difficult experiences Rick faced during his Timorese tour of duty was that of being away from his family—and Rick was not alone in finding that difficult!

At the time of his mission, Rick had two growing teenage boys. The task of raising the children and taking care of the household had suddenly fallen to his wife. While Rick was missing his family, other members of his team were trying to cope with their own family dramas at home. At least one Canadian contingent member, who was experiencing problems at home, later confessed that he had actually left for the mission without the full support of his spouse. Over time, the distance became an impediment, and the relationship worsened. In other missions that I was aware of, distance and lack of communication led some peacekeepers to separation and divorce.

In order to minimize the risk of a crisis at home while on a mission, it is crucial that family members support the decision for the peacekeeper to go on a mission. Not having familial support will most likely lead to some type of conflict while abroad.

While leaving for a mission is exciting, and can enlarge someone's horizons, it will not necessarily be the same for the spouse that remains behind. That spouse may have preferred to have the partner around to help when they need it, even if it were only for moral support. Leaving family behind may bring resentment from the loved one.

One peacekeeper once shared with me the difficulties his family had experienced while he was abroad: he had left Canada at the end of fall to arrive in a warm-weather country. Within a few months, full winter had settled in Canada, and with it, heavy colds and snowstorms. The spouse became the focal point of the family, having to deal with all emergencies, including shovelling heavy snow, dealing with a car that would not start due to extreme cold, taking a sick child to the hospital, and so forth. Even if the spouse had initially been supportive of the mission, she could not help but feel some resentment towards her far-away husband.

All the peacekeeper could do was to reassure his wife over the phone that he would soon be home to help her. I learned of another peacekeeper who, after an absence of nearly a year, had difficulty in fully reconnecting with his spouse and children. Even his faithful dog ignored him for some time.

However, do not be discouraged by some of the above tales! All of us who have been abroad have worried at one time or another about a spouse or family member at home. The good news, if I dare say, is that nowadays, with the Internet and software applications like Skype or FaceTime, communication between peacekeepers and their families is much easier.

According to author of *The Long Distance Romance Guide: Stay Close Whenever Apart*, Dr. Leslie Karsner, being apart from a loved one can even be healthy for a couple. For one, spending time away from a loved one can bring a greater appreciation for one another. It can also give someone the "space" the individual needs.[165]

However, there is no common recipe that can ensure a healthy relationship at home while a spouse or partner is away on a mission—that is up to the individual couple.

Despite some initial hiccups, the mission in East Timor helped Rick grow into a better person and police officer. Who could deny that? Within a few years after the completion of his tour of duty, Rick received two more promotions, and reached the coveted rank of Chief Superintendent.

In 2012, Rick retired from the RCMP and went on to a second career as the Executive Director (Chief Sheriff) of the Alberta Sheriffs and Security Operations Branch. Prestigious awards Rick received during his police career included: being appointed a Member of the Order of Merit of the Police Forces (MOM), in recognition for his service to the communities in Canada; and the

Queen's Golden and Diamond Jubilee medals, given to honour his career contributions to Canada.

In 2015, Rick completely retired from his laudable public safety career, and now operates a small security consulting firm in Alberta.

Rick's advice to anyone wishing to join a UN mission: do it for all the right reasons! Candidates must possess a spirit of adventure, have an inner desire to contribute to a better world, and be inspired to grow and develop as a person. Be flexible, open-minded, and willing to work both collaboratively and respectfully within an international team. For RCMP officers, adhering to the Core Values of the RCMP will help overcome many of the frustrations one may encounter on a mission.[166] They did for him.

6.

Blood Diamonds No More: Special Court for Sierra Leone, 2002-2013

It is July 2002, and a ceasefire agreement has been in place in Sierra Leone for the past three years. However, certain leaders of the Revolutionary United Front (RUF) have yet to comply. Motivated by this disregard for the ceasefire and continuous crimes against humanity, the Sierra Leone Government has obtained the assistance of the United Nations to set up a war crimes tribunal: the Special Court for Sierra Leone.

Its mandate is to prosecute those who bear the greatest responsibility for serious crimes against humanity, under both international and Sierra Leonean law. Although it is not directly overseen by the United Nations, the Special Court for Sierra Leone is funded by some of the most influential of the UN's member states, including Canada.

Four years later, in 2006, RCMP Corporal Kaare R. (Chuck) Kolot is set to land in Freetown, Sierra Leone. His mission, and that of his international colleagues, is to continue to gather evidence against erstwhile members of RUF and former Liberia President, Charles Taylor.

Chuck's mission in Sierra Leone will lead to an amazing feat for human rights crusaders: the convictions and sentencing of some of the new millennium's cruellest and most barbaric individuals.

SIERRA LEONE IS located in Western Africa; it borders the North Atlantic Ocean, between Guinea and Liberia. During the colonial period, this territory was part of British West Africa.[167]

In the 1780s, as the number of freed slaves grew in London, England, questions arose as to where they should best live. Granville Sharp, a British abolitionist and philanthropist of the time, suggested they should settle in the continent from which they or their ancestors had come.[168]

Figure 34: Sierra Leone. Map reproduced with permission of WorldAtlas.com

Twenty miles of hilly coast was secured with the agreement from the chief of a local indigenous tribe. The area, part of the north-western coast of what is known today as Sierra Leone, facilitated the integration of the freed slaves to their new home.

The first ship of freed slaves arrived from London in 1787.[169] Other ships arrived from Nova Scotia, Canada, in 1792, and later from Jamaica in 1800.

In 1807, the British government abolished the slave trade, and took responsibility for Sierra Leone (known then as Freetown colony) a year after. The area was used as a base in the campaign against slaving ships.[170]

From that point on, and over the next half-century, naval actions against other nations still trading slaves resulted in over 50,000 "recaptured slaves" being brought and freed into Sierra Leone. Anglican and Methodist missionaries in Freetown were then tasked with bridging the linguistic and cultural gaps between the different groups of freed slaves brought together in this new environment. This was accomplished by providing a shared new culture, through the promotion of the English language and the Christian religion.[171]

On April 27, 1961, after more than 150 years of British colonial rule, Sierra Leone became an independent state within the Commonwealth. With the election of a new government in 1967, and after only a few years of functioning democracy, Sierra Leone declined in a long era of repressive rules, military coups, and corruption.[172]

In 1989, an invasion from the Ivory Coast started a vicious war in Liberia that soon spilled into Sierra Leone.[173] The invasion force was led by Liberian rebel Charles Taylor, and his Libyan-trained group called the National Patriotic Front of Liberia (NPFL).

Initially, Sierra Leone's Army was deployed to the border region to fight off the incursion. However, the Sierra Leone Army (SLA) came under attack not only by the NPFL, but also by a Sierra Leone rebel group called the Revolutionary United Front (RUF), led by a former corporal in the SLA named Foday Sankoh.[174]

The RUF, backed up by Charles Taylor's NPFL, would lead

Sierra Leone into a 10-year campaign of terror. Part of their strategy was the misappropriation and control of the nation's most significant source of wealth: the diamond mines.[175]

Although the complexity of the Sierra Leone civil war goes well beyond what is depicted above, the conflict is notorious for the violence it engendered against civilians. For more than a decade, the RUF and other groups of thugs roamed the country's districts, wielding machetes, raping women, and often killing or crudely amputating the hands, feet, ears, and genitals of civilians, including children.[176]

The RUF was also infamous for barbarously subjugating children and turning them into child soldiers, capable of murdering even their own parents.[177] To this end, the UN estimates that 10,000 children participated in the conflict, some as young as seven years old.[178]

In July 1999, a peace agreement, the Lome Peace Accord[179], was signed by the warring factions to end the civil war. The agreement also provided for the demobilization and disarmament of combatants, as well as for assistance in their re-integration into civil society.[180] Further, the accord contained clauses that allowed for RUF members to hold public office, and assured them amnesty from persecution for war crimes.[181]

However, from a United Nations standpoint, the granting of amnesty for genocides, crimes against humanity, and other war crimes was highly objectionable. This resulted in the UN Secretary-General instructing his envoy to Lome to sign the Peace Agreement with a caveat, which explicitly stated that, as far as the UN was concerned, the amnesty could not cover the crimes enumerated above.[182] However, this caveat was not enforced when the UN sent troops under their new mission, the United Nations Mission in Sierra Leone (UNAMSIL), in November 1999.[183]

Unfortunately, by May 2000, UN troops had come under

attack by rebels, who renounced the ceasefire and refused to lay down their weapons and end hostilities. The situation deteriorated further when the RUF abducted hundreds of peacekeepers.[184]

Several hundred British paratroopers were sent to Freetown to help evacuate British citizens and assist in securing the airport. Given the blatant breach of the ceasefire, the international community put pressure on the rebels to obey the ceasefire and the imposed sanctions against RUF leaders.[185] By early 2002, UNAMSIL had disarmed and demobilized more than 75,000 fighters, including child soldiers, thus officially ending the war.[186] In July 2002, motivated by the disregard for the ceasefire and continued crimes against humanity by certain RUF leaders, the Special Court for Sierra Leone was established.[187] The Court was funded by voluntary contributions from certain member states, such as Great Britain, the United States, and Canada. As a result, the Court was not an organ of the UN, unlike the Court in Rwanda or in The Hague.

The Special Court of Sierra Leone's objectives were to try those who bore the greatest responsibility for serious violations of international humanitarian and Sierra Leonean laws during the conflict.[188] The war crime trials started in 2004, and were essentially divided into four prosecution lines. These were:

- The RUF Trials
- The AFRC (Armed Forces Revolutionary Council) Trials. This is the armed force that overthrew the government in 1997
- The Civil Defence Force (CDF), an ethnic militia that fought the RUF
- The trial of Charles Taylor, which was later moved to The Hague

As part of the Canadian contribution to the Special Court for Sierra Leone, six plainclothes Canadian police investigators were sent on a rotational basis to assist in gathering evidence of war crimes and crimes against humanity against the dozen people who were indicted.

As a note, there were another four Canadian police officers working for this mission, although their status was different: they were either retired officers or officers on leave without pay (LWOP).

In the later stages of the trials in 2006, Chuck Kolot, a 16-year veteran of the RCMP who had worked primarily in the economic crimes field, was selected for a one-year tour of duty that would start on May 01, 2006 and end on April 30, 2007.

Along with exhibiting a strong operational background, Chuck's Proceeds of Crime Section experience and his ability to drive vehicles with standard transmissions made him a successful candidate.[189] Although the ability to drive standard may have appeared like a frivolous requirement, Chuck would later discover that the Sierra Leone's landscape offered quite a challenge for drivers, even for the most seasoned off-road enthusiasts. In addition, joining the mission meant having to pass a number of medical and physical tests.

Pre-deployment training for the mission was held in Ottawa at RCMP headquarters, and lasted for a week. The training included lectures on health (with an emphasis on drinking several litres of water per day to prevent dehydration), appreciation of West African culture, UN conventions, war crimes, and crimes against humanity.

Among the most interesting lectures for Chuck was the one on the Sierra Leonean culture, and how to get ready to live in a country whose living conditions did not match those in North America. However, of most relevance was a situational briefing provided by an officer who had recently completed a rotation in

Sierra Leone. Though enlightening, the lectures and the briefing would not quite prepare Chuck for what was yet to come!

Chuck's arrival in Sierra Leone was anything but uneventful. Upon landing at the Lungi International Airport, the airfield serving Freetown and the rest of Sierra Leone, the first thing that struck him was the heat and extreme humidity of the place. One may think that, for someone coming from cold Canadian weather, ending up in a warm climate near the equator would be a paradisiac assignment. But wait a minute! As Chuck soon found out, the weather in Sierra Leone was so stifling that breathing alone was enough to make him sweat profusely. Admittedly, Chuck had better adapt to the weather very rapidly, or his year-long assignment could be most uncomfortable...

The capital city itself, Freetown, sits across a large bay from the airport. Due to the dilapidated state of the roads, it takes several hours to commute via vehicle. Because of this, the mode of transport of choice for peacekeepers and other Western visitors was the helicopter.

Once greeted by the UN welcoming committee, Chuck loaded his suitcases onto the UN helicopter, sat down, and buckled his belt for the trip across the bay. This was Chuck's first time in Sierra Leone and, as a matter of fact, his first time in Africa.

When they landed in Freetown, it was with haste that Chuck exited the helicopter, looking forward to breathing the fresh air of his new post. However, he almost gagged at the foul odour of garbage floating in the air, which instantly made him dearly miss the cleanliness he had left behind in North America.

As his colleagues drove him to the place he would call home for the next year, he could not help but think of how privileged he had been in Canada. Around him were dilapidated buildings, piles of garbage, dirt, extreme poverty, and a constant stench; all of which were strong reminders that the country had recently been through a civil war, and was currently one of the poorest countries in the world.

Once they arrived at his residence, Chuck was pleasantly surprised to find that the place was relatively new and very habitable, with its own electric generator and with some, but not all, of the amenities one would normally find in a modern home.

It may sound narcissistic, but it is a fact that many peacekeepers have shared: one of the most important aspects of a mission, from a personal standpoint, is how comfortable and homey the residence one lives in will be. Let's be honest! If the UN has established a mission in a country, it is because that country has major problems that it could not solve by itself. A mission's living and working conditions can be very demanding on an individual, especially when one is constantly exposed to extreme poverty and human suffering. As a peacekeeper, one needs a safe haven to replenish energy and be able to carry on helping the most disfavoured.

Chuck was luckier than most Canadian peace officers who serve overseas when it came to domestic arrangements. By the time he started his tour of duty in Sierra Leone, the other Canadian investigators attached to the Special Court had already banded together to rent a large house. All Chuck had to do was "show up" and "step into the shoes" of the Canadian peace officer who had preceded him. In his new accommodation, nicknamed the "Canada House", the atmosphere was convivial and almost frat-house like. But Chuck's living arrangement would not come cheap!

Living in conditions somewhat similar to North American standards meant having to pay a rent of $1,900.00 USD per month. This represented a sheer fortune for the average Sierra Leonean, whose yearly income was approximately $1,100.00 USD for men, and only $500.00 USD for women.

Since the $1,900.00 USD per month was actually divided among the six Canadians who resided in the house, each person paid approximately $316.00 USD.

The house was divided into five bedrooms, one of which was large enough to accommodate two beds. Because there was no washer and dryer, clothes had to be washed, hung to dry, and ironed as soon as possible in order to prevent insects from laying their eggs and ruining the fabric.

While the Canadian officers were at work, a housekeeper was hired to ensure the home was clean and that their clothing was free of insect eggs. It was with bemusement and some sadness that Chuck shared with me the salaries the residents of Canada House paid to their servants, which fell within the annual income range earlier discussed.

However, employment with the Canadians was a highly sought-after endeavour by the locals; it meant that they would receive a better salary than normal, and they could be truly appreciated. As an example, the main indoor servant working for the Canadians was earning more per year than a sergeant in the Sierra Leone police.

Thanks to one of Chuck's roommates, who particularly loved to cook, the culinary experiences during Chuck's stay in Sierra Leone were mostly good ones. Everyone in the house would take his turn cooking from time to time, but one individual particularly enjoyed the task, and would step forward for that duty most of the time.

Granted, the food markets in Freetown did not have as much choice as those in the developed world; nonetheless, chicken, rice, canned vegetables, and fresh fruits were readily available. Chuck would later jokingly admit that he somewhat enjoyed this Sierra Leone food, as he lost some weight. This may have also been due to the fact that he could not find a 7/11 or Mac's store nearby to buy the normal staples of a junk-food diet!

Upon his arrival, Chuck sought a UN identification badge and a Sierra Leonean driver's licence. However, the bureaucratic process to obtain the latter would prove to be a test of his patience.

Figure 35: City of Freetown, Sierra Leone. Photo courtesy of K. R. Kolot.

After waiting for what seemed like an eternity in line-ups that slowly took him from one booth to another, only to get approval stamps that all looked identical, Chuck was finally issued a Sierra Leone driver's licence.

Next, he would require a travel visa to Liberia in order to conduct witness interviews. These were needed as evidence for the trial of former Liberian President Charles Taylor. Taylor had been arrested only a few weeks prior to Chuck's arrival to Sierra Leone.

By the time Chuck arrived in Sierra Leone, some of the other trials were already in full swing. Therefore, his first few days were spent catching up with the rules of the mission, reading up on the history of the conflict, and learning about the structure of the Special Court for Sierra Leone.

An essential part of the police investigators' duties for the mission was to re-interview witnesses and victims of the conflict. In some cases, new witnesses had to be sought and located in order to obtain further ammunition to cross-examine at trial.

Interestingly, and for reasons particular to the Special Court, witnesses' statements were not recorded, but only taken down in handwritten format. This requirement initially caused concerns to some of the Canadian investigators, as it seemed to be out of step with the standards insisted upon in the Canadian criminal justice system.

In Canada, a statement being recorded for accuracy becomes even more of a requirement if the person being interviewed is an accused. With the availability of video recording, courts will question why an accused statement has not been videotaped, with the ultimate result that a statement could be ruled inadmissible if voluntariness and other strict conditions cannot be established.

Figure 36: A city square view in a remote village of Sierra Leone. Photo courtesy of K. R. Kolot.

Another aspect of the Sierra Leone mission that made it somewhat unique was that this was a plainclothes mission. In other words, it meant that the international police officers working in that mission did not wear police uniforms. Rather, they sported khakis and casual shirts most of the time.

It was also a mission where international police officers did not carry firearms. Further, officers attached to the mission were neither on the ground to teach nor to be a peacekeeper. Their principal duty was to investigate, gather evidence, and for some, be witness managers. To accomplish these tasks, Chuck and his colleagues relied on the assistance of Sierra Leonean police officers attached to the Special Court. For example, these officers could help translate from Krio, the local language, or from one of the tribal dialects into English.

Being a witness manager also required that officers keep in touch with witnesses and help facilitate their transport to Freetown in order to testify. In Chuck's case, his duty required occasional travel to Monrovia, Liberia; he would stay there up to a week at a time in order to interview more witnesses and obtain evidence on Charles Taylor's association to RUF. This was necessary in order to establish that Taylor was controlling the RUF, and thus responsible for many heinous crimes: Terrorizing the Civilian Population, Murder, Rape, Sexual Slavery, Outrages Upon Personal Dignity, Conscripting Children Under the Age of 15 (child soldier), and Enslavement.[190]

In the course of interviewing known witnesses, new names often surfaced. It was then the responsibility of the police investigators to identify, locate, and interview those new witnesses, which could be quite the challenge at times.

For example, many remote parts of Liberia had poor access roads and little to no communication assets. In order to interview a witness in one such location, a 4x4 vehicle had to be rented, and driven all the way out to see if the individual was there.

Often, after many hours of rough and bumpy driving, a peace officer would arrive at the witness' village, only to be told that they were away hunting, and would be back in several weeks. Then, the investigators had to drive back to the Liberian capital city, Monrovia, and pass on the interview request to the next visiting group of investigators, who would return a month or so later.

Under such circumstances, it was not uncommon for frustration to mount amongst the ranks of junior international police officers, who were not accustomed to such slow investigative progress. For that, they had to be reminded by senior colleagues that they were in the middle of the wilderness, and, as such, one could only do their best.

Figure 37: Actual courthouse building of the Special Court for Sierra Leone, Freetown. Photo courtesy of K. R. Kolot.

Although the safety situation in the country in 2006–2007 had improved drastically as a result of the rebels' disarmament, the general word of wisdom for the international staff was not to go anywhere alone. This word of caution was a wise one, given that mission police offers were not carrying weapons, and that neither were their Sierra Leonean counterparts.

On a late afternoon, just before Christmas 2006, Chuck decided to go for a run on the main beach after a long workday. This was not the first time he had run at that location, but it was the first time he'd done so alone, and at nightfall.

As he neared the end of his jog, he noticed three young males who were sitting in the sand suddenly get up and start following him. Chuck's feeling of apprehension heightened when he saw two of the young men run past him while the third one remained behind. Chuck did not have to rely on his inner sense as a street cop to realize he may be in trouble.

The two in front suddenly stopped running, did an about-face, and headed towards Chuck, while the one behind caught up to him. As the three converged, everything seemed to take place in slow motion: Chuck realized he was about to be robbed!

Now surrounded by the three youths, two of them started to pat him down in an obvious attempt to detect a wallet or some other valuable. Chuck had already observed that none of the males carried knives or firearms, although one of them brandished a sock filled with stones.

Chuck then yelled towards the road, as if he had colleagues waiting for him, and, at the same time, sprinted in the direction of his parked vehicle, a few hundred meters away. Luckily for Chuck, the manoeuvre seemed to be enough to scatter two of the culprits, while the third eventually slithered off across the road and into a mangrove swamp.

Chuck will later admit that this had been the only occasion he had exercised while carrying his wallet, mobile phone, and other valuables on his person…something he vowed not to do again!

Although Chuck got out of this experience unharmed, things could have turned out for the worse if the youths had been armed with more dangerous weapons. The experience Chuck went through was a reminder that he had to be constantly on guard when traveling in a foreign country.

But let's be honest! Canada and other developed countries also have plenty of thugs running around, and a similar scenario could have taken place back home as well—though North American muggers would have most likely traded the sock and stone for a real gun! In any event, the important lesson to learn here is that one must be constantly vigilant, carry the minimum personal goods, and whenever possible, not be alone in unknown places.

The Sierra Leone mission had other perils and dangers that were seldom fully assessed. For example, if caught off-guard driving down a muddy hill when heading to or from a witness interview, an officer could easily lose control and end up in a ditch, or worse. Imagine being stuck in the middle of the jungle with no radio access and no one around to help! It is not difficult to imagine that this sort of situation could easily become life-threatening. Fortunately, none of that happened when Chuck was on mission.

Poor road conditions may leave people isolated, but as Chuck came to realize, even in 2007, even people living in urban areas in Sierra Leone had very little exposure to the outside world. Chuck came to this realization during a visit to one of the larger cities in an outlying part of the country. This was his first encounter with Little Franklin.

Little Franklin was a two-year-old boy who was often near the local police station with his mother. The first time Little Franklin saw Chuck, he drew the attention of everyone around him with an intense scream and a terrified look in his eyes.

Chuck was not quite sure why Little Franklin was so afraid of him, especially since he had not said or done anything to the child. Was it Chuck's tall stature or baldness? Or both? Or perhaps his stern demeanour? Whatever it was, Little Franklin seemed scared to death.[191]

Chuck then learned from Little Franklin's mother that this had been the child's very first exposure to a "white man", and the experience was somewhat traumatizing for the boy. Feeling somewhat uneasy, Chuck tried to talk and calm down Little Franklin, but to no avail.

However, on Chuck's next visit to that village, Little Franklin seemed to have turned his fear into curiosity. He would now approach Chuck, size him up, smile, and even shake his hand, to the deep laughter of all those around.

One of the most notable episodes during Chuck's Sierra Leonean mission came from the incredible tale of human forgiveness that a local woman shared during an interview. During the conflict, RUF fighters had come to her small village. They had killed her husband, burned down her house, and raped her daughter. She recounted that, after the hostilities, one particular fighter amongst those who had been responsible had returned to her village.

The woman revealed that, despite her extreme grief, the extent of her anger translated into merely ignoring that person, and never talking to him ever again. Other than that, she seemed willing to take no further action against him. The cycle of anger and violence easily could have been perpetuated, but she chose to have it end with her.

This woman's tale is absolutely astonishing, and yet, it is also upsetting. Only a fraction of RUF fighters, those who had committed the worst atrocities, were criminally charged by the Special Court for Sierra Leone. This unfortunately left room for other criminals to roam around free, having received a pardon when the peace agreements were signed.

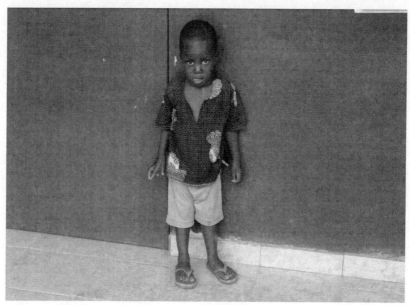

Figure 38: Little Franklin. Photo courtesy of K. R. Kolot.

It seems to me, as a peace officer, that the fighter who caused so much grief should have been held responsible for his actions, if indeed this was what happened. However, there were so many atrocities committed by RUF fighters during the war that perhaps the great majority of them would have had to be indicted…which may not have been a realistic option in getting the peace accords signed and bringing an end to the conflict.

One of the most challenging aspects of Chuck's work was appraising whether people he and his team interviewed were being truthful. Many human sources were utilized by police investigators in order to locate and identify witnesses of crimes against humanity. These human sources were often remunerated for the time and effort they invested. However, as little as they may have been paid (perhaps less than a hundred dollars each time), the amount represented a fortune in a land that ranked the poorest in the world on the United Nations Human Development Program

Index.[192] This created a challenge for the police investigators, who had to be on constant alert to ensure the information provided had not been made up only to receive money.

On one particular occasion, police investigators were attempting to track down an important witness in the war crimes case against former Liberian President, Charles Taylor. One of the human sources informed the officer that he could locate the witness and arrange a meeting between him and the officers.

After some time, the human source came back and provided further details on the witness. He then introduced the witness to police investigators, who found him to be a very cooperative individual. However, little did the officers know that the human source and the witness had been in collusion to elicit money from the officers.

During the interview, investigators realized that although the witness had provided information deemed useful, none of it could be immediately corroborated. As the investigators tried to authenticate the information, they realized that the person they had interviewed was an impostor.

In the end, no one got paid, but the episode was a sombre reminder to Chuck and his team that they operated in a very poor environment, and that they had to be constantly aware of the possibility that someone would try to swindle them. Distinguishing between individuals willing to provide pertinent, accurate, and honest information versus those attempting to deceive was a never-ending struggle.

The Sierra Leone mission taught Chuck many valuable lessons. For one, it taught him to be more appreciative and grateful for what he had. Social safety networks that we Canadians are used to and take for granted, such as unemployment insurance, the welfare system, health benefits, and others, were nonexistent in Sierra Leone. Even a mundane thing such as turning on a light switch was hit-and-miss! One never knew if the electricity would turn on, because the main power grid was shut down most of the time.

Second, the Special Court for Sierra Leone gave Chuck an opportunity to travel and live in a part of the world he would never have otherwise visited. From a personal perspective, the experience also provided him with the opportunity to get to know many Sierra Leoneans, whom, despite being extremely poor, taught him to take pleasure in life's simplest joys.

Figure 39: Chuck wearing African garb along with Sierra Leone police colleagues at a party at the Special Court compound. Photo courtesy of K. R. Kolot.

Chuck will later admit that one of the things he missed most from his adventure was the engaging and pleasant demeanour that Sierra Leoneans displayed. Their sense of communal values is something he will never forget.

However, not all features of the mission were necessarily positive. Some aspects of the work carried on by the mission were not as fulfilling from a modern policing perspective. Nevertheless, as a whole, Chuck's work with the Special Court for Sierra Leone was a great experience that contributed to the Court's quiet success in accomplishing its mission: to bring the perpetrators most responsible for the horrific crimes committed against the people of Sierra Leone to justice.

In April 2012, the International Criminal Court in The Hague found Charles Taylor guilty of 11 counts of Aiding and Abetting War Crimes and Crimes Against Humanity. Taylor is now serving a 50-year sentence in British custody.

7.

After the Sandstorm: UNMIS (United Nations Mission in Sudan), 2005-2011

It took nearly 23 hours, but you have finally arrived in Khartoum, Sudan. You are no tourist. Your mission here is an important one: to aid in the UN efforts to implement Comprehensive Peace Agreements between the fighting factions in the southern half of the country.

But that is a challenge for tomorrow. Today, you are hot, tired, and still feeling a little queasy from your hours of flight. You can't even have a shower: the facilities you find yourself in don't allow for it. The bed, at least, looks inviting, and you collapse on it to earn some much-needed rest.

Pteui! You wake up spitting sand from your mouth. The taste certainly is awful! While you were sleeping, a layer of sand has coated both you and the room. You try to clear your throat of a sharp, burning sensation, as if you have swallowed shards of glass. You look out the small window of your room. Must have been a storm...

This is the environment that Corporal Galib Bhayani found himself navigating in the summer of 2007. In a milieu where peacekeepers were frequently ambushed and killed by either rebels or government troops, Galib's perilous but heartening chronicles are a testament to UN efforts to stop the killing of civilians and bring peace to a war-torn region.

SUDAN IS LOCATED in north-eastern Africa. The country is bordered by nine countries, including Egypt to the north, Chad to the west, Ethiopia and the Red Sea to the east, and the Republic of

Congo to the south. In 2011, the southern part of the country held a referendum, and the area known as South Sudan won its secession from Sudan.[193]

The history of Sudan goes back thousands of years. It has been greatly influenced by Egypt and the later expansion of the Arab World in the 7th Century. The reign of the Ottoman Empire gave Egypt and North Sudan an Islamic flavour, while the South remained primarily Christian from the times of the Byzantine Empire.[194]

In 1798, France took control of Egypt following Napoleon Bonaparte's victory over the Ottoman Egyptian troops. By 1801, the Ottoman Empire had dispatched more troops, and, aided by the British, the French were defeated. A new Ottoman ruler of Egypt was declared.[195]

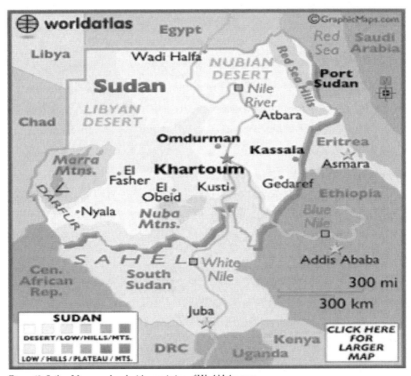

Figure 40: Sudan. Map reproduced with permission of WorldAtlas.com

Further south, the Sudanese territory still had no real central authority, and was the theatre of much tribal infighting. The Ottoman ruler of the time continued his conquests of southern regions of the Nile, where he established a military encampment. This encampment would eventually be named Khartoum, and become the administrative centre for Sudan.[196]

British influence in Egypt came about in the 19th Century, which later developed into a joint sovereignty; Sudan was to be administered by a governor-general, appointed by Egypt. In reality, Sudan was administered as a British imperial possession, much to the dismay of would-be Egyptian and Sudanese nationalists. In 1916, in the midst of World War I, the British invaded the region and incorporated the Darfur area into the Anglo-Egyptian Sudan.[197]

In the early 1950s, as many of its overseas colonies were gaining independence, Great Britain began to support Sudan's rights towards self-determination. However, the road to independence was marked by disturbance and bloodshed. The reason for the violence was that many of the non-Muslim Africans living in southern Sudan were alarmed at the thought of control by the more numerous Muslim Arabs of the northern regions.[198]

In hindsight, this event was a forewarning of the calamities that would afflict the new nation-to-be. For the rest of the century, the recurrent feature of the troubled political life of the area was the attempt by northern Muslim groups to transform Sudan into a fundamentalist Islamic state.[199]

The struggle for power in the north went through several distinct phases. After a spell of military rule (1958-64), elections in 1965 brought in a Muslim government. In the 70s, western countries, such as the United States, began to sell weapons to Sudan, hoping to counteract the Soviet support of neighbouring Ethiopia and Libya.[200] The 70s also saw the discovery of large oilfields in the

Upper Nile and southern region. These would eventually seduce the government of Khartoum to redraw the boundaries of South Sudan, effectively transferring oilfields to the north.

However, the attempt to redraw the boundaries failed, and Khartoum abrogated a previous agreement it had signed with the South that entitled the latter to more autonomy and a sharing of natural resources.[201] As Khartoum began annexing territories by force, civil unrest in the South led to a movement, the Sudanese People's Liberation Army (SPLA), to be born.[202]

The mid-80s were marked by civil war, waged by the SPLA and the government of Khartoum. At the same time, Khartoum imposed the Islamic Sharia law throughout the country.[203]

As the end of the decade approached, the Khartoum government moved towards signing some peace agreements with the South. However, before the signing, a coup d'état led by one Omar al-Bashir enabled him to seize power. His new government fiercely enforced the Islamic code throughout the country, banned trade unions, political parties, and other "non-religious" institutions. It also promoted the deployment of army militiamen, notoriously known as the People's Defense Forces, to raid villages in the South.[204]

The result was another reign of devastation and suffering, one of several which would last throughout the first decade of the millennium, and result in the deaths of about 1.4 million people and approximately one million displaced refugees.[205]

Beginning in February 2003, the Darfur region became the stage of a major armed conflict. The conflict would soon gain international attention for the violence engendered and for the ethnic cleansing taking place.[206]

The conflict in Darfur is seen as being entirely disconnected from the 22-year civil war that placed the Khartoum Muslim government against the Christians and Animists of the country's southern region. Clashes in Darfur started when the Sudan

Liberation Movement (SLM) and the Justice and Equality Movement (JEM) rebel groups accused the Sudanese government of marginalizing the region's non-Arab population, and took up arms against the government. [207]

The government responded to attacks by arming nomadic Arab tribes who were naturally at odds with Darfur's black African farmers. These nomadic Arabs, nicknamed "Janjaweed" (a word in the Arabic language meaning "Devil on horseback"), began pillaging towns and villages inhabited by non-Arabs. This resulted in the deaths of approximately 200,000 people, and caused an estimated 2.5 million refugees.[208]

The Darfur area was so dangerous that even African Union Mission in Sudan (AMIS) soldiers were unable to contain the violence. As a result of the atrocities committed in Darfur, and from UN recommendations to open a criminal investigation, the International Criminal Court (ICC) directly indicted Sudan's President Omar al-Bashir for his role in the commission of War Crimes and Crimes Against Humanity.

Back to the southern region, on March 24, 2005, the UN Security Council passed Resolution 1590 in order to establish the United Nations Mission in the Sudan (UNMIS) and support implementation of the Comprehensive Peace Agreement (CPA).[209]

Signed by the Government of Sudan and the Sudan People's Liberation Movement on January 9, 2005, the CPA called for UN assistance in the following: to facilitate and coordinate the voluntary return of refugees and other internally displaced people, to assist the signatory parties in the mine action sector, to conduct humanitarian assistance operations, and to promote human rights.[210] By September 2006, UNMIS military and police components were close to full strength with 8,727 troops, 695 military observers, 186 staff officers, and 666 police officers.[211]

Corporal Galib Bhayani's voyage to becoming a peacekeeper is an inspirational journey that illustrates the powers of determination and focus. I have known Galib since 2001. From 2001 to 2007, we both worked as uniformed patrolmen at the Richmond RCMP detachment in British Columbia.[212]

Our careers ran somewhat parallel until 2006, when we actually got to work alongside each other as junior supervisors on one of the detachment's four sentinels, called "watches". At night, Galib and I often got together for coffee, and we talked about our true passion: international policing. I had already completed my mission in Guatemala, while Galib was looking forward to an opportunity to participate in one.

However, uniform officer shortages and other impediments would prevent Galib from realizing his dream. As I've mentioned before, despite one having all the required experience and qualifications to be an excellent peacekeeper, good fortune and timing are often needed for one to be drafted.

Never give in. Never, never, never, never—in nothing, great or small, large or petty; never give in except to conviction of honour and good sense.

This famous quote was given by Sir Winston Churchill in 1941, during one of Britain's most harrowing times as the country suffered bombings from the Nazi Germany's Luftwaffe.[213] Britain never gave in, and the rest made history. If one person has been following Churchill's famous adage, it is Galib. Unlike many, who may see defeat in adversities, he sees opportunities. This is a trait I truly admire about him.

And so, after several unsuccessful attempts to be selected for a United Nations mission through the RCMP International Peacekeeping Operations Branch, Galib realized he might have to change his strategy to accomplish his goal.

Galib is a strategic planner. Well before his 2007 mission, he had already set his objective. He realized the selection process for peacekeepers was a difficult one. In order to make himself more competitive and increase his chances of completing a UN mission, he enrolled in a distance-education Master's Degree in International Diplomacy, with a focus on rebuilding torn countries.

Although he successfully completed his degree, his further attempts to be selected for a United Nations mission prior to 2007 kept being frustrated. But he did not give up! Armed with the Master's Degree and a solid police operational background, Galib sought other paths to his mission. The one he found would lead him to one of the most rewarding experiences of his career.

In early 2007, the United Nations had already established its mission in Sudan. There were only a handful of Canadian police officers embedded in the mission, and competition to join that mission was fierce. However, Galib learned that the United Nations was seeking a qualified security expert as part of its UN civilian program. The assignment called for a six-month tour-of-duty as a Regional Security Officer in South Sudan.

Galib jumped on the opportunity and applied. Shortly thereafter, he received the news that he was the number-one selected candidate for the job. But the story does not end here. Since this was an external employment, it meant that Galib would have to take a Leave of Absence Without Pay (LWOP) for six months.

After many attempts at convincing RCMP management that his "outside the police force" endeavour would actually benefit the RCMP in the long run, he was permitted to take a six-month LWOP to travel to Sudan.

For Galib, working as a peacekeeper in a United Nations mission was a dream, but what differentiated him from others is that he made that dream his goal. The ongoing pursuit of his objective, despite the many obstacles and hurdles he had to overcome, is an example to follow in order to accomplish one's own aspirations. Let us never give up on our dreams and ambitions!

Galib's UN mission was unique in comparison to the others described in this book, because he was directly hired by the UN Department of Safety and Security; he did not join through the RCMP International Peacekeeping Operations in Ottawa. This meant that, as a Regional Security Officer in South Sudan, Galib would be a civilian peacebuilder.[214] Therefore, he would not wear a police uniform, though he would still end up doing an analogous type of duty.

Similar to the RCMP, the UN required that a candidate heading for one of the missions around the world undergo an extensive medical examination. Assumedly, this was in order to ensure the individual could perform his duties under adverse conditions. Thankfully, Galib received a clean bill of health from his doctor and prepared for the next step.

Galib obtained a blue UN passport, also referred to as a "Laissez Passé". This travel document would provide his job description on the front page but, interestingly, would not mention his nationality. Galib later learned that one of the reasons the detail was omitted was because the UN did not wish to identify employees by nationality should one of them be kidnapped or otherwise involved in something serious. All it indicated was that the bearer was a UN employee. The passport also provided Galib with entry rights without a visa to some specific countries, such as Kenya.

For the length of his mission, Galib would be receiving a salary from the UN paid in USD. Medical benefits, such as dental and emergency health care, would also be looked after by the UN.

Civilian pre-deployment induction training was to take place in Brindisi, Italy, at the UN Logistics Base (UNLB). The UNLB was an Italian Air Force Base-turned-UN-training facility.

On April 21, 2007, about to realize his lifelong dream, an excited and apprehensive Galib boarded a Lufthansa flight in Vancouver, Canada, and headed for adventure.

After a 24-hour journey that took him through Frankfurt, Germany and Rome, Italy, he finally landed in Brindisi. There, Galib made his way to a hotel in the centre of town, where the UN had booked a room for him. A UN daily subsistence allowance of approximately $113 USD per day would compensate Galib for three meals, water, internet access, and other incidental expenses.

The next morning, Galib was picked up by a UN bus, where he and other civilian peacekeepers were taken to the training facility. It was exciting to see people from Russia, Australia, Ghana, France, Uganda, the United Kingdom, the United States, and other places around the world come together for training.

Figure 41: Galib (top centre) along with his international classmates at the Brindisi training facility, Italy. Photo courtesy of Galib Bhayani.

Interestingly, the classes taught at the UNLB were of a rather generic variety, and more macro-specific than what other officers in this book experienced. This was necessary because attendees were being sent to different missions around the world.

Classes would run an entire week, and started at 08:30 every day to end by 17:00. The training curriculum at the UNLB consisted of the following topics:

1. Introduction to the UN System, Benefits, and Responsibilities of Employees
2. Evolution of the UN and Development of Peacekeeping Operations Worldwide
3. Integrated Mission Components
4. Peacekeeping Doctrines and Principles
5. UN Phases of Security
6. Basic Security Skills. This included mine awareness, food and water safety, and a drill on what to do during a kidnapping or roadblock
7. Radio Communication
8. Gender Awareness Perspectives in the UN
9. Diversity and Cultural Sensitivity
10. Medical Briefings
11. Capacity Building
12. Sexual Exploitation and Abuse (SEA)
13. Life in Mission, including stress management
14. Performance Management and the UN EPAS (Electronic Performance Appraisal System), of how to document and complete a staff performance evaluation

Galib's most interesting and culturally rich discussions would most often take place after class, in a local restaurant. There, in a tranquil atmosphere over great Italian food and wine, classmates would exchange their individual stories as to the reasons they had joined the UN. Many admitted they had come for the excitement, others to change the world, and a few explicitly conceded that they had come for the money, since the UN paid quite well.

What Galib found most useful in the week of training were the actual hands-on exercises. For these, the UN brought in specialists from the field, such as ex-military, doctors, and senior managers, who put the participants through physical scenarios. These were very realistic and worthwhile.

Take the mock exercise on convoy security. Participants were engaged in role-playing UN personnel traveling in vehicles between two small villages in a remote area of conflict.

As the UN "convoy" traveled, it was attacked suddenly and without any provocation by a group of "rebel forces". The attackers had failed to realize that the people in the convoy were mainly peacekeepers, despite the distinctive UN markings.

All peacekeepers were forced out of their vehicles and forced to kneel beside the road with AK-47 machine guns pointed at their foreheads. Galib, who played one of the UN security officers, was shot first! Others who tried frantically to communicate with the rebels were also shot, or raped if they were women. None of the rebels seemed to understand that they were peacekeepers, and not a part of the government. No one listened, and no one seemed to care!

Despite the exercise being a scenario, and that no one was actually physically harmed, the intensity ran so high that some of the participants broke down and cried! Everything felt just too real for those who participated.

The exercise was meant to illustrate the many dangers one may face in the field. In the end, this particular exercise provided the participants with tools and an understanding as to how to avoid such situations in the first place.

The week-long training over, participants met for a final dinner and gathering. There, farewells and hugs were exchanged; some would depart the next day for missions in Liberia, Sierra Leone, Sudan, East Timor, the Democratic Republic of Congo (DRC), and other places around the world.

The training, the excitement, the novelty, the time difference, and the lack of sleep eventually took its toll on Galib. As he departed Italy for Sudan via a connecting flight through Jordan, Galib developed a serious stomach-ache. Embracing a bottle of Pepto-Bismol, Galib managed to endure the cramps until he landed in Khartoum at around 04:30, after a 22-hour journey.

The process through the Sudanese customs and immigration office turned out to be quite slow, despite the best efforts of a UN protocol officer present to greet Galib and other peacekeepers upon their arrival. Because alcohol was prohibited in Sudan, everyone was searched to ensure no one introduced this proscribed "elixir" to the country.

Eventually, Galib made it through customs and, along with the other newly arrived, bussed to a local hotel. There, they would spend their first night before attending the UN Headquarters in Khartoum the next day. Strangely, the UN did not pay for hotel accommodation. The peacekeepers were thus responsible for finding accommodation as soon as possible and at their own expense and time.

It was early morning in the city, and the thermometer already indicated a whopping 35 degrees Celsius. To the unaccustomed visitor, Khartoum could appear somewhat chaotic: cars driving on the wrong side of the road, a muggy atmosphere, heavy air pollution, a smell of smoke in the air, and a lot—a lot—of dust.

It was around 10:00 when a tired, sick, and sweaty Galib finally made it to his hotel. If the poor upkeep of the hotel Galib was staying at was a sign of things to come in Sudan, then his mission would be a difficult one! The hotel looked old and filthy. It would be a strong departure from the comfortable one he had left in Brindisi.

After he obtained his room keys from the reception, Galib rushed to his accommodation, looking forward to taking a refreshing shower after his long journey from Italy. To his dismay, Galib realized that the water pressure in his shower was so low, only a few drops of water came out of the faucet. There is no way he could take even a quick shower. Exhausted, Galib passed out on the dirty, stained bedsheets.

Galib managed to sleep a few hours before waking up and meeting a new acquaintance in the hotel lobby for a coffee. Perhaps inspired by the bravery of the great 19th century British explorer David Livingstone, Galib coaxed his new friend into taking a discovery walk of their surroundings.[215]

Not much had changed from the sight he had been exposed to earlier in the day as the UN bus took him from the airport to the hotel. The city was still dusty, and there were no sidewalks. The infrastructure was minimal.

Galib's expedition around the block was short-lived. Without sunscreen to protect themselves from the powerful UV rays of the afternoon sun, and with temperatures reaching 45 degrees Celsius, the new explorers' first priority suddenly shifted into returning to the hotel as soon as possible. The 10-minute walk had made both intrepid would-be-explorers very hot and sweaty.

As soon as he got back to the hotel, Galib headed to his room, and decided to take a quick nap before dinner. The jetlag was undeniably catching up! He soon passed out again on the bed.

Figure 42: Khartoum, the capital city of Sudan. The city is dirty, dusty, hot and polluted. Photo courtesy of Galib Bhayani.

When Galib woke up again, it was with the gritty taste of sand in his mouth. He had woken up to find layers of the stuff all over the bedroom—and on him. Literally, there was sand in every crevice imaginable: in his hair, his nose, his mouth, and even in his underwear. Sand had also managed to find its way into his suitcase.

Galib had been so tired that he had slept through a sandstorm, commonly referred to as a "haboob" in Sudan. Galib's bedroom had been hard-hit, even though the window had been closed. Sand had found its way through cracks, broken window seals, and from the air conditioning system. The room was filled with a thick haze that resembled smoke, except that this was no fire. It was sand dust—and lots of it![216]

After a frantic search for clean water through the sandy haze, Galib found an unopened bottle and vigorously rinsed his mouth to dislodge any sand particles left. He then headed out into the hotel corridor. There, the housekeeping staff were already at work mopping the entire hotel. By Galib's own estimate, there must have been one to three centimetres of sand covering every inch of the hotel floor and counter space.

What a way to start a new job! Needless to say, Galib's dinner that night was no gourmet food, with remnants of sand in almost every dish he had…

The next day, the first thing Galib did when he woke up was to peek under his bed and look in his shoes. No, he was not searching for sand, but rather for possible critters hiding there. Sudan is well-known for venomous snakes, scorpions, and other similar creatures that like to hide under beds or sneak into shoes.

Confident that no critters had invaded his space, Galib got dressed and prepared for his first meeting at the nearby UN headquarters in Khartoum.

After breakfast, Galib was picked up by a UN vehicle that drove around the city to pick up other colleagues. The smell of burnt garbage mixed with that of cooked meat from street vendors filled the air.

When Galib arrived at the UN headquarters, he and the other new arrivals were signed up for a week of induction training, this time with the UN police, UN Military, and other UN civilians. Topics such as landmine avoidance and food and water hygiene awareness were discussed. Tap water in Khartoum, and for that matter, in the whole of Sudan, was not very clean, and thus not recommended for consumption.

During his time in Khartoum, Galib opened a bank account with the UN, was assigned a radio, signed many waivers, and set up passwords to access the UN computer network.[217] Coming from an environment where efficiency was a trademark, Galib had to practice patience in dealing with the slow and at times bureaucratic UN process.

Figure 43: Tap water vs bottled water. Can you figure out which is which? Photo courtesy of Galib Bhayani.

Following the week-long induction, Galib would need to find a place to live until he knew which area of Sudan he would be deployed to. Staying at the hotel at $125.00 USD per night added up quickly, and was gouging his UN living allowance of only $113.00 per day.

At the UN headquarters, Galib met other Canadian military peacekeepers, who offered him hospitality at their residence. And just like that, Galib got an army cot and shared an apartment with eight Canadian Forces soldiers whose mission was to be advisors to the Sudanese government. As a result of the hospitality of his new colleagues, Galib did not have to worry about finding a place to live for the three weeks he would spend in Khartoum until his deployment to a region.

Personally, I hold much admiration for our Canadian soldiers. Not only are they well-trained, but those I have had the pleasure to meet in the field, whether it was in Guatemala during my UN mission in 1999, in the Dominican Republic and Haiti after the 2010 earthquake, or here in Canada, were extremely professional and always prepared to render assistance to anyone who needed help.

Figure 44: UN headquarters in Khartoum, Sudan. Photo courtesy of Galib Bhayani.

After three weeks spent in Khartoum learning more about the mission and security plans in preparation for his deployment, Galib finally received his assignment. He would be posted to Ad-Damazin, a difficult to access area located in southeast Sudan, near Ethiopia. The only method to access the area from Khartoum was by small plane or helicopter. This was an exciting post, for sure. Would he be safe in such a remote area? Only time would tell!

Upon arrival in Ad-Damazin, the first thing Galib did was look for a place to stay. As luck would have it, a fellow RCMP officer from Vancouver, British Columbia was departing the mission at the time Galib was arriving, and offered him an opportunity to take over his austere accommodations…which he was sharing with a group of Canadian military and Brazilian Air Force officers. Thankful for the offer, Galib readily accepted and moved into what he would call home for the next six months.

Figure 45: A PUMA utility helicopter Galib would use to travel to remote areas during his mission. Photo courtesy of Galib Bhayani.

For a reasonable $150 USD per month, Galib would enjoy a room in a secure compound that also included a barrel of water for washing and a somewhat modern, clean, and comfortable bathroom (by local standards, of course). The accommodation boasted a "beautiful" open-air dining room that came with a full complement of mosquitos and flies. It soon became imperative for Galib to use a mosquito net at night if he did not want to be "eaten alive", or risk catching malaria.

With seven individuals living under one roof, house rules were mandatory in order to keep a sustainable harmony between the tenants. To this end, everyone did his share of chores and other maintenance. Each week a schedule would be put up for one of the roommates to visit the market and buy fresh supplies (usually tinned goods) and cook a meal for the rest of the roommates.

In the capital city of Khartoum, one could find a variety of food items available, including fast-food restaurants. However, in the field, away from the capital city, food choice was much more restrictive, and they had to be content with the basics, such as vegetables, rice, and canned food.

Figure 46: The clean and comfortable bathroom located at Galib's residence. Note the squat toilet and the abundance of toilet paper. Photo courtesy of Galib Bhayani.

Since Galib was the latest addition to the household, his turn to shop and cook took place during his first week. Excitedly, Galib proclaimed that the night's meal would be chili and rice. And with that, he was off to the local market, where he found chunks of beef for his recipe.[218]

Upon returning home, eager to demonstrate his culinary savoir-faire, Galib grabbed a manual meat grinder and started his preparations.

A few problems soon arose. First, the residential compound had been without electrical power for the last thirty-six hours. Second, the quality of the tap water was so poor that it abounded with fecal matter and other pollutants, making it barely acceptable for showers—if one dared. There was no way Galib would cook rice or beans with such dirty water.

Thanks to available bottled water and a gas stove, Galib's first meal at the residence turned out to be a success (so he says!).

Like many low-income countries, domestic assistance was something quite affordable in Ad-Damazin. At their residence, Galib and his roommates enjoyed the services of a local cleaning lady, who came four times a week to wash dishes, dust the floor, and do the laundry.

As the roommates soon found out, washing methods turned out to differ slightly from what they had expected. The results: underwear, shirts, and other garments often shrank, or doubled in size following a washing.

Friday night at the movies, whenever electricity was available, would be a fun event that bonded "the boys" at the house. It would be under a clear sky and temperatures in the mid-thirties that Galib and his roommates would set up a projector on the rooftop of their home. Watching DVDs or photos of friends and families back home would understandably make them a little homesick at times!

Figure 47: Chef Galib's cooking facility. Photo courtesy of Galib Bhayani.

One morning, Galib woke up and stepped out of his mosquito tent only to land in a huge puddle of water on the floor. There had been a rainstorm overnight, and water had entered their accommodation. There was so much water in Galib's room that some of his clothes were actually floating.

Ad-Damazin, also known as the Blue Nile, is an area covered by the UN Sector V headquarters. This is the area where Galib had been assigned to be the UN team leader for safety, security, and analysis of the local situation.

Galib's duties encompassed the administration and overseeing of a team of 75 UN peacekeepers, who would report daily to the UN Headquarters in Khartoum on the security situation on the ground.

Galib's team was also responsible for other duties, including tracking the movements of UN personnel assigned to the area, as well as assisting non-government organizations (NGO's) in their work, ensuring their safety.

Galib informed me that the road between his residence and his workplace was built by Osama Bin Laden in the 1990s. Even though the drive from his residence to the UN Sector V office was only 6 km, he admitted that at times, especially after a rainstorm, parts of the road could get quite muddy and difficult.

A day at the office would normally start around 07:00 and would often last until 19:00, six days a week. In the morning, Galib would start with an instant coffee and one piece of dry bread. Plodding through the mud around the office, he would find the generator and fire up the air conditioner. He would then start reviewing emails, followed by attending a plethora of meetings, including daily briefings. Galib would prepare daily situational reports on mines and other security threats; most of his information was gained from liaising with the local police and army.

Figure 48: Some of the muddy terrain that Galib had to drive through to get to some of the villages in his area. This is the reason the UN insists everyone must know how to drive a standard transmission. Photo courtesy of Galib Bhayani.

One of the first initiatives Galib participated in when he arrived at his post was to assist the UN Camp Head to teach local Sudanese how to use a toilet. This was no lie! Unaccustomed to the western-style porcelain toilet, villagers using these novelties would tend to stand on the seat and then squat to do their business.

This often caused the low-end porcelain to break and embed shards of porcelain in the persons' behinds. It must have been painful for sure! Victims were easily identified, since they would not sit down and would walk around very slowly, often still bleeding from their wounds.

Seeing this as a scourge, the UN Engineering Division, along with the General Services, put a western-style toilet in the UN compound square and tasked Galib to demonstrate how to sit and conduct business. It must have been quite entertaining to watch Galib teach "Toilet Etiquette 101" to the villagers! [219]

Figure 49: Toilet Etiquette 101 taught by Galib. Diagram reproduced with permission of Mt. Rigi Railways, Switzerland.

There was a multitude of perils and dangers in Galib's corner of the world. Some were natural. Venomous snakes such as the African Cobra, arachnids like the Camel Spider (a spider the size of an open palm), and mosquito-borne diseases such as malaria and dengue fever accounted for most of such dangers one would encounter.

Of course, there were plenty of man-made threats as well. Landmines and other unexploded remnants of war also compelled them to remain vigilant.

39 degrees 77-776 E; 14 degrees 06-811 N; GR 719922

60MM unexploded mortar found near Kurmuk! It is marked and fenced! All stay clear of the area!

...urgently radioed Galib to his area staff one day. Heavy rain had exposed an unexploded 60 mm mortar shell near the village of Kurmuk, 100 km south of Ad-Damazin. The unexploded bomb had been lying on a track that peacekeepers used every day. It was a miracle no one had been killed.

In August 2007, Galib received an assignment to provide security to a group of doctors from the World Health Organization (WHO). They needed to conduct an assessment in a remote area, where a dam had burst. Over a thousand families, including children, had been flooded and further isolated in a village named Bout. Initial reports coming from the area identified serious health concerns for the inhabitants, who faced starvation and diseases. The WHO team of doctors were pressing Galib to organize a trip to the region so that the situation could be further assessed.

Figure 50: Unexploded mortar shell located by a patrolling Pakistani Army platoon. Note how the colour blends with the ground, which makes it dreadfully difficult to spot. Photo courtesy of Galib Bhayani.

Arranging travel to the village where the flood had taken place was not necessarily a difficult task. All Galib had to do was provide details of the trip to the UN HQ in Khartoum and request a UN helicopter.

However, providing security for that mission was another story! Galib felt that flying to the area to provide security would be beyond the capacity of his office. None of his staff were armed, and the area was still under rebel control. Furthermore, Galib was terrified at the thought of the helicopter landing in a minefield.

With pressure mounting from HQ and the doctors, who wanted to conduct their assessment and save as many lives as possible, Galib obliged, and organized a mission to the village.

In addition to being in rebel territory, the 1.5 hour helicopter ride from Ad Damazin to the village of Bout was that much more dangerous due to poor visibility in the rainy season. Helicopters had been known to crash in bad weather near the south Sudanese mountain range.

On a warm and cloudy day in August, a UN PUMA helicopter landed at the Ad Damazin airport, where it was met by Galib, members of his security detail, and a group of approximately 10 WHO doctors.

Anticipating a rough and bumpy ride, Galib had skipped breakfast just in case it came back up during the flight.

With all its passengers on board, in a roar of sheer power the twin-turbine helicopter lifted from the runway and headed towards the village of Bout. Although he would not admit it to anyone, Galib was still apprehensive about the whole mission.

The flight, even though bumpy at times, turned out to be uneventful. As the helicopter approached its final destination, one of the pilots identified a soccer field where they could land. The pilot explained to Galib that this would be the safest place.[220] It would fall on Galib to be the first one to jump out and assess the terrain. He had to be sure to remain bent over while doing so, because the blades would still be turning!

The landing manoeuvre was necessary to prevent the full weight of the helicopter from resting on the ground and risking getting stuck in the thick mud. However, this manoeuvre was not at all reassuring to Galib, who now had to beware of two major dangers: rotating helicopter blades and possible unexploded mines or other ordnance hidden in the mud. By the time they were ready to land, he was already nauseated.

As the chopper hovered over the muddy soccer field, Galib opened the side door. The chopper slowly touched down. As instructed, Galib jumped out of the helicopter and immediately sank to his ankles in the mud! High on adrenaline and bent over, Galib kept on running away from the helicopter and the revolving blades. It was with a sigh of relief that Galib turned around and signalled to the pilots that everything was okay.

But wait! Galib suddenly felt a cool sensation engulfing his feet. As he looked down, he noticed that he was barefoot! His brand-new hiking shoes had gotten stuck in the mud as he jumped out of the aircraft, and his momentum had been such that his feet came right out of the shoes.

Galib grinned as he eventually found and picked up his hiking footwear, now covered inside and out with mud. The rest of his assessment in Bout would be a wet one!

Once everybody was out of the helicopter, the doctors started their health assessment. They had brought medical supplies, which they used as they met children and families in need of attention. Meanwhile, Galib met with the village elders and chief for a walking tour of the surroundings to assess the damages caused by the flood.

Figure 51: A barefoot child in the muddy village of Bout, South Sudan. Photo courtesy of Galib Bhayani.

The conditions in and around the village were atrocious. Not only was the village engulfed in thick mud, but the smell of stagnant water was pungent. These were also potential breeding grounds for health hazards such as malaria and dengue fever.

Back at the soccer field where they had landed, Galib heard a familiar sound overhead. He looked up to see the approach of a Sudanese Army helicopter, getting ready to land beside them.

The sight of the Sudanese Army helicopter made Galib somewhat uneasy; its presence in the area had not been anticipated. As it turned out, the helicopter and crew were also on a reconnaissance mission to assess damages to the region and provide food assistance to the devastated village.

Their mission in Bout over, Galib and the doctors flew back to Ad Damazin without incident. Very tired and completely covered with mud after his 12-hour journey, Galib managed to head home and take a pail shower before returning to the office to write his report on the situation. It comes as no surprise that he recommended further assistance from the Sudanese government to help the people of Bout, whose livelihood had been literally wiped-out.

One area of Sudan that was still extremely dangerous at the time of Galib's mission was Darfur, because the war there was still ongoing. Although he did not have to work in that area, he kept hearing tales of atrocities from other peacekeepers. The Janjaweed, the Arab militia backed by the Sudanese government, was mainly operating in the Darfur area, and was particularly ruthless towards black ethnic Sudanese.

For instance, some of the accounts of violence depicted attackers raping women in front of other villagers, and even in front of the victims' fathers and children. But the viciousness of the attacks did not stop there. After a woman was raped vaginally, her breasts were often slashed, and a stick shoved into her privates.[221] The same fate would happen to teenaged girls or pregnant women. Few would survive.[222]

After much international reporting on allegations of ethnic cleansing, the activities of the Janjaweed were curtailed by the African Union and UN peacekeepers. However, this did not happen before a number of peacekeepers became victims of Janjaweed ambushes.[223]

For these crimes against humanity, the International Criminal Court charged President Omar Al-Bashir on Commission of War Crimes for his support of the militia. Although Al-Bashir was still President of Sudan as of the writing of this book, he was a wanted man by the ICC. With two International arrest warrants issued against him, Al-Bashir is unlikely to travel abroad to states that are party to the Rome Statute of the ICC.[224]

Situations that Galib encountered in Sudan may not have been as deadly as those faced by peacekeepers in Darfur, but many could nonetheless land a peacekeeper in a lot of trouble, or with a ticket home well before the end of a mission. Like I mentioned, alcoholic beverages were prohibited in Sudan, and attempts to bring in liquor placed some UN staff in precarious situations.

Galib recalled a Turkish police officer getting his luggage x-rayed upon landing in Khartoum. When a bottle of wine was found in the Turkish national's luggage, he was repatriated immediately. Had he not been a member of the UN, he might have gone to jail. Why a peacekeeper would take that sort of risk when they must have been forewarned prior to departure is beyond me!

Do you want to scare Galib to death? If yes, then place him face to face with a snake! Within a week of Galib's arrival to Ad Damazin, sixteen venomous snakes had already been killed, all within a few feet from the UN compound where he worked.

On one occasion, a duty guard caught one alive, bagged it in a Ziploc, and brought it into Galib's office—who, needless to say, freaked out! The snake was only three feet long (small compared to the norm) but was large enough to scare Galib and many of his colleagues. It is suspected that the UN office where Galib worked might have been built near the migration path of these limbless reptiles.

Figure 52: One of the many snakes roaming near Galib's compound at night. Photo courtesy of Galib Bhayani.

There is no doubt that the people Galib met and worked with during his assignment in Sudan made his mission memorable. One of his most vivid experiences was a canoe trip down the River Nile with two UN colleagues. One of them, Mark, an avid canoeist from Australia, would take his canoe out on the weekends down the Nile, to the convergence of the Blue Nile and the White Nile near Khartoum.

The waters from the White Nile travel from Lake Victoria, in Uganda. The river makes its way north and meets up with the waters of the Blue Nile, which originate at Lake Tana in Ethiopia. Both the White and the Blue Nile come together near Khartoum, Sudan, and become The Nile, the longest river in the world.[225]

On a sunny Saturday in August, Galib and another UN colleague were invited by Mark to join him for a canoe ride on the Nile. The quietude, the beauty of the landscape, the African wildlife, and the camaraderie all made the adventure an unforgettable experience.

During the time Galib was in Sudan, he was inundated with daily reports of shootings, murders, arrests of UN staff members, and warning broadcasts of unexploded mines.

In one particular incident, Galib responded to a call in the small village of Kurmuk, near the Ethiopian border. The village of Kurmuk was known to be a stronghold for the Sudan People's Liberation Army (SPLA).[226] There had been a shooting that had taken place there a week after Galib's arrival in Ad-Damazin. Up until that time, it had been difficult to obtain updates on the situation, due to poor communications and lack of cell phone coverage.

It would take at least 8 hours by car to drive the 100 km that separate Kurmuk and Ad-Damazin. In the 10 days following Galib's arrival, there had been a total of two shootings. The first one was by SPLA soldiers who were upset that they had not been paid their due salaries, while the second was committed by an SPLA soldier involved in a domestic dispute.

The events that led to the second incident were as follows: An SPLA soldier had befriended a village girl, but her relatives (two women) had rejected his proposal to marry her (permission to marry was obtained from the family, not given by the prospective bride). On several occasions, he had approached the relatives and tried to convince them to allow him to marry the village girl; alas, to no avail. So on the fateful day, the soldier returned to the homestead of the relatives in Kurmuk and found the two ladies seated outside, along with their two children at their side.

The soldier shot the ladies on sight, also injuring one of the children as he tried to flee. Another woman came out of one of the nearby huts after hearing the shots fired, and courageously grabbed the soldier's gun. Members of the community soon joined the scuffle, and eventually managed to disarm the soldier.

After a short time, the SPLA arrived at the scene, confiscated the suspect's gun, took him into custody, and transported him to their base. The victims were rushed to the Kurmuk Health Centre, where they were admitted, both in critical condition after sustaining the gunshot wounds.

Apart from being a horrible tragedy, Galib described a major problem with the scenario that affected the performance of his duties. Whenever people heard shooting, they would run into their huts, start digging into the muddy ground, and pull out hidden AK-47s and other weapons because they thought the civil war was starting up again. In this regard, Galib and the UN were continuously struggling to disarm local populations as part of their UN mandate.

Towards the end of his mission, Galib attended the living quarters of the local Dutch and Bosnian contingents for a barbecue (BBQ). Contrary to popular belief, setting up a BBQ in Sudan is no simple endeavour!

In Sudan, a BBQ starts with a visit to the sheep market. There, one finds a selection of hundreds of sheep and goats to choose from: all alive, of course! Next, one chooses the animal and witnesses it being skinned right in front of the buyer's eyes. For $63.00 USD, one gets enough meat to feed 20 people.

So for the BBQ, it would be sheep meat, veggies, and Sprite. Cigars were provided by another peacekeeper, thanks to a recent visit to Entebbe, Uganda. This was "decompression time" after a hard week of work, Sudanese-style!

But what made the experience particularly unforgettable, other than witnessing the poor animal being decapitated for the occasion, was that the great camaraderie around the BBQ came to a sudden halt when the event turned into a vomit-fest! Yes, our intrepid Galib and two of his colleagues were mistakenly given a sheep burger with a part of the animal that was not for human consumption. The result was that the three of them started to throw up violently.

All were rushed to a nearby UN Pakistani military hospital, where they tried in vain to communicate their woes in English, Croat, and Dutch to a doctor that only spoke Urdu. When the doctor finally figured out what had taken place, one of them had already been treated for malaria, the other for dysentery, and the third, Galib, for fever!

Then came the end of Galib's six-month mission. Not because of the earlier food poisoning, but rather because his contract was over. Time had just flown by!

To anyone wishing to complete a tour of duty with the UN, Galib's advice is to "be patient!" There is so much to learn about the UN, and the area where one is seeking a posting that, without patience, one will simply not survive.

This is not an exaggeration: shortly before completing his mission, Galib sent out an email to selected friends and colleagues, detailing some of the "lessons learned" on his trip. Though he felt that the UN experience was, in his words, "Awesome!", in comparison Galib felt that the RCMP "ran like a precision Swiss watch".

From his perspective, there was always the worry about how long the help they were giving the Sudanese people would last. How long before the people would find themselves back at war with one another? What was the UN doing to help in the long run? Only time would tell.

Galib's e-mail ended with a reflection on how the differences in quality of life between Sudan and North America had really impressed themselves upon him while he was in Africa. He could foresee some changes in the future regarding his personal consumption rates, certainly.

Honestly, I find Galib's journey very inspiring. The goals he attained did not happen overnight. Time after time, his efforts to be selected for a mission were frustrated. However, Galib being the strategic planner that he is, he never gave up. He set goals and reached them one at a time. Whether it was going back to school or gaining experience in a certain area of policing, all was mapped out to help him reach his objectives.

Not surprisingly, the experience he gained from his mission opened doors to new opportunities he'd never dreamt of. He began a part-time international teaching career, helping police officers from countries such as Turkey, Kenya, Malawi, and Zambia learn about democratic policing, the rule of law, and human rights.

Galib eventually moved his teaching passion closer to home, at a Canadian university where he taught Criminology. His passion for policing and education continues to this date.

Galib's desire to make a difference did not stop with his teaching. Soon after his mission to Sudan in 2007, he and his former colleagues set up a charity organization for the Sudanese people called "Someday is Now International".

Figure 53: From left to right, Galib, two Halifax Police Department officers, and an RCMP colleague. Photo courtesy of Galib Bhayani.

The charity ran until 2016 and helped fund projects in Sudan in the areas of education, maternal help, and vulnerable children. Projects like helping a 72-year-old Sudanese woman care for abandoned or orphaned children in her community were examples of the many undertakings the charity addressed. These made a positive difference in the life of otherwise disfavoured individuals.

Often, when I face a roadblock, I think of Galib and get my inspiration from his actions. I often say to myself, "If he did it, I can too; as long as I am as willing to discipline and apply myself just as much as he did."

Within five years of completing his Sudanese mission, Galib went on to acquire a Ph.D. in Security Studies. Two years later, he became a Commissioned Officer within the RCMP. In 2016, he left for another adventure: a one-year capacity building mission in Bagdad, Iraq. He completed the mission in 2017, contributing to rebuilding Iraqi policing services. Shortly after returning from his Iraqi mission, Galib got another promotion, this one to the coveted rank of Superintendent.

Keeping up with Galib's accomplishments will undoubtedly be a challenge of scale for me, but by applying his methodology, I am positive that chances at success will greatly be increased. The same can be true for you![227] As Thomas Edison once said, "If we did all the things we are capable of doing, we would literally astound ourselves."

Galib encourages everyone to have an open mind, to be receptive to how others function and live in this world, and just to enjoy each moment of a peace mission. He also champions anyone keen on doing something different to at least "give it a try", whether it is a UN mission or any other personal ambition. Obviously, living in harsh conditions in a mission somewhere around the world may not be for everyone. However, one will never know without experiencing it.

The UNMIS ended in 2011, with elections that saw South Sudan winning its independence from Sudan.[228] As the UNMIS mandate ended, the United Nations Mission in South Sudan (UNMISS) was established to help consolidate the newfound peace and security, and to help establish conditions of development in the new country.

Sadly, Galib's worries and foresight about the flaring of war in South Sudan were not farfetched. Less than two years after its independence, the world's youngest country propelled itself back into civil war when two of its top SPLA politicians bitterly split; one of the two became the leader of a new rebel group.[229] It happened despite the best efforts of the UN to maintain a fragile peace in the area. At the time of this writing, UNMISS efforts to bring peace and security to the country are ongoing.

By the time I was finalizing this book, Galib had become the Chief of Police of the RCMP North Vancouver Detachment.

"Safe journey and continued success to you, my friend!"

8.

Of Biblical Proportion: EUPOL COPPS (European Police Coordinating Office for Palestinian Police Support), Palestine 2006- Present

Palestine: a region that has yet to be officially defined as either country or state, despite being occupied for over 3,000 years; a land that has been conquered by not only its native Israelite population, but by the Philistines, the Assyrians, the Babylonians, the Persians, and the Greeks as well – all before what is considered the "Common Era"; a realm that is home to not one, but three of the largest organized religions in the world; a holy land where Jews, Muslims, and Christians compete for prominence; and, most recently, a territory where Israelis and Arabs violently clash for their rightful home.

This is the location of the EUPOL COPPS mission. Unlike the other missions discussed in this book, EUPOL COPPS was not a UN mission, but rather, a European Union (EU) initiative. Its objectives, however, are comparable in that it mandated international police and civilians to provide support in order to reform and rebuild the police force in the Palestinian Territories of West Bank and Gaza.[230]

Like the UN, the EU has been at the forefront of lasting peace efforts in the Middle East by contributing to the strengthening of law and order.[231] *The mission started at a time when tensions were at an apogee between two main Palestinian parties, FATAH and HAMAS, whose past and current efforts to liberate Palestine from Israeli occupation have brought much violence and destruction to the area.*[232]

BEN J.S. MAURE, M.S.C.

RCMP Inspector Walt Sutherland's participation in EUPOL COPPS in the West Bank took place between August 2008 and August 2009. His tale takes the reader to a fascinating land, rich in history, but also crippled with a thousand-year-old conflict that seems to have no end in sight. Despite the best efforts by the international community to bring peace to the area, much remains to be done in this Holy Land.

AT THE ESSENCE of the Palestinian-Israeli conflict is a question of land and who controls it.[233] Historians believe that the area known as Palestine is one of the oldest continuously inhabited areas in the world, with evidence of settlement going back as far as 9000 BCE.[234] With such a lengthy and at times abstruse history, I have made my best attempt to present a reliable yet simplified portrait of some of the most important events that led to the current conflict.

Strategically located at the joining of Africa and Southwest Asia, the area presently called Palestine comprises the state of Israel and two other territories: The Gaza Strip and the West Bank.

The southern limit of the Gaza Strip borders with Egypt, while the northern and eastern frontiers border with Israel. The territory is delimited by the Mediterranean Sea to the west.[235]

For its part, the West Bank is delimited by Jordan to the east, with a significant coastline along the western bank of the Dead Sea. The West Bank shares the rest of its borders to the north, west, and south with Israel.[236]

Both Gaza and the West Bank are also commonly referred to as "occupied territories". These areas were captured and annexed by Israel in 1967, an addition that has never been recognized by the UN.[237]

Although historians place the Israelite tribes' arrival to Palestine before the late Bronze Age, between 1400 and 1300 BCE, they did not become firmly established in their new territories until 1200 BCE.[238]

Around this time, the land was invaded by the Philistines people (the word Palestine is believed to be derived from it). Economic life continued to flourish for nearly a century, until the region split into two separate kingdoms, Israel and Judah.

Even then, contention for control of this land was fierce, and both kingdoms fell under a succession of more powerful neighbours, including the Greek Army of Alexander the Great.[239]

Figure 54: Israel. Map reproduced with permission of WorldAtlas.com

During this period of war, many Jews were forced into exile, to cities as far away as Babylon. By the beginning of the Common

Era, the region had become a part of the Roman Empire.[240]

Even so, inhabitants of the kingdoms aspired again to political independence. By the middle of the second century CE, an estimated half-million Jewish people had been killed by the Romans following two Jewish rebellions against the regime. With the take-over of the Byzantine Empire (Eastern Roman Empire) and its conversion to Christianity on or about the 4th century CE, Palestine, and the City of Jerusalem, became centres of Christian pilgrimage.[241]

Between 632 and 640 CE, a unification of the Arabian Peninsula took place under Islam rule. Parts of the Byzantine Empire fell to the Arabs, including the Palestine region and what is known today as Syria; both were now under Muslim rule.[242]

With the Arab conquest began 1,300 years of Muslim presence in the area. Interestingly, the take-over and subsequent surrender of Jerusalem was negotiated by the Arabs without bloodshed or massacre. Those who wanted to leave were allowed to do so with all their goods intact, while those who wished to stay were guaranteed protection for their lives, their property, and places of worship.[243]

Over time, some Christians converted to Islam for either convenience or conviction. At the same time, a small permanent Jewish population returned to Jerusalem after more than 500 years of exile. Except for a period of approximately 100 years of Christian dominance during a time called "the Crusades", Palestine remained under Muslim control.[244]

From the 16th century until the end of WWI in 1918, the Muslim Ottoman Empire ruled the region. It is believed that the tolerance that Turkish Ottoman rule displayed towards other religious beliefs contributed to the Jewish migration to Palestine. By 1914, their number approximated 85,000 people.[245] It is also during the first decade of the 20th century that a Jewish congress decided that the Jewish homeland should be in Palestine.[246]

Following the defeat of Germany and the collapse of the

Ottoman Empire after WWI, Great Britain was awarded the right to administer Palestine under a League of Nations mandate; British interests were in assisting the growth of the Jewish population through immigration, so that it would eventually form a majority and gain self-rule.

Therefore, the Jewish population soared from approximately 85,000 inhabitants at the end of WWI to 174,606 by 1931, bringing its total to 16% of the entire Palestinian population.[247]

During this period, attacks on Jews led by Arabs became more prevalent, largely sparked by disputes over the use of a holy site, namely the Western Wall of the Al-Aqsa Mosque.[248]

In the early 30s, German and European Jews began to enter Palestine in more significant numbers. This was a consequence of the German Nazi party coming into power and initiating persecution of Jews throughout Europe.

By 1941, approximately 474,100 Jewish inhabitants were in Palestine. The large influx of Jewish immigration during that period did not please Palestinian Arabs, who feared losing their majority as well as their land to a Jewish national home. An Arab revolt against the British administration, and consequentially, Jewish settlements within Palestine, ensued.[249]

Great Britain eventually curtailed its Jewish immigration and Jewish land purchase policy in Palestine, most likely to gain Arab support throughout the Middle-East for the Second World War. However, this move was not taken well by some Jewish extremists, who formed terrorist groups and launched attacks against both the British and Arabs.[250]

Around the same time, the British administration realized that its obligations towards Arabs and Jews would likely never be reconcilable, and came to the conclusion that the region should eventually be divided.

During the war years, moderate Jewish wings and Palestinian

Arabs alike supported the British. It was also during this time that the Jewish ammunition industry peaked in order to support the British. The discovery of Nazi extermination camps and the Holocaust at the end of WWII brought back the agenda of Jewish immigration to Palestine, this time with some US support.

By 1947, the number of Jewish settlers in Palestine was still on the rise. A slowly withdrawing British administration then referred the Palestinian matter to the United Nations.

On May 14, 1948, the State of Israel was proclaimed.[251] The very next day, military units from Syria, Egypt, Iraq, Lebanon and Transjordan (now Jordan) crossed into Palestine and joined other Arab guerrillas in an attempt to crush the new State of Israel.

This initiated a series of military engagements, which ended with Israel gaining more territory and a truce being agreed upon in 1949. This also left Egypt with control of the Gaza Strip, while Jordan retained the land known as the West Bank.[252] Alas, the conflict also left hundreds of thousands of Palestinian Arabs homeless, many ending up in refugee camps scattered throughout the West Bank, the Gaza Strip, Lebanon, and Syria.[253]

Exile soon defined Palestinian political and cultural activity, which generated and fostered the emergence of movements seeking to reclaim Palestine and an end to the existence of the Jewish state.

As a result, a number of Palestinian guerrilla organizations emerged in the late 50s and 60s, including the Palestine National Liberation Movement (known as FATAH). One such group, the Palestine Liberation Organization, claimed to be the sole representative of the Palestinians. It soon promoted terrorist attacks against Israel, with the goal of liberating Palestine and fostering the return of Palestinian refugees to their homeland.

This caused another Arab-Israeli war to break out in 1967. This time, Israel, Egypt, Syria, and Jordan fought intensely for six days, which culminated with another victory for Israel. Militarily,

Israel now occupied East Jerusalem, the West Bank, the Gaza Strip, and Golan Heights. [254]

Soon after the war, racial tensions between Palestinians and Israelis rose again, this time as a result of Jewish migration to the occupied territories.[255] In 1987, widespread anti-Jewish settler riots erupted within the occupied territories. The uprising became known as the "Intifada".[256] HAMAS, an extremist Palestinian Islamic movement dedicated to the destruction of Israel, came into existence that same year.

From 1988 up until 2006, violence continued to plague the area, which at times was characterized by Palestinian suicide bombers targeting Israeli citizens. The attacks were often followed by swift and severe reprisals by Israel. [257]

As Peace Talks efforts continued throughout the decades, some progress was made. On or about 2003, the United States, the European Union, Russia, and the United Nations formally introduced a "Road Map to Peace" plan that called for a Palestinian state to be established.

In 2005 the Israelis withdrew soldiers and settlers from all of the Gaza Strip and parts of the West Bank.[258] With this move, and a take-over of the territories by the Palestinian Authority, new hopes for peace were raised.

Alas, in 2006, another blow to the peace process took place with the surprise election victory of HAMAS candidates, who won the majority of seats in the Palestinian legislature. As a result, HAMAS formed a coalition government with FATAH, the organization that had dominated Palestinian politics for decades.

A year later, after violent clashes between the two groups, a state of emergency was declared, and the government was dissolved. HAMAS was left in control of the Gaza Strip, and FATAH of the West Bank. Since, HAMAS has continued its attacks on Israel, which have been retaliated through Israeli airstrikes and ground campaigns on the Gaza strip.

The European Union (EU)'s political engagement in Palestine was minimal until the last decade of the 20th century.[259] Starting in the 1990s, the EU took a more prominent role in the politics of the region, using its mediating powers between the Arab states and Israel.[260]

As part of the EU's commitment towards a lasting Middle Eastern peace, the EU agreed to take the lead in strengthening the rule-of-law in the Palestinian territories, as well as working with the Palestinian Authority to improve its civilian police.[261]

At the end of the Intifada in 2005, and following an invitation from the Palestinian Authority, the EU established the European Union Police Co-ordinating Office for Palestinian Police Support, (EUPOL COPPS). Through EUPOL COPPS, a competent Palestinian Civil Police (PCP) would be developed, along with infrastructure and an improved criminal justice system. All of this was in anticipation of the creation of a future Palestinian State.[262]

EUPOL COPPS's multi-pronged approach was therefore focused on providing support and development to seven main areas:

1. Criminal Investigations: development in crime scene investigations and forensic laboratories
2. Prosecution: improving investigational structure within prosecution
3. Courts: improving the work of judges on several social justice issues
4. Defense Rights: fostering the right of defense to ensure the Criminal Justice System complies with international standards
5. Human Rights: basic training curriculum on Human Rights for the PCP, creating an oversight mechanism for grievance and Human Rights within the PCP

6. The Correctional System: developing a penitentiary system that is a part of the justice system
7. Ministerial Administration: providing expert advice and capacity building at a government level

To deliver its support initiative, the EUPOL COPPS relied on police advisors coming from 17 EU member states. Canada was also invited to participate, and contributed by sending two RCMP police officers, one of them being RCMP Inspector Walt Sutherland.

One of the factors that fostered Canada's involvement in this EU mission was that, at the time, Canada was investing a significant amount of money into the region. Since Canada had a vested interest in Palestine, it seemed a natural evolution to join forces with the EU.

In his police training advisory role, Walt would assess the training needs of the PCP and assist with mentoring, training, equipping, and professionalizing PCP members.[263] Mission staff in 2009 stood at 42 internationals (EU, Canada, and Norway) and 19 locals.

Selection of candidates for this mission was based on the need for a senior officer, for someone who held a strong and diversified police background, police training, career development experience, and, of course, being releasable from operational duties. Because Walt met the entire set of criteria, he was selected for this unique mission.

It was Canada's first attendance in this mission, and the role that the Canadian officers would play was yet to be ironed out. Thus, in July 2008, Walt and two RCMP members from the International Policing Operations Branch traveled to Israel and the West Bank for a one-week reconnaissance trip.

Once they arrived, they met with the Head of Mission, the Security Officer, and the Intelligence Officer. During this trip,

Walt learned that Canada would be providing additional police support. This would mean that he and another RCMP colleague, Corporal John Pullen, would assist with implementing a modern police training curriculum for the Palestinian police.

Upon his return to Canada, Walt debriefed the RCMP management on the role Canadians were expected to play and prepared to head back for his one-year assignment.

Pre-deployment training took place in Ottawa and lasted three days. As Walt's contingent was rather small (only he and Cpl. Pullen were going to Jerusalem), they were grouped with four other RCMP officers who were preparing to leave for Lebanon to provide assistance on an investigation.

Because the six were going to a relatively similar region (Lebanon borders Israel to the north), the six officers were lumped into an intensive three days of training. During that time, Walt reviewed the usual administrative functions, such as expense claims and the likes. A session with the RCMP Health Service head nurse was also on the agenda to discuss medical matters relative to the area.

A cultural and historical information session on Palestine was then presented to the group by an RCMP officer who was well acquainted with the region. Although the training normally afforded to larger troops was missed because of the tight schedule, Walt and his colleagues nonetheless felt that the three-day training they had received provided them with enough information to start their mission safely.

Travel to Tel Aviv, Israel, from Toronto, Canada was a relatively easy endeavour, given the fact that there were regular direct flights between the two cities.

After 12 hours spent in the relative comfort of an Air Canada jetliner, Walt and John landed in Tel Aviv. Unlike other mission arrivals previously described, I jokingly compare Walt's landing in Tel Aviv to that of a tourist arriving at his destination.

A modern city located on the Israel Mediterranean coastline, Tel Aviv boasts beautiful beaches, warm weather, cafés, bars, parks, and great restaurants. It can be easily compared to any global city, such as San Francisco.[264]

Therefore, the cultural shock that many peacekeepers experience upon landing in a new country was definitely not as "pronounced" for Walt and John. Nonetheless, the harsh reality of life in the West Bank would soon catch up with them.

At the Ben Gurion International Airport in Tel Aviv, Walt and John were picked up by EUPOL COPPS colleagues, who drove them directly to Jerusalem, approximately an hour-and-a-half drive from Tel Aviv. Jerusalem is the centre to three major Abrahamic religions: Judaism, Christianity, and Islam.[265] The Holy City would become Walt's home for the next year.

The status of Jerusalem is one of the areas of contention in the Israeli-Palestinian conflict. During Walt's mission, Jerusalem was still under Israeli control. Prior to 1967, an unofficial border called "The Green Line" had divided Jerusalem in half, separating East Jerusalem (mainly populated by Muslim and Christian Palestinians) and West Jerusalem (mainly populated by Jews). This demarcation had been the result of a 1949 Armistice Agreement between Israel and its neighbours: Jordan, Egypt, Lebanon, and Syria.[266]

When Walt and John arrived in Jerusalem, EUPOL COPPS staff facilitated their stay by booking rooms in a hotel located in the former East Jerusalem. Because he had arrived in Israel on a Friday, Walt enjoyed the weekend to tour one of mankind's most holy sites: The Old City of Jerusalem, only a few blocks away from his hotel.

But despite its sheer beauty and historical magnificence, social tensions between Palestinians and Jews in Jerusalem would soon give Walt a foretaste of the true reasons he had travelled to the region.

With the first day of work at the EUPOL COPPS headquarters in Ramallah, Walt's weekend spent as a "tourist", suddenly ended, to reveal the harsh reality of life in this conflict zone.

After being picked up at his hotel by EUPOL COPPS staff and driven to Ramallah through the Kalandia Israeli checkpoint, Walt's first day started with his induction into the mission. During the induction, which lasted four days, topics like mission administration, security, intelligence gathering, communication strategies, and the current situation in the West Bank were discussed.

At EUPOL COPPS HQ, Walt and John were assigned to the Program Unit. Their task was to assess the current Palestinian Civil Police Training and provide recommendations to EUPOL COPPS and the Commissioner of the Palestinian Civilian Police on how to enhance, improve, and support police training.

Although he held a Bachelor's Degree in Physical Education and a strong operational background supported by 33 years of policing, Walt's experience in police training was limited. John, on the other hand, had extensive knowledge in the matter, having been an RCMP Depot Regina Training Academy instructor.

Figure 55: Photo of the Kalandia Israeli military checkpoint, where Palestinians holding permits can leave the West Bank and enter Israel. This checkpoint, like many others, has been fire-bombed. It is located between Ramallah and Jerusalem. Photo courtesy of Walt Sutherland.

One of the first priorities Walt addressed when he arrived at the mission was to find accommodation. Although the hotel where Walt was staying in Jerusalem was comfortable, remaining at the hotel for the entire duration of the mission was not an enviable option from either an economical perspective or a practical one. As such, with the assistance of mission staff, Walt and other newly arrived officers started to search the city of Jerusalem for apartments.

After about a week of inquiries, Walt was referred by a colleague to the owner of an apartment who wished to rent his place for $2,500.00 USD per month. The place boasted two bedrooms, two bathrooms, a kitchen, a living room, a balcony, a terrace, and came very decently furnished. Being clean, well-maintained, and fairly close to the checkpoint that Walt had to cross to go to work every day, he and John decided to rent the apartment.

That said, $2,500.00 USD is an expensive rent. Thankfully, the Memorandum of Agreement between the Government of Canada and EUPOL COPPS stipulated that Canada was responsible for covering accommodation, meals, and allowances for its members at the rate prescribed by the Government of Canada Treasury Board. This arrangement was similar to the mission allowance that European Police were getting from the EU.

In order to gather data for his duties of police training needs assessment, Walt first attended the training academy in Jericho, and made note of the living and learning conditions.

Walt's visits to the Jericho training facility always started with a stop at the Commander's office to pay his respects. The latter would return the courtesy by serving Walt a cup of strong, but delicious, Arabic coffee and a cup of very hot, sweet tea. Formalities over, Walt would be allowed to continue his assessment of the facility.

Walt recalled that the training methods that were currently in place (with a minimum number of trainers) required that hundreds of recruits be trained at the same time…in a facility that could realistically accommodate roughly 70 cadets at a time. Completing military marches and other physical activities in temperatures ranging anywhere between 40-50 degrees Celsius was the norm. Being void of showers and a laundry area, the stench of perspiration often floated in the air.

Despite the difficult conditions at the academy, they did not deter the pride and commitment of the young recruits, whose drop-out rate was an astonishing 0 %!

Walt and John also travelled to all of the 13 Palestinian police districts. There, they met District Commanders and sought their input insofar as to what they saw as being paramount to their training needs.

Walt also canvassed the other EU police officers and obtained an opinion from them as to what they perceived were the gaps or shortcomings of the Palestinian police in matters of training.

In all, Walt met with a variety of stakeholders, including the public, which enabled him and John to put together a comprehensive report to EU management on the training needs of the Palestinian police.

It took Walt roughly three months to complete the evaluation. In the end, he provided a number of recommendations in terms of what he believed the Palestinian police needed in the context of law enforcement formation.

As you might have guessed, one of the recommendations he suggested was to provide better living conditions at the Jericho Palestinian Police Training Centre. Imagine how difficult police training was in the rudimentary facilities the Palestinian cadets were provided: small classrooms, crammed dormitories, no shower, and having to stay for weeks at a time—it is not surprising that the place was not conducive to efficient learning. Because of these difficult living conditions, it was imperative that something be done in that area as soon as possible.

Since most Palestinian police officers only spoke Arabic, Walt and his colleague worked with interpreters hired by the EU. In

Walt's opinion, the challenges with the Palestinian police were very interesting. It was a police force unlike any other. It did not have to be started from the ground up, unlike other police forces, such as that in Afghanistan.

However, the Palestinian police was not a modern police organization. Most of the police officers within the force came from the military. Their training was militarized, and consisted of marching, physical fitness, and largely geared towards crowd control.

Interestingly, even though the climate of the area was highly volatile, and some districts held terrorist factions, the Palestinian police proudly boasted a section it called "Tourist Police". Some members of the force were also dedicated to traffic law enforcement and criminal investigations, even though officers assigned to those areas seldom had the required skills or equipment to perform their duties.

For example, the Palestinian police did not have a Forensic Identification Section where fingerprints could be lifted, DNA collected, and crime scene photos taken: all of which are a must-have to assist in many criminal investigations. The police also faced a dilemma in that they did not possess a laboratory where seized drugs could be analyzed or identified.

Clearly, one of the biggest problems the area had to contend with was the fact that the Palestinian territories were neither considered a country nor a state. Some of the laws the police enforced were either adapted or borrowed from neighbouring countries, such as Jordan or Egypt.

Walt provided the example of traffic law enforcement. Because the territories had no traffic laws, officers could not issue tickets. Many cars found on the street were heavily dented and lacked mirrors, headlights, or turn signals, making them a hazard to other vehicles and pedestrians. Driving was mostly a survival exercise, where the biggest and the fastest vehicle got the right-of-way.

A typical day in Walt's mission would start from his home in Jerusalem, where he would jump into his vehicle and head into the West Bank. He would cross the Kalandia checkpoint and head into the EUPOL headquarters in Ramallah, where he would pick up his translator. At the office, he would read the latest correspondence that had come in.

Every day, Walt had to write a trip plan to be remitted to the EUPOL security officer. This document explained in detail the places Walt would travel to, the reasons thereof, and the radio channel he would be monitoring.

More often than not, Walt would find himself in the city of Jericho, an hour's drive from Ramallah. There, he would spend the day with the Palestinian police training school staff. In the first three months, this meant assessing the school facilities and finding out what kind of training was being offered to the officers.

Walt spent most of the remaining nine months of his mission implementing all of the recommendations he and his team had identified. Further, a kitchen and a new training office were constructed in the building that housed the academy. Eventually, the EU would start building a new police academy to accommodate training needs.

Parallel to Walt's endeavours to identify training needs for the police were efforts by the EU to establish the rule of law in the territories. To this end, the EU had fostered the coming of EU judges, prosecutors, lawyers, and correction officers so that the territories could develop some of their own laws, and establish their own court procedures and rules of evidence.

Throughout the mission, Walt's work was complicated by the fact that Israel controlled everything that entered or exited the West Bank. This was due to Israel's "war on terrorism". This translated into barriers and checkpoints being erected all around the West Bank, in order to prevent the supply of armaments from reaching terrorists hiding within the confines of the West Bank. All equipment for the Palestinian police had to come through Israel.

Many communities within the West Bank were isolated, because checkpoints and borders were set up in such a way that one could not simply travel from one village to another.

When the EUPOL COPPS mission was established, officers were also assigned to the Gaza Strip of the Palestinian territories. However, the military group in charge of the area, HAMAS, was considered by international communities as a terrorist entity. In the end, EUPOL COPPS left the area and concentrated its efforts in the West Bank, under the control of FATAH, led by President Mahmoud Abbas.

Alas, even though HAMAS was mainly confined to the Gaza Strip, its terrorist methods and open threats against the sovereignty of Israel would make Walt's efforts and training assessments a much more challenging endeavour.

Although food and water in Israel were very clean, and food inspection standards were similar to those we are accustomed to in North America, there were areas in the West Bank that were not so hygienic. For example, it was not uncommon in the West Bank to come across a butchered cow hanging from a post, with meat being hacked out of it.

Walt would go to the training school and share meals with the recruits. That meant that he ate what they ate. Walt admits that he would have felt bad if he had said "no" to eating the same food as the Palestinian recruits. As such, he ventured to taste Palestinian cuisine. Eventually, he came to enjoy it, but not before he lost 25 pounds and remained in bed for a few days…

Despite acts of terrorism plaguing the region for decades, Walt and other EUPOL COPPS staff felt a relative safety living on the heavily secured Israeli side of Jerusalem. Each day, however, Walt had to travel to the West Bank, where he could potentially become the unintended target of a terrorist attacker.

At the time, security intelligence did not identify EUPOL COPPS as the intended target of terrorists. That said, it was the constant element of the unknown that made the places Walt visited a potential graveyard. Even with trip planning in place, the best advice mission security could give Walt was: "Don't be at the wrong place at the wrong time." How can one prepare for that? This would become a daily challenge!

During Walt's mission, the Israeli Army was on high alert, and conducted incursion operations in the West Bank. This was in an effort to remove individuals of interest, members of HAMAS, and anybody the Israeli authorities believed was a threat to its sovereignty.

As such, Walt kept in contact with the EUPOL COPPS Intelligence, which worked closely with the Israeli Army and the Palestinian Authorities. This enabled EUPOL COPPS Intelligence to warn its officers when to stay away from certain areas.

Ensuring that unnecessary risks were not taken was thus part of Walt's regular duties. However, as good and effective as the EUPOL COPPS Intelligence could be, it could not prepare its officers for the eventuality of a rocket attack. At the time, these were coming in from Hezbollah operatives located in Lebanon.[267] Rock throwing incidents against the Israeli Army were also common occurrences, and EUPOL COPPS officers had to be vigilant not to find themselves in the middle of an attack.

In December 2008, as random rocket attacks against Israel intensified, Israel launched bomb strikes of its own at Gaza, targeting HAMAS-controlled locations, and invaded the territory. Although these events were taking place in the Gaza Strip, they strongly influenced the mood against Israel in the West Bank. That translated into Walt's mission becoming that much more dangerous and risky, as the odds increased that he would inadvertently find himself in a conflict zone.

On a day-to-day basis, Walt would travel to Ramallah to arrive at the EUPOL COPPS office by 08:00. At the latest, Walt had to be out of the West Bank by 20:00, as many border checkpoints would prevent cross-border travel after that time.

Walt had been working alone one day at the EUPOL COPPS office in Ramallah, when he suddenly realized it was getting late. It was already dark outside, and he needed to get back to Jerusalem before the border checkpoint closed. So he hopped in his vehicle and headed straight to the checkpoint. He had little time left before 20:00. As he neared the checkpoint, he realized that, to his dismay, it was blocked.

Figure 56: EUPOL COPPS vehicle driven by Walt. Walt (to the left) is seen here with a colleague in the desert area of the West Bank. Photo courtesy of Walt Sutherland.

Traffic was at a standstill! Walt noted a large Palestinian youth protest nearby. As vehicles honked, the youths started to throw large rocks haphazardly towards them. These rocks were large enough to break a windshield and seriously injure an occupant.

Seeing the danger, Walt put his vehicle into reverse and managed to quickly get away from the demonstration. Even though

Walt was unhurt, and no youth had targeted his marked EUPOL COPPS vehicle, the fact that he found himself in the middle of a volatile demonstration was quite unnerving.

It was with a sigh of relief that Walt found himself at a safe distance from the demonstration. However, with nowhere to go, darkness all around, and no road signs anywhere in sight, his anxiety ramped up again. He was lost!

Taking a deep breath to calm down, Walt reached a colleague on the radio and provided him with some reference points. The colleague eventually appeared in a vehicle, and from that time on, Walt followed him through a maze of roads. In the course of time, both reached an alternate checkpoint and safely crossed into Israel.

The war in Gaza really raised EUPOL COPPS's security awareness, and placed many of its staff on high alert. The threat to the safety of its employees was such that EUPOL COPPS headquarters in Ramallah had to increase its security and build bomb shelters for its personnel. Movements of EUPOL COPPS officers also became restricted to certain areas known to be safer.

As a note, EUPOL COPPS officers were not armed. In an area that harboured so much violence and danger, one could wonder about the logic of not having EUPOL COPPS carry personal weapons. The reason, according to Walt, was very simple: if EUPOL COPPS officers had been armed, they would have been severely underpowered. Consider the incommensurable difference of carrying a police pistol versus the automatic rifle favoured by both Israelis and Palestinians. Being neutral and unarmed was the safest approach.

The best experience Walt got out of his mission was that of working with other EU police officers. They upheld similar values and operated in a comparable fashion; therefore, carrying out assignments with them and learning how they enforced the law in their native countries was a truly enriching venture. Throughout his mission, Walt worked with Danish, Swedish, and Czech Republic officers, with whom he developed a strong friendship.

Despite the many dangers lurking there, working in the Middle East had its reward: the ability to travel in some of the world's most historically rich regions! Walter recalls that on one occasion, during his assessment of the Palestinian Civil Police training, he travelled to Bethlehem to meet with the Tourist Police division. The Tourist Police were in Bethlehem to provide assistance and security to the hundreds of thousands of tourists who visited the city every year.

Although Bethlehem was a short distance from Jerusalem, it took quite some time to travel to the area, as Walt had to proceed through several Israeli checkpoints to get beyond the separation wall bordering Israel.

After some driving through the twisted, narrow streets of Bethlehem, Walt and a colleague arrived at their destination. There, they met with the head of the Tourist Police to discuss training needs. At the end of the meeting, Walt was asked if he would like to see the place where Jesus was born.

Raised as a Christian, this was an unbelievable opportunity for Walt: to see one of the most sacred sites on Earth. It was also quite apparent that Walt was not the only one who wanted to see the place where Jesus was born. Tourist line-ups appeared to stretch for hundreds of metres from the site.

Walt would have loved to visit, but it was getting late, and they would have to leave soon to make it through the Israeli checkpoints on time. When Walt explained the matter, the head of the Tourist Police casually told him not to worry. He then led Walt and his colleague through a small doorway known as the Door of Humility, which led directly into the Church of the Nativity.

Walt had to bend down for the low doorway. And just that quickly, Walt was inside the famous ornate church, with its hanging lights and mosaic floors. To him, the scene felt simply surreal.

Next, the Tourist Police led Walt to a rear stairway, which connected to an underground crypt. And there it was: the Grotto of the Nativity, the place where Jesus was born! As he admired the sanctity of the place, Walt realized with embarrassment that the tourist police had held back the long line trying to get a glimpse of this very place.

Surrounded by altars, a large silver star held centrepiece on the floor of the crypt. There, it is believed, was the spot where the baby Jesus was born. The officer quietly indicated that Walt could touch it, if he wished.

Walt knelt down and touched the star. The moment sent shivers up his spine. It felt nearly hypnagogic! The significance of visiting a place so central to his own religion would never escape him.

On another occasion, Walt and a Czech colleague took a well-deserved mini-holiday to neighbouring Jordan, where they visited the ancient city of Petra. In addition to being famous for its rock-cut architecture, the ancient city was the set of blockbuster movies such as *Indiana Jones and the Last Crusade*, *Transformers: Revenge of the Fallen*, and a number of other, lesser known motion pictures.[268]

Figure 57: Inspector Walt Sutherland on leave in the ancient city of Petra, Jordan. Photo courtesy of Walt Sutherland.

Perhaps one of Walt's most challenging tasks during his mission was to get the Palestinian police to think like a modern police force. Because senior officers within the Palestinian police came from a military background, they did not think like police officers, but rather like military ones. Although there was nothing wrong with the latter, applying policing principles and techniques without the benefit of training in the police vision to serve and protect turned out to be tricky.

For example, the management of the Palestinian police had unrealistic expectations about what police work was all about. They saw the television crime show *CSI* as being the norm in police investigations, without realizing that what took an hour to investigate on a show may have actually taken several months to do.

At the time of Walt's mission, Canada was considering building a forensic crime laboratory for the Palestinian police. Building the facility was one thing, but educating the police on how to collect and handle police evidence was another story. No procedures had been established to deal with the seizure and handling of police exhibits. Therefore, police investigative thinking would first need to be worked out.

For instance, the Palestinian police's way of solving a crime might have been by obtaining a forced confession from an accused, rather than by looking for and amassing other evidence of the crime. Public trust and apparent support of the police was also very low, thus preventing many citizens from approaching the police and providing witness evidence.

Visiting a police station could sometimes turn into a frustrating endeavour, as Palestinian officers would be at their posts smoking cigarettes and drinking coffee instead of being proactive and conducting vehicle or foot patrols.

Since they were not getting calls from the public, if an incident occurred, five to six officers would jump in a vehicle and attend the scene. Once arrived, there was no protocol as to how to secure the area and gather evidence. If there was evidence, the police had no tools to collect it in a manner that satisfied court exigency and minimize contamination (i.e. no gloves to prevent contamination of exhibits, no fingerprint collecting kit, and no exhibit bags to tag and separate evidence).

For example, after seeing a law enforcement television show, the Palestinian Traffic police approached the EU in order to obtain sophisticated radar sets that took photographs of offending vehicles. Alas, their wishes might have been premature, as there were no laws in the West Bank that governed the speed of vehicles. Obtaining such equipment would have been futile until traffic laws and regulations in the West Bank had been established.

The Palestinian police's authority to stop vehicles can be epitomized in one sentence, which was once shared with Walt by a senior Palestinian officer: "We are the police, stop!" To show Walt that he meant business, the police officer took him on a ride-along to introduce him to a "vehicle stop, Palestinian police style".

On a routine patrol, officers, armed to the teeth and riding in the back of a pick-up truck, first came up behind a car they wanted to stop. They overtook the car, cut it off, and all the officers jumped off the back, pointing their AK-47s at the driver and passengers. Then, for no apparent reasons, all were ordered out of the offending vehicle. Walt felt a measure of sympathy for the occupants, who must have had the scare of their life.

But this was a routine check, and no occupant seemed otherwise surprised or worried! After his story, I kind of feared to question Walt as to how his police counterparts conducted high-risk takedowns! In a part of the world where suicide bombers once thrived, I could only imagine that such takedowns would end up with casualties…or at best, an extremely unpleasant experience for drivers and passengers alike.

Challenges were not only with the Palestinians. They also existed with the Israelis. For instance, the high level of security surrounding the checkpoints and what could be brought into Palestinian territories only added to the existing difficulties in providing adequate training to the Palestinian police recruits.

For instance, recruits only disposed of ten bullets each to complete firearms training. This was the maximum quota the Israeli Army allowed the police to practice with, perhaps out of a belief that those same bullets could eventually be used against the army. When compared to the firearms training Canadian police go through, using thousands of bullets with proper shooting ranges and targets, there was no wonder the Palestinian police were undertrained, with their ten bullets and improvised riverbed firing range!

Perhaps the greatest struggle Walt had to deal with was in convincing the Palestinian police to change its methodology, thus developing it into a modern police organization. This was not an impossible mission, but one that would require effort and follow-up from the EU for years to come.

Patience is a virtue that one should possess if considering working in the developing world. As Walt put it, things do not simply happen overnight. Change comes in very slowly. Therefore, one's expectations to contribute to societies with human rights issues should be adjusted accordingly. If views or visions are not well received by the host, one should not necessarily give up, but instead introduce them in another way.

For example, we saw earlier that stopping a vehicle in the way the Palestinian police did would be somewhat unacceptable in Western society. Imposing our values to their actions in the name of democracy might not be practical in a world where terrorism is almost a part of daily life.

Figure 58: From left to right: Insp. Walt Sutherland, Major Omar (Head of Police Training), Lt. Col. Zahir Sabba (Commander of the Police College) and Corporal John Pullen. Photo courtesy of Walt Sutherland.

Walt's admiration for the Palestinian and the Israeli people was evident. He truly enjoyed working and being in the company of both. Yet, the reasons that kept the two nations apart from each other remained very difficult to conceive for a Westerner. The conflict in Palestine has its roots so deeply entrenched in history that it may, unfortunately, not be solved any time soon.

In the meantime, owing to the work of people like Walt, a lasting peace in this incredibly beautiful and historically rich part of the world is what we can hope for!

9.

Defying the Taliban: ISAF (International Security Assistance Force), Afghanistan 2001-2013

It is summer. The temperature under the sun reaches a suffocating heat of more than 40 degrees. You are hot and thirsty under your heavy military gear. Gusts of wind blow desert sands into your face. But these are the least of your worries.

As you walk on patrols with your team on the streets of Kandahar, you can't help but feel the uneasy sensation that you are being watched: here, you are unwelcome!

The local population acts hostile towards you, as if you were the enemy, the invader. As you advance, you look over your shoulder for any signs of an ambush. Your heart is racing as you think of four of your comrades, who perished a few days earlier when their vehicle hit an Improvised Explosive Device not too far from where you now stand…

Welcome to Constable Gregor Aitken's mission with the International Security Assistance Force (ISAF) in Kandahar, Afghanistan. Gregor's story in Afghanistan, from March to December of 2009, is a tribute to the courage, dedication, and determination of all those who, like him, participated in the endeavour to bring peace to and rebuild this broken land. Gregor's tale in Kandahar will give you a front-row seat to one of the most dangerous places on earth.

BRIDGING CRUCIAL TRADE routes between southern and eastern Asia to Europe and the Middle East, Afghanistan has long been a sought-after kingdom by empire builders. For millennia, great armies have attempted to subdue its territories, leaving traces of their efforts in great monuments now fallen to ruin.[269]

Slightly bigger than France, modern-day Afghanistan is a mountainous country delimited to the east and south by Pakistan, to the west by Iran, and to the north by the former Soviet Union constituent states of Turkmenistan, Uzbekistan, and Tajikistan. About half of the country's territory is more than 2,000 metres above sea level.[270]

Figure 59: Afghanistan. Map reproduced with permission of WorldAtlas.com

For a good part of its history, the region known as Afghanistan was part of the Persian Empire. The area was also occupied in different epochs by the Indian Mughal dynasty, various Muslim dynasties, the Mongols, and the armies of Alexander the Great, among others.[271]

The beginning of modern Afghanistan can be traced back to 1747, when a tribal chief named Ahmad Khan Abdali was elected king of the Afghans in Kandahar.[272]

In 1818, the capital city of Kabul was taken by a different Afghan tribe, named Barakzai, led by one Dost Mohammed.[273] After many years of civil war against the Afghans of Kandahar, the country was divided amongst Mohammed and some of his brothers.

Eventually, Mohammed became the accepted leader, or emir, of most Afghan tribes and by foreign states. Because of their strategic location for trade with India, Kabul and other Afghan areas soon find themselves at odds with both Russia and Great Britain.

Around December of 1838, the British Army assembled in India for an Afghan invasion. By April 1839, the British had captured the city of Kandahar; Kabul was conquered four months later.[274]

During the campaign, Mohammed was taken prisoner by the British, and he and his family were exiled to India. However, it was not long before Afghan tribes' resentment over the British take-over grew. By 1842, war forced the British to withdraw from Kabul.[275] However, within a year, Kabul was re-captured by the British, who returned this time with Mohammed as an ally, restoring him to his throne.[276]

By 1875, Russian influence was growing in Afghanistan. Attempts were made by the British Crown to reaffirm its power over the country by force. However, in 1878, another violent incident forced the British to accept a new local emir as ruler of the area, since he was the popular choice among many Afghan tribes.[277]

It was under this latter emir that the boundaries of modern

Afghanistan were drawn, to affix the limits of British, Afghan, and Soviet spheres of influence in the region.[278]

The emir was eventually succeeded by three generations of his family, which reigned over an authoritarian regime. During that time, many economic investments in mining and small factories (candles, soap, etc.) were made. However, "modernization" was not always welcomed by the tribal Afghans, and attempts were often frustrated by anarchy and violence.[279]

WWI brought wide support to the Turkish Ottoman regime, although the country was able to maintain a policy of non-involvement throughout the hostilities. After the war, the independence of Afghanistan was recognized by Great Britain.

By the turn of the decade in the 1920s, the Afghans concluded a treaty of friendship with the new Bolshevik regime in the Soviet Union. This resulted in the country becoming one of the first states to recognize the Soviet government. As a result, a "special relationship" between the two governments was born.[280]

Although Afghanistan remained neutral during WWII, the country got a taste of the global conflict when some of its frontiers were prepared with anti-tank mines. This was in a bid to prepare its borders in the event the German army defeated Russian forces and pushed eastwards.[281]

Relations between the Soviet Union and Afghanistan continued to flourish until 1978, when a violent revolution set the latter upon an entirely new direction.[282]

In 1978, a coup d'état saw a pro-Soviet Union, a left-wing faction of the Afghan Army take control of the country, which promoted an increased Soviet presence. Soon, a guerrilla movement known as the Afghan Mujahedeen started to rebel against the army.

In December 1979, in an attempt to render assistance to the army and fight the Mujahedeen, Soviet troops entered Kabul. It was not long before Cold War circumstances fostered covert military aid to the Mujahedeen from the United States, Great Britain, and other allies that had feared a Soviet control over Afghanistan.[283]

It is also during this time that a young Saudi man named Osama bin-Laden started to bring contingents of Arab fighters to Afghanistan in order to wage a war against communist Russia and its Afghan Army allies.[284]

Russian intervention in Afghanistan came to an end in 1988, when Soviet leader Mikhail Gorbachev announced a pull-out of Soviet forces from the country; Osama bin-Laden eventually returned to Saudi Arabia.[285]

Ten years of warfare in Afghanistan truly devastated this already poor country. During that time, nearly 2 million refugees fled into Pakistan, while another 1.8 million fled into Iran.[286] The United Nations oversaw the agreements between the United States, the Soviet Union, Pakistan, and Afghanistan on the settlement of the situation in the country. The Mujahedeen, however, were not party to the accord. As such, they continued to wage their fight against the government of Kabul, and the civil war continued until Kabul fell to the Mujahedeen in 1992.[287]

From the continuing chaos and violence emerged a group of fundamentalist Islamic Sunni students in 1994, who were followers of the Quran. These were orphan Afghan-war refugees, who had been raised in Islamic religious schools spread across northern Pakistan.[288] They were raised to hate and fight a "Holy War" that aimed to restore Afghanistan to its people.[289]

The Taliban (the word "Talib" means "student" in the Pashto language), as it became known, showed little tolerance for other forms of Islam, and viewed democracy or any other secular political process as an offence to Islam.[290]

By late 1996, popular support for the Taliban among some Afghan tribes was growing. Kabul eventually fell to the Taliban, and with it came an effective control of nearly 90% of the country.

However, Afghans would soon realize that the price for the imposition of Muslim fundamentalism was very high. Under the regime, women were forced to wear a veil in public, were denied access to education, were only allowed to go shopping if accompanied by a male relative, and were prevented from seeking employment other than working at home.[291]

With the strictest version of Islamic law came harsh criminal punishments, where hand amputations for theft, public executions, and floggings became common sights.[292] It was during this time that the Taliban regime opened its doors to Islamic militants from around the world. Among those who used the country as a place to hide and set up terrorist training camps were Osama bin-Laden and his al-Qaeda followers.[293]

On September 11, 2001, four commercial airplanes were hijacked by 19 al-Qaeda terrorists. Two of them were deliberately crashed into the World Trade Center towers in New York.[294] A third one crashed into the Pentagon in Virginia, while the last one burst into flames in an open field in the state of Pennsylvania.[295]

The attacks, which caused tremendous destruction to infrastructures and occasioned the death of nearly 3,000 people, triggered colossal efforts from the United States and its allies to find those responsible.[296]

It was not long before American authorities figured out who was behind the plot and attacks. In the aftermath of September 11th, one of the first countries to be hailed responsible for the outrageous events was Afghanistan. For its ruling authority, the Taliban, to allow the terrorist organization al-Qaeda the right to use the country, set up terrorist training camps, and provide asylum to its leader, Osama bin-Laden, Afghanistan soon became the focal point of the global "War on Terror".[297]

The Taliban leadership in Kabul rejected international pressure to surrender al-Qaeda's Mogul and his troops. On October 7th,

2001, the United States and its allies invaded the country in an offensive it named "Operation Enduring Freedom."[298] The invasion soon forced the collapse of the Taliban government, but not before its leaders and those of al-Qaeda, including Osama bin-Laden, escaped.[299]

United Nations involvement in Afghanistan can be traced back to the early 1980s, when it denounced the Soviet invasion, called for a withdrawal of all international military troops, and sought support from the involved states to contribute humanitarian assistance. Efforts to have the military abandon their campaign were somewhat in vain.[300]

It was not until 1988, with the beginning of the withdrawal of foreign military forces, that the United Nations set up a mission in Afghanistan.[301] The mission, then named United Nations Good Offices Mission in Afghanistan and Pakistan (UNGOMAP), was mandated to overview the withdrawal process and make plans to support an anticipated return of refugees to their country.[302]

In the early 1990s, the United Nations continued to provide agricultural assistance, food aid, and health services to Afghans, despite a civil war raging and a new refugee crisis. In 1993, a Peace Accord was negotiated between the tribes involved in the civil war, and refugees began to return.

Alas, the Peace Accord did not totally prevent hostilities from continuing. By 1995, the Taliban had taken control over much of the southern and western areas of the country. Kabul and most of the country fell a year later. Under the Taliban, all humanitarian aid offices were compelled to relocate to Kabul.[303]

The 1998 bombings of the United States embassies in Kenya and Tanzania by al-Qaeda's effectives were landmark events. They compelled the UN to denounce the Taliban for allowing international terrorists the use of the country, both as a sanctuary and training ground.

At the same time, the UN, which still had a small mission (UNSMA) and other humanitarian agencies working in the country, faulted Taliban authorities for their inability to protect UN staff. Notable during that time were the killings of three UN employees, including a military attaché in Kabul.[304]

Although the US invasion of Afghanistan ousted the Taliban regime, the political, military, and humanitarian situation in the country continued to deteriorate. In order to help maintain a degree of security and help Afghan opposition leaders to rebuild their country, the UN Security Council authorized the establishment of the International Security Assistance Force through UN Resolution 1386 in December 2001.[305] With the setup of a new government structure, the Afghan Transitional Authority, hopes were raised for peace and development in the country.

As time went by, new partnerships were created, so that the ISAF, the United Nations Assistance Mission in Afghanistan (UNAMA), and the Afghan Transitional Authority would join efforts to rebuild the nation.

As a new Afghan government was formed, namely the Government of the Islamic Republic of Afghanistan, the ISAF's role continued to be that of conducting military operations throughout the country. This was both to reduce the capability and will of the Taliban insurgency, and support the growth of state agencies such as the police, the army, and national security.

Furthermore, the ISAF would play an important role in facilitating improvements in governance and socio-economic development. Providing a secure environment for sustainable stability that was observable to the general population was a primary objective.[306]

Alas, in the eleven years since its inception, the ISAF mission has been anything but smooth. Frequent insurgent attacks and suicide bombings have made the mission particularly lethal to its members.[307]

As of September 2012, there had been more than 3,024 coalition force deaths, including 2,000 U.S. troops and 158 Canadian soldiers. These high numbers propelled the Afghanistan campaign to the top of the most dangerous UN-mandated missions.[308]

Therefore, the ISAF mission was firmly a peacemaking operation. With police officers wearing full army combat gear, their mission hardly resembled anything else; the daily dangers and challenges they faced were truly phenomenal.

In Afghanistan, civilian and military worked in tandem to restore the rule of law and governance under what was known as "the whole of government approach". From a Canadian perspective, this meant that the Department of Foreign Affairs and International Trade (DFAIT), the Canadian Forces (CF), and Canadian civilian police were working together.

Part of this approach was to help rebuild infrastructure. Police Operational Mentoring and Liaison Teams were tasked with rebuilding the very weak institution of the Afghanistan National Police (ANP). Operational Mentoring Teams were doing the same for the Afghanistan National Army (ANA). At the same time, Canadian battle groups and other allied nations sought out and destroyed the Taliban.

With more than 15 years of combined police and armed forces service, RCMP Constable Gregor Aitken was an ideal candidate for a mission in Kandahar. He had many years of police operational experience, plus an excellent knowledge and understanding of the military.

Despite his experience, Gregor's biggest obstacle to being drafted for the Afghan mission would be to obtain support from RCMP management so that he could be released from his current duties. Let us not forget that, during the first decade of the new millennium, many RCMP detachments, especially those in British Columbia, were already understaffed. This situation made it more difficult for police officers to be released from duties and participate in an overseas mission.

Thus, most RCMP managers would only consider good performers to apply for a UN tour of duty once they had discussed potential issues such as: the impact a prolonged absence would have on the family, the change of climate, and the difficult reality of some missions. To managers, it was important to determine that a candidate's motivation was the right one, and not solely based on obtaining a medal, earning money, or, worse, escaping from work or home realities.

For Gregor, a mission meant an opportunity to make a difference, as small as it might be. At the time he applied for Afghanistan, he was an investigator at the Surrey detachment Drug Section in British Columbia. Having received the blessings to apply from the detachment's higher hierarchy, Gregor could only wait until "all the stars lined up" in his favour.

And soon they did! Being mature, an excellent performer, and mentally and physically fit, the RCMP International Peacekeeping Operations Section would eventually facilitate his candidacy. However, despite the many layers of checks set up to ensure that candidates selected for that mission would be adept, not everyone drafted would turn out well-prepared.

Pre-deployment training for this mission lasted six weeks and took place in two locations: Chilliwack, British Columbia and Ottawa, Ontario. The first part of the pre-deployment exercise, which comprised four weeks of theory, commenced in Ottawa at the Canadian Police College. There, Gregor met the other members selected for the mission, many of whom would later become his emotional and physical lifelines in Kandahar. Other CF and United States military personnel, whom Gregor would meet later on his tour-of-duty, also played a crucial supportive role.[309]

In Ottawa, Gregor was exposed to informative sessions on:

administrative requirements, the use of force, war crimes, and child soldiers. A hand-out on the mission was provided, as well as a very brief overview of the police mandate.

However, this overview was, in the opinion of many attendees, short in many important areas. Receiving more cross-cultural training about Afghanistan, its people, its customs, the region as a whole, and learning more about the challenges the Afghan National Police (ANP) faced would have been an asset. Furthermore, acquiring information about the mandate of the mission and what might be expected in-theatre would have been an advantage.

Mentoring ANP officers was a dangerous endeavour. Taliban infiltration within the ANP occurred occasionally, and would often result in the death of one or more foreign police trainers. Consequently, a stronger emphasis on tactical and survival skills, an in-depth look at the mission's mandate, the role that each partner and coalition forces played on the ground (i.e.: ANP, ANA, CF, US Forces, etc.), would have better prepared the candidates to face the daunting challenges ahead.

In spite of the absence of the material mentioned above, a thorough review of the different use-of-force levels was afforded. This was done with an emphasis on non-lethal approaches and directions on how to diffuse conflicts through communications and respect.

However, in Afghanistan, where death or grievous injury happened at the most unexpected moment, constantly keeping a tactical mindset was of paramount importance. This ought to be the norm to survive, even if it meant that some well-intended community policing concepts might suffer in the process.

As a case in point, take the chilling example of what happened to a CF officer in 2006. The officer, who was leading a civilian and military mission in a remote Southern Afghanistan village, removed his helmet as a sign of respect to the village elders whom he had come to visit. Alas, at that moment, he was savagely attacked from behind by a youth, who buried an axe in the officer's head.

Life-threateningly wounded, the officer fell unconscious into a pool of blood. The youth, who continued his attack, was eventually shot dead.[310]

To this effect, the second phase of pre-deployment training involved a crash course on how to operate assault rifles, namely the C-7. This phase took place in Chilliwack, British Columbia. There, officers would also get to practice drills and obtain a basic introduction on the way the CF operated.[311]

By all accounts, this two-week training was insufficient for those police officers without previous military experience. With CF soldiers undergoing a six-month preparation before leaving for the Afghan campaign, the police candidates were at a bit of a disadvantage. This became quite obvious later in-theatre, as some officers handling C-7s were jokingly referred to as being more dangerous than the Taliban insurgents.

On a brighter side, this shortcoming was quickly identified from candidate feedback, and subsequent rotations of officers benefitted from a more thorough military preparation.

Once the Chilliwack training was over, candidates returned home for a week to be with their families. They later flew to Ottawa one last time to prepare for their departure overseas.

Leaving a daughter and a wife behind to go to a war zone was no easy task. What could have possibly motivated Gregor to sign up for such a dangerous endeavour? One of the driving forces behind the decision was his desire to make a positive difference in the world. A proud father of a one-year-old girl at the time, Gregor was aware of how women in Afghanistan were so poorly treated, and as such, he believed his contribution would aid in paving the road for the betterment of women's rights and conditions in Afghanistan.

On a sunny but cool day in March 2009, Gregor left Ottawa

and flew to Toronto, where he embarked on a 72-hour journey that would take him to Kandahar.

In Toronto, the voyage started with a business seat to Dubai on Emirates Airlines.[312] Business class dining on Emirates Airlines turned out to be an experience out-of-this-world! On long-haul flights, Emirates Airlines offered five-course lunches and dinners, with a great choice of hors d'oeuvres, entrees, steaks, cheeses, and vintage wines.

Unable to resist the temptation, Gregor ordered curried prawn and a vintage white wine, which he bragged was one of the best meals of his entire life. Then, as he was grinning and enjoying his dish, he suddenly had an obscure thought: what if this dinner turned out to be his last meal?

Thankfully, it was not! However, Gregor would come across a few situations within his first 48-hours in Afghanistan that would make him wonder whether the gourmet meal he had enjoyed on Emirates Airlines would indeed be his last.

Once he arrived in Dubai, Gregor continued his journey on to an undisclosed location in the Middle-East, which we will refer to as "Host Nation", or HN. At HN, Gregor waited for a further two days for a Royal Netherlands Air Force Hercules plane to transport him, members of his tour, and other international soldiers to Kandahar Airfield (KAF) in Afghanistan.

Riding on a military transport cargo plane after the lush transatlantic voyage on Emirates Airlines was a harsh return to reality for Gregor. Heavy noise from the engines, vibrations, uncomfortable webbed jump-seats, freezing temperatures, and the sight of cargo instead of a blockbuster movie reminded him of the true nature of his endeavour.

At about the four-hour flight mark, still well into the night, the Dutch Hercules plane started its descent to the Kandahar Airfield. Without any warnings, perhaps to avoid potential surface-to-air missile attacks, the plane abruptly nose-dived. Before Gregor had a chance to recover from the shock, it quickly banked to the left, then to the right, and to the left again.

Dizzy and about to throw up, Gregor let out a sigh of relief when the plane finally touched down. Still feeling some mild nausea caused by their unexpected "roller-coaster" ride, Gregor and the other CIVPOL officers rushed out of the plane. They were brought to an area where they briefly greeted the outgoing RCMP contingent commander.

"Dispiriting" is a word that described Gregor and others' first hours in Afghanistan. Miscommunication within the CIVPOL administration as to the exact arrival time of Gregor and his companions resulted in their accommodation not being ready. Fortunately, a vacant tent with bunk beds was identified and made available for the fatigued crew, who managed to catch a few hours' sleep before daybreak.

When Gregor woke up a few hours later and walked out of the tent, the scope of what he and others had gotten themselves into revealed itself: dust blowing, dark and grim perimeter fences, bunkers, anti-blast walls, the deafening drone of helicopters coming and going, the loud roar of turbine jets taking off…such grim and alien surroundings could only mean one thing: he was in a war zone!

Despite first impressions, Kandahar Airfield revealed itself to be a fascinating place to be. Over thirty thousand people lived on the base, including military, police, and other civilian support staff, all hailing from over thirty countries.

Later that morning, Gregor and his companions met their CIVPOL mentor, another Canadian police officer who had been in Afghanistan for some time. He informed the newly arrived that the noise they may have heard overnight was the sound of sirens warning of a rocket attack. Apparently, the base had briefly come under an offensive from insurgents firing rockets. Albeit well after the fact, Gregor and his comrades were informed of the location of the nearest bunker, should the warning sirens be heard again. Although no one's fault, Gregor was bothered by the fact that such pertinent information was not communicated at an earlier time.

Next, Gregor and his colleagues were led to the quartermaster store, where they received their ISAF photo identification and desert-coloured equipment to replace the green ones that had been issued at the HN base. At HN, a pistol, body armour, and helmet had already been issued, as this was mandatory equipment to fly in a Hercules troop transport plane.

As Gregor and others were getting their equipment, soldiers around them talked about the previous day's blast, which had injured and killed Canadian soldiers. With that incident had come a "Communication Lockdown" until the families of the wounded and the deceased were advised at home.

The situation unfortunately temporarily prevented Gregor and the other newly arrived from notifying their own worried families that they had landed safely in the country, a situation that only added more stress to them. Sadly, "Communication Lockdown" would become a common occurrence during the course of Gregor's mission.

Details of the previous day's incident were pretty grim. Two soldiers had died while on patrol when their 17-tonne Light Armoured Vehicle (LAV)[313] hit an Improvised Explosive Device, or IED. The force of the blast had been so powerful that it flipped the heavy vehicle into a ditch.

Gregor later learned that the same LAV was also supposed to carry an RCMP officer. It was only by a pure twist of fate that the RCMP member had escaped grievous injuries or death: at the last minute, the RCMP officer was asked to board the LAV behind the first one for strategic reasons, saving him from the explosion.[314]

Of course, the incident did not do much to reassure Gregor and those who had just arrived that they had made a good decision by accepting to travel to Afghanistan. Being happily married and the father of a one-year-old girl, Gregor had put a lot at stake for his journey into Afghanistan. Indeed, the likelihood of coming back home gravely injured, or worse, was increasingly becoming a stronger probability.

But being at Kandahar Airfield revealed another facet: one of an incredible story of life, death, camaraderie, and adventure. Among the uproar of gunship choppers taking off every few minutes, medical evacuation helicopters bringing in wounded, military jets screeching on the tarmac, and the scramble of soldiers running in all directions, Gregor could not help but feel constantly in suspense. One thing was undeniable: the mission promised to be packed with adventure and challenges.

Kandahar Airfield was also the place where Canadians stationed there had formed what they called a "Canada House": a building dedicated to giving Canadians a piece of home. In that building, staff could relax, watch satellite television, play video games, read books, and socialize.

The Canada House was designed to be a "home away from home". It was also a rallying point where Canadian convoys arrived and departed from the Kandahar Airfield.

Kandahar Airfield was not Gregor's final assignment, but a transition point before he arrived at Camp Nathan Smith (CNS). CNS was a former food factory that had been damaged during the civil war, and later turned into an American military base in the middle of Kandahar City.[315] It was there that Gregor was to really start his mission—although for him the adventure had started the moment he landed.

As Gregor and his comrades prepared to embark on their journey to CNS, a Canadian Forces Master Corporal approached. In a loud, no-nonsense tone, he explained that they were about to leave the camp. He understood that most of those he was addressing were not military, but rather civilians or police—it did not matter! Everyone would die the same if they got hit by a bomb. In the field, it was everyone's responsibility to take care of everybody else.

With those encouraging words, Gregor looked out at the four vehicles that would take him and the company to CNS: three RG-31s and one LAV. Owing to his military training, Gregor knew that someone traveling in a 4x4, mine-protected, Armoured Personnel Carrier RG-31 theoretically had a much better chance of surviving a bomb blast than someone riding in a LAV.

Still weighing heavily on his mind was the tragedy of the Canadian Forces soldiers who had succumbed in a LAV a few days earlier. Regardless, at 3 to 1, the odds were pretty good that Gregor would end up traveling in an RG-31.

"Aitken!" shouted the Master Corporal. "You'll sit in the LAV!" Not having much choice, Gregor entered the vehicle and sat on a bench.

Beside him was a comrade who had already been in a shooting confrontation with insurgents. Noticing that Gregor was not totally at ease, he smiled and told him that everything would be fine.

Despite the kind words of his comrade, Gregor was not reassured at all. In fact, his knees started to shake, while his mind raced to evoke some of the worse scenarios possible. As fear engulfed him, he cringed at the thought of letting his companions, family, and the country down.

And then, something amazing took place: instead of becoming paralyzed, Gregor took a deep breath, held on to it for a moment, and let go. He did that a few times. His knees stopped shaking. He felt at peace.

Gregor had managed to restrain his apprehensions by forcing himself to confront the situation he feared. Knowingly or not,

Gregor was practicing courage. Like renowned 19th Century American author Mark Twain once said: "Do the thing you fear most, and the death of fear is certain." In Afghanistan, Gregor and many of his colleagues developed the habit of courage by practicing it over and over again.[316]

Practicing courage whenever it was required was the key. By acting courageously when called for, as though they already possessed such bravery, they actually earned it![317] Not to say that Gregor or others were not brave to start with, but by confronting their fears whenever they arose, they were able to overcome their apprehension and fully function in a highly dangerous environment.

Thankfully, the ride to Camp Nathan Smith (CNS) was uneventful. Gregor would later recall that due to a mishap, assault rifles had not been issued to any newcomers for their trip to CNS. Here they were, in the middle of the desert, in a war zone, armed only with small handguns holding more or less 15 rounds of ammunition. Thankfully, they were informed that the situation would be rectified in the future, so that no newcomers would be left under-powered on the trip from the Kandahar Airfield to CNS.

Figure 60: Gregor Aitken ground guiding an RG-31 Nayala Armoured Patrol Vehicle. This occurred later on in the mission, while conducting a presence patrol in the desert north of Kandahar City. Photo courtesy of Gregor Aitken.

Despite Gregor's first 48-hours in the country being a roller coaster of emotions, it would not be long before he and the others would fully adapt to the harsh and dangerous realities of the mission.

Camp Nathan Smith would be Gregor's base camp for the first few days of his mission. It was there that Gregor and other officers were issued military assault rifles, more combat gear, and night-vision goggles.[318]

In addition, at CNS, newcomers would be provided with mandatory "in-theatre training". This local grounding provided specific knowledge and information on how to deal with unexploded IEDs, major trauma first aid, and military vehicle familiarization (LAVs and RGs).

As a safety measure, all mission participants had to attend variations of the above lectures every time they returned to the country from leave, regardless of how long they were away. This was to ensure that a peacemaker was constantly updated on current policy and ever-changing safety measures.

His induction training completed, Gregor went on to his first assignment as police mentor with the CF, on what was called a "presence patrol". This assignment consisted of going out on foot patrol with a Canadian military platoon of approximately 30 soldiers. The company also included two international civilian police (Gregor and a colleague named Andy Johnstone), translators, and ANP effectives.

These patrols, which stretched at times almost two city blocks, were conducted during the day and took the troops through the many sand-and-dust filled streets and alleys of Kandahar. The idea behind the patrols was to go out with the ANP and find out where crimes occurred.

For example, this meant that Gregor would help the ANP in identifying who stole bicycles, who built homemade bombs, who sold drugs, and who committed crime in general.

Furthermore, the exercise was meant to reinforce the idea with the local populace that the Afghan Government and the ISAF were not afraid to go where they were needed, whenever they wanted, despite Taliban claims to the contrary.

In addition, as a police mentor Gregor had to overview how the ANP officers reacted to certain situations in order to better elevate ANP policing skills. For instance, he supervised how they conducted themselves with the public, how they interviewed people, and how they gathered evidence and made notes (most ANP officers did not know how to read and write, which made it somewhat complicated when it came time to make notes and gather evidence).[319]

On Gregor's initial patrol, he had been out walking for less than ten minutes when an engine was heard revving up. A man on a dilapidated motorcycle raced towards him and his company. Alarmed at the thought that this could be a suicide bomber, all raised their weapons and aimed at the oncoming driver. Quickly realizing that his life was in danger, the motorcyclist put on the brakes and abruptly came to a full stop in a cloud of dust.

The next seconds would be nerve-racking! With weapons aimed at the motorcyclist, Gregor and others from the CF contingent cautiously approached the individual, who was ordered to keep his hands visible and well above his head.

Gregor then summoned an ANP officer, who started to question the man. In the local language, Pashtun, they asked him his name, where he was from, and why he had raced towards the platoon.

The man, who admitted to carrying a concealed pistol, initially advised he was a security guard at one of the nearby allied troops training centres. The man was nonetheless searched by ANP officers under Gregor's watchful eye. An expired security guard identification tag was located on the motorcyclist, who later admitted to no longer being employed at the camp.

Discussing regulations regarding the carrying of firearms, and learning that the man was an ex-guard for the coalition—which meant certain death to him if the insurgency found out—Gregor and the ANP officers came to the conclusion that the man was no threat, and that he carried the weapon for the sole purpose of personal protection.

Gregor then unloaded the man's weapon, and through an interpreter, informed him he could have his gun and ammunitions back once the entire Canadian patrol had gone by. Leaving the man without his gun could mean his death at the hands of insurgents; but allowing him to carry the weapon in the presence of the patrol could also mean death or serious injuries to members of the company.

Gregor and the CF had barely finished dealing with the man on the motorcycle when a nearby farmer frantically waved at them in an effort to get noticed. When asked what was wrong, the farmer

Figure 61: Gregor Aitken on a foot patrol through a bazaar in northern Kandahar City. The area was known as a pro-Taliban neighbourhood. Photo courtesy of Gregor Aitken.

pointed to a wall ahead of the troop, where a live IED had been concealed by insurgents. Faced with the possibility of grievous harm or death, Gregor's heartbeat revved up yet again.

A safety perimeter was soon set up around the wall where the IED had been spotted. With many members of the team only days away from completing their Afghan mission, volunteering for the duty of approaching the wall and assessing the threat was not a popular idea. However, this task had to be done, and the troop remained at a safe distance while a few daring Canadian soldiers walked up to the wall.

KA BOOM!

A huge explosion rocked the ground, and sent almost everyone still standing running for cover. In the backdrop, Gregor noticed a large column of smoke rising, and thought his brave colleagues had surely perished.

The sounds of a nearby gun battle broke the deathly silence that followed the explosion. However, as far as Gregor could tell from first reports coming in, no members of his patrol had yet been injured, including the audacious soldiers that had approached the wall.

Soon, all learnt that two suicide bombers on motorcycles had blown themselves up at the entrance to the headquarters of the National Directorate of Security, the Afghan security agency. The headquarters, located less than a kilometre away from Gregor's patrol, was now under siege by a wave of insurgents, who were trying to enter the building through a large breach caused by the explosion.

In the chaos, Gregor and his patrol attempted to respond and provide support to the distressed security office. They were instead ordered back by their base. An American unit with embedded RCMP members, known by the codename "Warhog", responded to the call instead, since their unit was closer to the building being attacked. All Gregor's company could do was mark the location of the found IED.

Picture this: US Army Hummer vehicles zipping by a graveyard of Russian tanks. This was the scene that Gregor and his troop saw as they hurried back to Camp Nathan Smith.

Running for a few kilometres with heavy military gear in hot weather was no easy task. Tired but rewarded by the sight of the nearby base gates, Gregor paused for a moment to catch his breath. From the corner of his eye, he noticed another potential threat: an unknown civilian vehicle, loudly racing towards his foot patrol.

As it sped towards the patrol and, fearing that the vehicle might be another suicide bomber part of a larger coordinated attack, a soldier fired a few rounds at it. One of the rounds hit the windshield, and caused the driver to lose control. He crashed into a ditch.

As it turned out, the driver was not an insurgent. Scared but unhurt, the driver apologized to the patrol commander for his erratic driving.

Later, in the safety of the base, after all the commotion had stopped, a colleague ran up to Gregor to ask him how he liked his first foot patrol. Apparently, action like this was commonplace. With a casual "high five", he congratulated Gregor for getting out of there alive, and continued on his way. At this, Gregor couldn't help but wonder just what he had gotten himself into!

But things would soon get even more intense for Gregor. Remember that unit of American Hummer vehicles that raced to support the security headquarters after it was attacked? Well, two weeks later, Gregor became an integral part of that team… acting as a Police Mentor for the Afghan police.

The roles of the Canadian police assigned to the Kandahar mission were numerous, but not all involved walking on military patrols. Functions such as Intelligence Analysts and Policy Directors were also important, albeit obviously less dangerous.

The crucial intelligence that Gregor and members of his patrol would dig up with the ANP during his first two weeks in-theatre would turn out to be of great assistance in order to continue monitoring criminal gangs and Taliban insurgency. The day after Gregor's first patrol, a Quick Response Force neutralized the hidden IED that the farmer had pointed out to them.

Gregor spent nearly two months with the American Police Mentor Team (PMT) Warhog before being transferred to a Police Operational Mentor and Liaison Team for another five months. Gregor completed his Afghan tour-of-duty assigned to a Counter Narcotics Police unit. Although no longer attached to Warhog, Gregor still conducted the occasional patrol with the team and other American units such as PMT GridIron.

Figure 62: Top left, Cst. Gregor Aitken with the U.S. Police Mentoring Team (PMT) Warhog. Photo courtesy of Gregor Aitken.

The food at Camp Nathan Smith was okay, but it was definitely a far cry from what Gregor had experienced on Emirates Airlines. At least bottled water was readily available. Once one left the camp, reverting to military rations was the only way to avoid getting sick. Poor general hygiene in town meant that anyone not accustomed to the local food could get very sick from catching intestinal parasites.

The accommodation at CNS was decent, although quite basic. Gregor slept in an 8- by 5-foot plywood room that fit a single bed and a desk. Hot and cold showers were available in the complex, as well as Internet access.

Nonetheless, Gregor and his patrol comrades often slept at a Police Sub-Station that was known as Kandahar PSS-9. This outskirt office accommodated the patrol officers for four days at a time before they returned to CNS to resupply.

The reason they overnighted at PSS-9 was in an effort to be in the presence of the Afghan police, whom Gregor and his troop field-coached, as much as possible. At PSS-9, Gregor and his team slept "under the stars" in army cots most of the time. An equipment supply room was also taken over and turned into a makeshift bedroom for the times the soldiers needed to sleep under a roof.

Despite making do with the available space, the sleeping quarters in the police building were not at all safe. This was because they only offered one exit to escape. With the constant threat of being targeted by insurgents, sleeping in these quarters was less than ideal.

Without a shadow of a doubt, IEDs and suicide bomber attacks were the number-one threat to coalition soldiers in Afghanistan. Of the 158 Canadian military deaths that had occurred during the Afghan campaign, well over 100 were the direct result of suicide bombers or IEDs going off.[320]

Still worse was the United States servicemen's number of casualties in Afghanistan. As of July 31, 2014, the Defense Manpower Data Center reported a staggering 2,334 deaths, 78% of which were attributed to hostile activities.[321] Of the number of fatalities attributed to these hostile activities, which include a range of "in combat" causes of death (e.g. grenade attacks, machine gun fights, mortar attacks, landmines, bombs, helicopter crashes, IEDs, etc.), nearly 50% were the result of IEDs.[322]

Then there were the "Taliban implants". This term referred to Afghan National Police officers or Afghan National Army officers who were pro-Taliban. These were particularly vicious as they would, without warning, commit mutiny, sometimes killing colleague officers and coalition trainers.

Another danger that would sneak up unnoticed upon its victims was heatstroke. In Kandahar, under scorching heat of 40-plus degrees, topped by irritating, dusty desert wind, heatstroke was a disaster waiting to happen.[323]

Danger was truly everywhere in that mission. If Gregor and his coalition soldier colleagues did not have to worry about suicide attacks, IEDs, heatstroke, rocket attacks, or Taliban implants, then they had to worry about being ambushed in an insurgent gunfight. Simply put, no one could afford to become complacent during the mission.

Figure 63: Some of the sleeping arrangements at Police Sub-Station 9, where Gregor and his colleagues spent nights following patrols. Photo courtesy of Gregor Aitken.

Roughly five months into his mission, Gregor was assigned to work as an Afghan police Field Coach, embedded with a Canadian Forces Police Operational Mentoring and Liaison Team. His task consisted of overseeing Afghan police officers also embedded with the unit, and ensuring they acted safely and in accordance with local laws. This was particularly necessary when dealing with the general public and when searching for suspect insurgents or criminals.

On one particular occasion, Gregor was on foot patrol in Kandahar with the unit (which was made up of Military Police and infantry from the 22nd Regiment, the "Van-Doos"), when he came across a young boy, aged roughly between 12 and 14 years old. The boy was standing on a sidewalk directly across the patrol, and it was obvious by his demeanour that he wanted to cross the street and go somewhere.

Tired from the exhausting heat and the heavy gear he was carrying, Gregor reverted to a community policing behaviour: he waved to the boy in a friendly manner, and allowed him to cross through the walking patrol.

Then Gregor had a startling thought: despite the boy's seemingly young age, what if he was a suicide bomber? Part of the vulnerability of a foot patrol was that they could never anticipate who was a potential bomber and who was not. They had to consider almost all individuals as a potential threat, which clashed with the police officers' "serve and protect" maxim.

Remembering a post-blast scene he had attended earlier in the mission where the body parts of a 12-year-old male suicide bomber were recovered, Gregor suddenly realized the imprudence of his decision to let the boy through.

But who could fault him? His police mindset of being friendly and accommodating had taken over. The sad reality was that in a war zone, this seemingly cordial action had little to no place, as it could have gotten several members of the platoon killed.

In fact, immediately upon return to the police station where he and the troop were temporarily staying, Gregor called for a debriefing and apologized to his teammates for his action. Although some of his platoon comrades were obviously very irritated, they were quick to brush off the mishap as part of a greater learning experience.

Figure 64: The remains of a truck in Kandahar after a suicide driver at the wheel of a Vehicle Borne Improvised Explosive Device (VBIED) struck a coalition convoy. Photo courtesy of Gregor Aitken.

In a place where death lurked at the most unanticipated moment, one had to be consistently in a tactical mindset. On a positive side, the incident with the young boy made Gregor even more aware of his surroundings. He did not make the same mistake twice!

Even though a tactical mindset was needed to survive, one still had to mitigate risks. There was simply no other way around it. This aspect made the mission even more dangerous. Keeping a combative attitude at all times towards everyone was not practical, especially if one wished to earn the support and trust of the general public. So Gregor and his team learned to take calculated risks, whether it was through mingling with children or by paying their respects and visiting village elders.

Figure 65: Gregor Aitken on a search mission to locate Taliban insurgents that had been reported by an informant. The mission was abruptly aborted due to the high presence of Taliban supporters unfriendly to the ISAF coalition. Photo courtesy of G. Aitken.

The Afghan campaign was full of unique experiences: some were very memorable, while there were others Gregor would rather forget. Alas, amongst the latter stood a peculiar one that Gregor could simply not let slip from his memory. Let me introduce you to Sergeant X (name withheld), the "Taliban implant".

Sergeant X was a member of the Afghanistan National Police, who was being trained and facilitated by Gregor and his coalition colleagues. Amongst a range of not-so-glamorous rumours surrounding the sergeant's training was that he was an insurgent facilitator, who provided coalition intelligence to the Taliban.

Although the information had not been substantiated, Gregor and his colleagues were always highly suspicious of Sergeant X. Even though they had to train him, their trust towards the individual was very low.

Soon, their distrust of the man would intensify even more. On one occasion during a night patrol involving Gregor, the CF, ANP officers, and Sergeant X, the team heard a large explosion in its vicinity. As it turned out, an IED had prematurely exploded ahead of the patrol, and was traced to a nearby compound.

Being already near the scene of the blast, Gregor and his team contained the area; indications were that the insurgent who detonated the device was hiding nearby.

Figure 66: From left to right: CF Corporal Alex Caron, 22nd Regiment; ANP Sergeant X; and Gregor Aitken. Photo courtesy of Gregor Aitken.

At the same time, the team received a radio communication that stated another coalition special force unit was in the area, about to make an arrest on a bomb-maker. It did not take much reasoning to figure out that the blast and the pending arrest were related incidents.

As teams closed in on the hiding insurgent, Sergeant X tried to convince the teams that no one was in the area, and that all should move on to other areas. Ignoring the advice of Sergeant X, a nearby compound was searched, and the bomb-maker was located and captured.

Other incidents related to Sergeant X included the continuous disappearance of ammunition from police stations. Every time he was confronted, Sergeant X came up with an excuse to explain the missing ammunitions.

As time went by, the situation with Sergeant X became so awkward that Gregor and his team decided it would be safer to withhold any classified information from Sergeant X and any ANP members who befriended him. This made working with the ANP officers quite difficult. Sensitive information would only be shared once the team reached a final destination.

Figure 67: Outside view of Police Sub-Station 9, (PSS-9), on the outskirts of Kandahar City. Photo courtesy of Gregor Aitken.

Thankfully, Sergeant X was not the only ANP whom Gregor trained and walked patrol with. As such, Sergeant X was not always with the team.

But Gregor's suspicions about him were not farfetched. Sometime after Gregor left the mission, he learned through a colleague still in-theatre that Sergeant X had poisoned some of his ANP comrades, stolen weapons and a police vehicle, and fled the area, only to turn over the stolen goods to the Taliban insurgency.

Even though Gregor had always displayed incertitude over Sergeant X, the news of his latest escapade made him feel betrayed. After all, he had spent time patrolling Kandahar with the man, and even risked his life on some of the patrols where Sergeant X was also present. Being betrayed by a comrade would become one of Gregor's most significant ordeals. Thankfully, not all of Gregor's experiences were as negative as this one.

During one of his patrol missions with the Counter-Narcotics Police, Gregor and his team decommissioned several hundred kilos of raw opium and heroin, likely destined for European and North American markets.

The seizure and destruction of the drugs was indeed another unique experience that gave a more positive outlook to Gregor's mission, especially since he had been a former Drug Section investigator.

Figure 68: Gregor Aitken with a translator and a member of the Counter-Narcotics Police. The photo was taken after the seizure of several hundred kilos of raw opium and heroin. Photo courtesy of Gregor Aitken.

Who would have thought that drinking a few beers could be a challenging experience? In Afghanistan, it was! Alcohol was banned in the country, in following with strict Muslim rules. However, alcoholic beverages, such as beer, could still be consumed on-base on special occasions, such as on Canada Day, St-Jean Baptiste Day, and during the Grey Cup.

But even during those special days, alcohol consumption would be restricted. Beer was dispensed from a cold refrigeration unit, and each Canadian on base was only allowed to consume two. Furthermore, these had to be signed-off by the military Quartermaster and opened in front of him to ensure they were not stashed and kept for a later time.

This meant that an individual had to drink his alcoholic beverages quickly, so as to enjoy their refreshing coolness before they got warm. What a drag! Not even a chance to sit back and chat with friends over a few cold brews.

"Insha Allah!" At the grace of God! These words would be repeated over and over again by Afghan police officers who often appeared to submit themselves to the "will of God" for plans or activities they undertook.

Although there was nothing wrong on the surface with such philosophy, at times, the mere utterance of these words would become a source of frustration for the ISAF and coalition forces personnel, some of whom did not share the same beliefs. Right or wrong, the utterance of the words was in many instances interpreted by ISAF personnel as a way for the speaker to dodge responsibilities.

For example, a police debriefing would be scheduled for 08:00. By that time, everybody present would have to be ready and in uniform. But…Insha Allah! This meant that some officers would show up at 09:30–10:00. Some explanations for being late were legitimate, while some others were improbable. Regardless, to the speaker, whatever misfortune happened was never his or her fault, but "God's will".

A more serious example of the cultural gap between the Afghan police and its ISAF trainers is demonstrated by the following case: during an attack at a police checkpoint, one of Gregor's trainees was killed after being hit in the chest with a fragment from a grenade. ISAF investigators discovered that not only was the victim not wearing his issued body armour, but that all of the brand-new body armours issued to that police team had been thrown in a garbage bin! They were furious. To make matters worse, when questioned, the checkpoint commander responsible for the safety of the officer answered that the death of his subordinate had been "God's will".

Whether the officer's death had been a twist of fate did not matter! Gregor and other coalition force members were incensed with the attitude of the checkpoint commander. Gregor and ISAF investigators believed that the officer's injuries might not have been fatal had he been wearing his bulletproof vest.

Still unsettled by the checkpoint commander's absence of empathy and lack of judgment, Gregor publicly berated him in front of his subordinates, and held him personally responsible for the death of his officer. Gregor held a firm conviction that holding the officer accountable was the right thing to do to prevent further unnecessary deaths; however, the humiliation suffered by the checkpoint commander could have compelled him to lash out at Gregor.

Fortunately, Gregor did not become the target of a vengeful Afghan officer. On the contrary, the checkpoint commander became one of the most vigilant and well-turned-out officers Gregor worked with. Ensuring his team was well-equipped and prepared became the norm for the checkpoint commander when heading out for patrols or setting up roadblocks. Sadly, "God's will" claimed the commander's life just two months later, when he was killed in an IED incident.

Of utmost challenge was Gregor's busy working schedule in Kandahar. Long working days, often exceeding ten hours under scorching heat, meant that he arrived at base camp or at the police sub-station office pretty much exhausted.

Despite the fatigue, Gregor took the time to wrap his mind

around setting personal goals, some of which he achieved illustriously. For example, one of his ambitions was to be promoted to the next rank of Corporal upon returning to Canada.

Figure 69: A once-new ANP body armour thrown in a garbage heap at a checkpoint. Photo courtesy of Gregor Aitken.

To achieve his objective, Gregor would have to discipline himself, overcome tiredness, and make time to dedicate himself to the RCMP promotional process. This also meant he would write down examples of the day-to-day activities he believed were relevant to his advancement.

A lot is to be said about Gregor's motivation and willingness to sacrifice in order to reach his goal. Many of us dream about what we would like to do or accomplish, but we do not have a roadmap to find our way there. But what is a roadmap?[324] In this context, a roadmap is essentially words written down. According to internationally renowned speaker and motivator Peter Legge, the difference between a dream and a goal is just that: the written words.[325]

However, as Peter Legge points out, there is more to do than simply scribbling down some ideas on a piece of paper. Without putting some real thought and energy into devising each goal, people are simply making a wish.[326] Goals need to be clear, complete and focussed.

For Gregor, this meant that on his roadmap to a promotion, he had set up times to write about his activities and read about the required steps for his promotional process. He further set up deadlines for each, and never gave up on his final objective.

On the last day of his mission, as he waited to fly back to Canada, Gregor learnt that he had been promoted to the rank of Corporal. Gregor would later tell me that this day had been one of the best of his life. Not only had he made it out of Afghanistan alive, he had also achieved his goal and been promoted. As Peter Legge has said, "Goals give life its flavour! They also provide a sense of direction and purpose."[327] [328]

By all accounts, Gregor's mission in Kandahar was stressful, difficult, frustrating, and above all, very dangerous! One frustration that Gregor and others experienced from time to time was the arrival of new police officers in-theatre, who were "shocked" to find themselves in the middle of an active war zone.

Individuals who had not done their "homework" often became poor performers, and were poisonous to the morale of the mission. As such, Gregor's advice is to do your due diligence, and inquire about all aspects of the mission you apply for.

Gregor's other recommendation to anyone wanting to do a similar mission is to question the true personal motive behind the desire to volunteer for such an endeavour. As noted above, conducting some research on the particular mission one wishes to join is paramount.

As he admitted, Gregor conducted his due diligence before he went on his assignment. This included discussions with returning officers and the like. In spite of his preparation, Gregor felt that the pre-training and research he conducted were only partially adequate; nothing could have prepared him sufficiently for what he would face when he arrived in Afghanistan: the insurgents, the language barrier, the high level of illiteracy of Afghan Security forces, the drug trade, Afghan politics, mission politics, and so on.

As to whether his contribution to the mission made a difference in the life of Afghans, Gregor's sentiments are divided. On the one hand, his personal interactions with Afghans may have influenced many to persevere and work towards building a better and safer country. On the other hand, the difficulties in bringing together the many cultures that make up Afghanistan remains an issue for which he is not yet sure his contribution made any difference.

Fostering peace and education will be crucial to rebuilding this country ravaged by sustained conflicts. Despite the difficulties and challenges ahead, world nations must not give up on Afghanistan. But Afghans themselves must work together to find solutions for their internal conflicts; otherwise, many years may go by before we see true changes in that fascinating part of our planet.

A word about terrorism:

Through this chapter and previous ones, the topic of terrorism has been discussed, but not necessarily developed. At the time of this writing, terror groups such as al-Qaeda, the Islamic State (IS), al-Shabaab, and al-Qaeda in the Islamic Maghreb were doing all they could to create havoc around the world, by cowardly targeting and killing civilians. Many countries, including Belgium, Burkina Faso, France, Indonesia, Kenya, Mali, Spain, Turkey, and the United Kingdom, have become the targets of these groups, who have attacked and tried to destroy the makeup of our democracy.

Sadly, we have now entered an era where terrorist organizations have a propensity to hit anywhere around the world (either through coordinated attacks or by influencing lone-wolf attackers). If one looks at some of the current terrorism strongholds around the world, (e.g.

Libya, Nigeria, Syria, Afghanistan, Iraq), one cannot help but note that they appear to be either failed states or neophyte democracies.

In a world where terrorism has become frontline news, it is crucial that the international community work together to fight against it. Through peacebuilding operations, I believe those weak or failed states could be assisted into strengthening their rule of law and internal capacity to fight terrorism.

However, for this happen, these operations would have to include a mandate that allows specific powers to the peacebuilders to enable them to act in cases of terrorism and other international crimes. It would also be crucial that the countries participating in such operations send troops or police with training and expertise concerning counter-terrorism.

We have seen in some missions that sending a miss-match of countries to perform long-term support to state functions may not necessarily work all of the time. Specific mandates to specific nations within a mission may be the key.

Some countries may benefit from an overt approach, others covert, and still more from something in between. For instance, nations can provide capacity training and expertise to a country in dire need of improving its security or developing a counter-terrorism apparatus while an overt peacekeeping presence is still maintained.

The particular role of the police in those operations would also be crucial, and could include building a country's capacity to investigate terrorism, develop bomb disposal experts, promote Human Rights and so forth.

Canada's international reputation as a peacekeeping nation is sewn in its citizen's personal identity and held dear by many. With threats from stateless terrorist actors threatening world order and global politics, I do not think that Canada can afford *not* to join in the global fight against terrorism.

10.

The Ultimate Sacrifice: MINUSTAH (United Nations Stabilization Mission in Haiti), 2004-2017

Never in his 28-years of service with the Service de Police de la Ville de Montréal (SPVM) would Detective Lieutenant Serge Boulianne have imagined having to deal with the type of calamities he faced during his nine-month tour of duty in Haiti. Peacekeepers are generally well-prepared for harsh conditions and dangers when they sign up for a UN mission. A peacekeeper going to a mission in a tropical zone might have expected to deal with poverty, flooding, hurricanes, dengue, and malaria. However, no one would expect to face multiple calamities all at once, including a devastating earthquake!

Established in 2004 to provide a secure and stable environment to a new transitional government, MINUSTAH had evolved by 2010 into the fourth largest UN mission, only behind Darfur, Congo, and Lebanon.[329]

From the monitoring of the Haitian National Police reform, the fostering of the rule of law, supporting the constitutional process, and promoting recovery and reconstruction efforts in the wake of the earthquake, MINUSTAH mission objectives continuously adapted to the changing needs of Haiti.

Serge's mission, which began in October 2009 and ended in July 2010, would bring him face-to-face with situations that attacked the core of his police ethics. I am hoping that, like me, you will find his tale in this impoverished nation something truly inspiring. In my opinion, Serge's mission gave true meaning to the adage "To Serve and Protect".

SITUATED BETWEEN THE Caribbean Sea and the North Atlantic Ocean, Haiti occupies the western third of the Island of Hispaniola, which it shares with its eastern neighbour, the Dominican Republic.[330]

The modern history of Haiti starts on December 5, 1492, with the arrival of Christopher Columbus to the New World. Columbus and his fleet landed on the "Island of Hispaniola" (the Spanish Island), which he claimed and named on behalf of the Spanish Crown.[331]

Prior to Columbus' arrival, the island had been inhabited by indigenous tribes, namely the "Tainos" and the "Caribes".[332] Amongst its many native names, the island was called "Ayiti" and "Quisqueya".

Within a century, the indigenous population of Hispaniola was literally annihilated by European diseases and harsh working conditions, the latter as a result of Spanish settlers using them as slaves to mine gold.[333]

In the mid-16th century, French pirates and buccaneers settled on the western end of Hispaniola and nearby islands. They were followed by French settlers.[334] As sugar, cacao, coffee, and tobacco plantations developed on the western side, so did the need for a free labour force.

Soon French landowners in western Hispaniola imported an increased number of African slaves, whose population neared 5,000 by the late 17th century.[335]

In 1697, Spain formally conceded the western third of Hispaniola to France as a result of the Treaty of Ryswick.[336] France renamed the area Saint-Domingue and the territory became France's most prosperous overseas possession.[337]

By 1789, the population of Saint-Domingue had reached 556,000 inhabitants, 500,000 of whom were African slaves, while the rest were divided between the European colonists (approx.

32,000) and free mulattoes (approx. 24,000). [338]

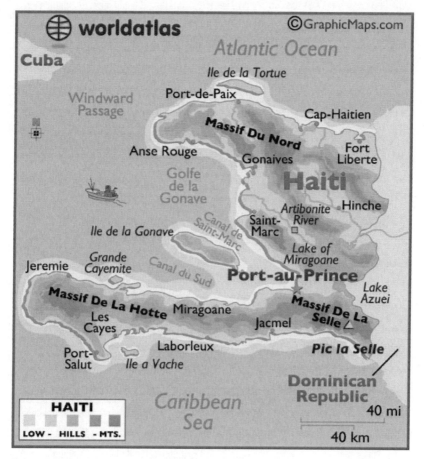

Figure 70: Haiti. Map reproduced with permission of WorldAtlas.com

The treatment of slaves and their living conditions in the plantations were, for the most part, brutal. In the field, slaves endured beatings, whippings, and rapes. Some were crucified on planks, buried alive, or even thrown into boiling cauldrons of cane syrup.[339] In general, slaves had such miserable lives that death was seen as a welcome release.[340]

In the late 18th century, a slave by the name of Toussaint L'Ouverture, who had managed to achieve some degree of literacy by serving a

French master, rose as the leader of the first independence movement.[341]

Through a series of rebellions against the French masters, L'Ouverture succeeded by 1800 in taking control of the whole of Saint-Domingue (Haiti).[342] A year later, his liberation force invaded the Spanish side of the island and freed more slaves.[343]

However, the conquest of the city of Santo Domingo was of a short duration. France sent more troops with General Leclerc to quash the black rebellion and recapture the island.[344]

L'Ouverture was captured in 1802 by Leclerc. He was sent to France, where he died in 1803. However, L'Ouverture's independence movement did not die with him; on the contrary, it was revived by Jean-Jacques Dessalines, who led another Negro revolt the same year, and proclaimed the independence of Haiti on January 1, 1804, thus becoming its first ruler.[345]

Dessalines died in 1806 and a general by the name of Henri Christophe took the reign of power. Over the years, Haiti attained some degree of stability, and by 1822, under the leadership of a mulatto named Jean-Pierre Boyer, the entire island of Hispaniola was once again under Haitian control.[346]

Boyer ruled French-speaking Haiti and governed Spanish-speaking Santo Domingo as a conquered territory until 1843, when he was overthrown. An independence movement, led by Juan Pablo Duarte, saw the eastern part of the Island (Dominican Republic) gain its freedom from Haiti on February 27, 1844.[347]

Within Haiti, a profound hostility continued to develop between racial groups: the mulattoes, who were economically more stable, and the poorer blacks, who were direct descendants of the island's slaves.[348]

Like the eastern part of the island, 19th century Haiti saw a succession of coups d'états and political instability, which culminated in 1915 with a US Marines invasion to safeguard American interests on that side of the island.[349] The US military government remained in Haiti until 1934, after which it departed.

The following years might be considered as "déjà vu" politics; the country reverted to its customary chaos with one military coup after another until 1957, when a medical doctor named Francois Duvalier was elected president of the country by an overwhelming majority.[350]

Francois Duvalier's ascent to the presidency was welcome news. He was a prominent doctor (who was later nicknamed Papa Doc) and as such, optimism was high among Haitians that his election would bring an era of stability and democracy to Haiti.

Unfortunately, this could not be further from the truth.[351] Seeing the Haitian army as a threat to his leadership, Duvalier reduced its size, created his own "watchdog" militia called "Tontons Macoutes [352]", and used autocratic and corrupt measures to make himself president for life.[353]

After Francois Duvalier's death in 1971, his nineteen-year old son, Jean-Claude Duvalier, dubbed "Baby Doc", was sworn in as president of Haiti. He would remain in power for another 15 years, until he was ousted during a 1986 popular uprising.[354]

During his reign, Jean-Claude Duvalier relied on the ruthless "Tontons Macoutes" to support his dictatorship. His departure in 1986 did little to stimulate Haiti's struggling attempts at democracy, and the country was soon again to be plunged into a pattern of turmoil.[355] Within the first four years of Duvalier's departure, Haiti saw five different governments come and go, no one better than the other.

The United Nations involvement in Haiti started in 1990, when a provisional government requested UN presence to monitor elections. The campaign was won by a Catholic priest by the name of Jean-Bertrand Aristide, and with his arrival came new hopes for democracy. Alas, his reign was short-lived. A year later, his government fell to a military coup that ended democratic rule. Aristide sought asylum in the United States.

Haiti reverted once again to chaos. In February 1993, the UN attempted to deploy peacekeepers to the country under UNMIH (United Nations Mission in Haiti). This was under an agreement that a Security Council oil and arms embargo would be lifted if democracy was restored, the Haitian Armed Forces modernized, and a new police force created.[356]

Alas, the non-cooperation of the Haitian military made it impossible for UNMIH to fully deploy and carry out its mandate. Anti-UN demonstrations held in October 1993 were orchestrated by the Haitian army and led to the premature departure of 51 RCMP peacekeepers that had arrived in Haiti a week earlier.

The retreat of the RCMP and other UN international staff crumbled hopes of restoring democracy in the tiny Caribbean nation. Soon UN sanctions were re-imposed.[357]

With several thousand pro-democracy activists being murdered within the following three years of Aristide's departure, economic pressures from the United States led the de-facto government to step down. In 1994, twenty thousand US troops were allowed in to occupy the country.[358] Aristide then returned under UN protection.[359] Taking advantage of the presence of the US troops, Aristide dismantled the Haitian Army, initiated free-market reforms, and held new elections, which were won by a coalition associated with him.[360]

From 1994 to 2000, a series of UN peacekeeping missions took place in Haiti, including UNMIH, UNSMIH (United Nations Support Mission in Haiti), UNTMIH (United Nations Transition Mission in Haiti), and MIPONUH (translated in English as: United Nations Civilian Police Mission in Haiti).[361] Throughout this period, positive developments were made, including the creation of a national civil police and the return to some democratic rules.[362]

Unfortunately, by the turn of the new millennium, Haiti's political situation had deteriorated. Political infighting amongst groups that had supported Aristide soon led parliament to be dissolved. Despite the turmoil, Aristide was re-elected president. In 2004, in a growing climate of lawlessness, violence, rising cases of AIDS, and accusations that his administration had become corrupt, Aristide fled the country. Once again, Haiti plunged into chaos.[363]

However, this chaos would not be tolerated by the UN Security Council, which soon passed UN Resolution 1529, sending a Multinational Interim Force (MIF) to Haiti in a bid to re-establish law and order. The United Nations Stabilisation Mission in Haiti (MINUSTAH) took over from MIF in June 2004.[364]

Originally set up to support a transitional government, ensure public safety, and reform the Haitian National Police (HNP),[365] MINUSTAH counted on nearly 6,700 military personnel, 1,622 police officers, and more than 550 international civilians to accomplish its tasks. From 2004 to early January 2010, MINUSTAH's mandates were adjusted to reflect the ever-changing political climate and socio-economic situation.

The development of the HNP was an important part of MINUSTAH's day-to-day functions. UN peacekeepers helped build the capacity of the police force, and accompanied and supervised HNP officers in their many daily tasks and operations. Despite major challenges, hopes were high that Haiti could eventually offer a more promising future to its citizens.[366]

It was in Montréal in early 2009 that SPVM Detective Lieutenant Serge Boulianne and his family made the decision for him to participate in a UN mission. Serge, an enthusiast hunter and fisherman with experience living in the wild, was well aware that going on a UN mission could bring some harsh conditions. It was thus with an open mind and a desire to learn about a new culture that Serge applied for the Haitian mission through his police service.

The selection of candidates for this mission was based on the need for experienced police officers in addition to a demonstrated ability to speak French. Similar to most missions, officers had to be open-minded to principles of diversity, and be willing to accept living in arduous conditions.

Other traits that were highly sought-after from potential candidates were motivation, leadership, and initiative. Obviously, being able to adapt to harsh living conditions was a true asset for the Haitian mission. This was especially the case for those peacekeepers who would be assigned to rural areas, where amenities were at an even lower level than those in the capital city of Port-au-Prince.

It comes as no surprise that Serge's 27 years of operational police experience, and his obvious ability to speak French, would put him in an enviable position in getting a "seat" for the Haitian mission.

At the SPVM, through its International Mission Department, Serge benefitted from several sessions of pre-deployment training.[367] Capitalizing on the experience its officers gained with their presence in thirteen international peacekeeping missions since 1995, the SPVM International Mission Department offered its candidates a qualitative mission overview. They brought in field experts to discuss assignment types and the conditions the selected officers would likely endure during their respective missions.

After that, Serge completed another 12 days of pre-deployment training in Ottawa. This would be done in the company of other candidates (a total of twenty in Serge's contingent) who came from other police organizations.

The Ottawa training approach would at times include sessions that were similar to that facilitated by the SPVM International Mission department. Regardless, the sessions would serve to reinforce Serge's mission preparedness, and as he will later attest, there could not have been sufficient training to prepare him for what he was about to face in Haiti!

Figure 71: Preparing for the Haiti assignment. New friendships are made, and all expect to face some adverse conditions. Serge is in the bottom-row centre. Photo courtesy of Serge Boulianne.

Serge described his arrival in Haiti as euphoric. In October 2009, when Serge arrived, the thermometer in Port-au-Prince reached more than 30 degrees. One can easily understand the delight of being in a warm place, especially after leaving behind the cold nights of Québec's fall season.

The most memorable moment Serge recalls from his arrival in Haiti was the way he and his contingent were welcomed at the airport by his Canadian UN colleagues. He was able to renew his friendship with some of his colleagues from the Montréal Police, who were already deployed to Haiti.

The Canadian peacekeepers already in-theatre had taken care of all issues related to immigration, customs, luggage pick up, and transport to the hotel, for their incoming colleagues. Talk about VIP service and a trouble-free arrival!

Perhaps due to the size of the Canadian contingent (just under 100 members when Serge arrived), camaraderie was high. Newly arrived troops would often be matched with a sponsor (a Canadian UNPOL) in an effort to acquaint the newcomer to Haitian life as soon as possible. The mentorship also served to help the novices find a place to stay until their final regional assignment. In Serge's case, he and the other newcomers were lodged in a local hotel known as "The Montana".

A day after his arrival, Serge was driven to MINUSTAH's headquarters, where he received his mission identification cards and got acquainted with the mission UNPOL management.

There was a certain anxiety in the air during Serge's first 48 hours. He and his contingent took the opportunity to speak at length with those who had been at the mission for some time. Being unaware of the type of duties or the area of the country where they would be assigned to was a little unnerving. Merely being posted to a rural area meant more adversities than others, let alone the specific challenges the area could possibly offer.

After receiving mission identifications, Serge prepared to attend a ten-day mission induction. This introduction, provided by the UN, would address topics such as UN mission process, administrative policies, country history, mission security, and other topics related to duties and mission management. Officers would receive their assigned duties only after the induction.

Figure 72: The Hotel Montana, a five-storey, 144 room luxury hotel: the pride of Port-au-Prince. Photo taken in October 2009 courtesy of Serge Boulianne.

At this point, Serge had some assumptions as to what his duties would entail. Prior to their departure, Serge and his colleagues had been asked to supply a Curriculum Vitae to the UN. He assumed that this initiative was aimed at identifying the expertise of an arriving peacekeeper, and therefore matching that officer to suitable duties.

Further to the submission of a CV, there was a pre-arrival personal phone interview conducted by a UN staff member, which further seemed to indicate a desire to identify a particular member's expertise.

Serge had over twenty years' experience as a Serious Crime Section investigator, fifteen of which had been spent investigating sexual aggressions against women. He definitely had something to offer in that field.

However, despite his experience in major crime and the UN's multi-step screening process, once his induction was over Serge learned he would be assigned to the Intelligence Section in Port-au-Prince, doing data entry and analysis.

Compared to the emotions he had been used to in dealing with victims and offenders as the leader of a 40-investigator sex crime team, Serge's duties entering and analyzing data lacked lustre. By Serge's own admission, not being able to work in his area of expertise was somewhat disappointing.

Nonetheless, Serge kept an open mind, and applied himself to his new role. Soon, he learned to use special analysis software, link criminal events, and build profiles on individuals of interests (e.g. street gang members).

Personally, I understand Serge's initial disappointment. Even though both the SPVM and the RCMP had warned him that one's expertise may or may not be used during a mission, Serge had built up some expectations.

My understanding of the situation at the time, based on my frequent visits as a diplomat liaising with the Haitian police, was that the force would certainly have benefitted from Serge's advanced knowledge in the investigation of violence against women. Regardless, Serge was assigned to intelligence work. The fact that Serge kept a positive attitude and applied himself to his new duties reflected highly upon him. His professionalism and willingness to undertake new challenges were, simply put, commendable.

Figure 73: From left to right: Québec Provincial Police Inspector Michel Martin and Montréal Police (SPVM) Detective Lieutenant Serge Boulianne. Both were photographed in front of the Christopher Hotel in late 2009. Photo courtesy of Serge Boulianne.

I have heard several tales where peacekeepers had anticipated assignments in their areas of expertise and ended up working in other fields. Although many were disappointed, and perhaps upset at first, most kept an open mind and performed admirably in their new functions.

I also learned of officers who were assigned duties relevant to their field of expertise and who ended up extremely frustrated and bitter. In the latter cases, frustration set in as a result of situations not moving as fast or not heading in the direction the experts would have liked to see.

As an example, Serge confessed that if he had worked as a sex crime investigator and experienced a cultural unwillingness from local authorities to consider women as equals, he may have been more frustrated than having to learn new duties.

The bottom line is to be prepared to face different assignments when one signs up for a UN mission. Keeping a positive attitude, regardless of the duties one may be performing, is paramount to making the overseas stay a unique and worthwhile experience.

As Serge would later attest, despite his initial disappointment, his experience as an intelligence officer turned out to be a very rewarding and satisfying undertaking. He worked side-by-side with civilians and armed forces intelligence experts from many nations. It also turned out that Serge's CV pointed to a number of aptitudes that were deemed necessary to be a thorough intelligence analyst. In the end, the CV and interview Serge completed were not in vain.

The training in Ottawa had well-prepared Serge and others to some of the adversities they would encounter with regards to food, water, and accommodation. For example, in some rural parts of Haiti, there were places where meat was sold on the street, without any method of conservation or protection against flies or other parasites.

However, for those who would be fortunate enough to be assigned to larger centres, such as Port-au-Prince, modern grocery stores were available. Many of those stores carried North American food products and other similar items. Bottled water was readily available in most parts of the city, and was deemed the only safe water to drink.

When it came to accommodation, Serge will admit that he was very fortunate to have ended up with his roommates, Sergeant Mychel Girard from the Québec Provincial Police and Inspector

Serge Fyfe from the SPVM. All were around the same age and shared many traits and common interests. Serge advises looking for compatible colleagues whenever possible, in the eventuality that sharing accommodations is required. Such an endeavour could even start during a pre-training session.

Sharing accommodation can be a rewarding experience, but it can also lead to conflicts if a roommate is not willing to compromise. Serge will admit that he was lucky with Mychel and Serge. They had met in pre-training, got along well, and ended up being assigned to the same region.

Serge was indeed fortunate to have identified good roommates, but it was not only luck. He turned down an offer for accommodation that was five minutes away from his workplace in order to be in the same residence as Mychel and Serge. Though the three of them had most amenities a modern Haitian home had to offer (gas stove, refrigerator, washing machine, and an electrical inverter for power shortages), they lived almost an hour away. To Serge, however, having reliable roommates was more important than the convenience of location.

Soon, the trio hired a maid who would cook, clean the home, and do their laundry. Having to work shifts of ten or more hours a day under scorching heat, coming home to a freshly cooked meal was worth gold.

Most peacekeepers expect to encounter some type of adversities when they sign up for a mission: confronting insurgents if one is in Afghanistan, facing a severe drought if one is in Sudan, or, like the peacekeepers who enrolled for the Haitian mission, to recover from hurricanes and floods. But no one was prepared for a murderess of an earthquake.

On January 12, 2010, a magnitude 7.0 earthquake struck the country.[368] 220,000 Haitian civilians reportedly perished, many buried alive, while over one million people instantly became homeless and began a struggle to survive.

On that fateful day, 102 UN personnel lost their lives, including RCMP Chief Superintendent Doug Coates and Sgt. Mark Gallagher.[369] With hundreds of casualties, MINUSTAH was not in good shape: in fact, it was decimated! Never in its 62 years of history had the UN faced such a great loss of staff in one single event.[370]

But with the bravery of those UN staff who survived, MINUSTAH would soon get back on its feet. With the assistance of member states, MINUSTAH launched emergency relief operations within hours.[371] Later, on February 19, 2010, the UN Security Council approved Resolution 1908. This allowed for an additional 2,000 soldiers and 1,500 police officers to be sent to Haiti, bringing the total of uniformed staff to just over 13,000.[372]

It is no surprise that the magnitude 7.0 earthquake that hit the country would test Serge's survival and 27 years of policing skills to their limit, in an incredible saga of life, death, and constant peril.

January 12th started off as a beautiful, hot, and sunny afternoon in Port-au-Prince. At twelve minutes to five, Serge emerged from his office in the Christopher Hotel with a grin on his face. After a 10-hour day, it was time to go home and enjoy a cold "Prestige" beer with the roommates.

As he walked to the parking lot to await a ride, he could not help but think how fortunate he was to be in a warm climate, avoiding the bitter January Canadian cold. Serge's attention caught on the picturesque Haitian village that could be seen far off on a hill.

Without any warning, the ground started to shake violently. It took Serge a few seconds to realize that this was an earthquake. He had better brace himself!

The shaking intensified. In a sharply surreal moment, Serge saw roofs and structures collapse under a huge cloud of dust from what, only a moment ago, had been the picturesque Haitian village.

Closer to him, he saw parked UN Toyota 4x4 vehicles start to bounce up and down like rubber balls, crushing everything in their path. The shaking and waving motion of the soil beneath him was so intense that Serge was forced to his knees, dropping one hand to the ground to try and keep some balance.

That was when the fear sank in. He could practically imagine a crater opening up beneath him and sucking him into the abyss. Serge closed his eyes and braced for more shocks. A loud, thunderous roar engulfed him, quickly followed by a huge cloud of dust.

The ground had been shaking for what felt like an eternity when, abruptly, it all stopped. Serge wiped the dust off his face and opened his eyes. An unbelievable spectacle unfolded in front of him. The once five-storey Christopher Hotel had been rendered into a giant ski slope; an entire wing of the hotel had collapsed onto itself, with the top floors stacked on each other like pancakes.

In the chaos of the moment, Serge's years of police training kicked in. He was safe and sound, but he knew many of his UN colleagues had to be trapped inside the flattened hotel. He had to help them!

But first, anticipating that what had just happened would make the news around the world, Serge tried to use his cellular phone to call and reassure his family in Canada. Alas, he would soon discover that all communications had been cut off. It would take several agonizing hours before Serge's loved ones in Canada learned through intermediaries that he was safe and sound.

The chaos in Port-au-Prince and at the scene of the collapsed Christopher Hotel was hard to describe. Echoes of moans and cries could be heard coming from the ruins of the tumbled hotel. To make things worse, clouds of concrete dust hung over the whole city, making it difficult for anyone to breathe, and instantly turning the day into the night. Despite being a victim of the earthquake himself, Serge was quick to get back on his feet and put his altruistic values first.

This meant that he would put all his efforts into helping friends, colleagues, and the general Haitian population before himself. In the minutes that followed the earthquake, he and a small team of UN soldiers who had escaped the collapse of the building bravely entered the crumbled wing. Through their efforts, they managed to locate other personnel, including Serge's own contingent commander, who were still alive. After Serge helped them out of the ruins and into safety, he kept on working tirelessly.

Throughout the evening, aftershocks were hampering rescue efforts. As Serge explained, parts of the ground floor where the hotel wing had collapsed had withstood the weight of the upper stories. This had created pockets where survivors might have been. However, with several thousand tonnes of concrete lying on top, what was left standing threatened to come down with each new tremor.

With the collapse of its headquarters and the death of many of its staff, including its Chief of Mission, the MINUSTAH mission was decimated. By midnight on January 12th, most surviving peacekeepers had regrouped with their own contingents and contacted their embassy.

Serge and other Canadian peacekeepers were no exception. Using UN vehicles that had not been destroyed, he and his Canadian colleagues regrouped and started looking for missing Canadian contingent members in diverse areas of Port-au-Prince. High on adrenaline, and with people screaming for help in all parts of the city, he would not get any chance to sleep for another 72 hours.

The stress and intensity of the second day were, in many ways, comparable to that of the first day. While driving though the ruined city, Serge and two of his colleagues came across a woman who had miraculously survived the collapse of her home. In a desperate attempt to get some help, her frantic husband waved at Serge's vehicle.

Figure 74: The Christopher Hotel less than an hour after the earthquake. A courageous UN soldier is seen walking on the hotel's flattened fifth floor in a desperate attempt to locate surviving and stranded colleagues. Photo courtesy of Serge Boulianne.

It was with horror that Serge realized the predicament the woman was in. To reach his wife, the husband had crawled into a small hole, no bigger than 2 by 2 feet, that narrowly extended a few metres within the collapsed structure. He hoped Serge and his colleagues could help him free her.

Only equipped with an improvised rope (a thick electrical cord they had salvaged out of some rubble), Serge and his team had a colossal task in front of them: moving several thousand pounds of concrete to clear a passage and free the woman.

Alas, after much effort to clean up some of the rubble, Serge discovered that one of the woman's legs rested under a piece of concrete that supported the entire weight of the collapsed roof, itself weighing several tonnes. Hydraulic equipment to lift the concrete, and having paramedics to perform a leg amputation, were the lady's only hope of getting out alive.

Despite the pleas of her husband for Serge and his colleagues to stay, he and his team could do little more but move on. Serge radioed the couple's location coordinates for an eventual search and rescue team. However, being powerless and having to abandon the woman with her husband shook him to the core of his ethics. There was nothing else he could do! Without the proper tools that search and rescue teams possessed, Serge would only have put his life and that of his team at risk by trying to get her out of the crumbled building.

Readers with a law enforcement background may frown and suggest that someone from Serge's team should have stayed with the lady until rescue arrived. At home in our developed country, that is what might have happened. Imagine for an instant the scene of a serious traffic accident, where drivers or passengers are seriously hurt and trapped in their vehicles. The police officer attending would in most instances be talking to victims, assessing their conditions, and reporting it to a rescue team on its way. Meanwhile, the officer would be reassuring the victims and staying close to them until help arrived.

In Haiti, in the hours after the quake, this was simply not possible. All that remained around Serge was the gloomy spectacle of an entire city crying, with thousands of people trapped under collapsed structures and begging for help. With their limited means, Serge and his colleagues had to move on and look for the ones they might be able to actually assist.

Then, only a few hundred metres away, another woman could be heard crying for help. Among the rubble of what used to be a middle-class home, Serge could see an arm coming out of a small hole, waving at him frantically. The arm was all that could be seen; the rest of her body was behind a barrier of rubble.

Her house, located on a slope, had totally caved in under the strength of the tremors. The collapsed structure appeared extremely unstable, and anyone trying to enter risked being crushed alive.

Again, the only thing Serge could do was to comfort the woman by telling her that help would eventually be on the way. Heartbroken, he had to leave.

With so many people injured and in need of medical attention, one of the UN bases that had not been damaged in the quake was soon turned into an emergency care clinic. Thus, on the second day, Serge and some of his colleagues were summoned by UN medical staff to provide security at the UN clinic "Log Base", located near the Port-au-Prince International Airport.

As it turned out, his duties at the clinic would engage him in making some of the most heart-wrenching decisions of his policing career, and would put yet another unwanted twist into his ethical value system.

For example, in a desperate attempt to obtain medical care, many surviving civilians had made their way to the facility. It was not long before the constant influx of gravely hurt people overwhelmed the small medical clinic, which soon faced a dilemma. There was simply not enough room for new patients.

To make matters worse, the small back-up of medical supplies was quickly running out. Acting on instructions from doctors not to let more patients in, Serge and his colleagues had no other choice but to turn newcomers away.

Serge's actions were not without consequences; he was well aware that some of the people he turned away would not survive another day unless cared for. Conditioned to serve, protect, and save lives, never in his career as a police officer had Serge faced such a dilemma. The necessity to turn away people who desperately needed his help deeply hurt him. It was with little consolation that doctors at the clinic reminded him that his actions had helped saved the lives of the patients who were already there and in urgent need of care.

In the evening on the second day, Serge and other Canadian

contingent members arrived at the secured compound of the Embassy of Canada, in downtown Port-au-Prince. The Embassy building had suffered quite a hit from the earthquake. Although the building was standing, its roof helipad had caved in, and was unsafe to use.

At the Embassy, Serge's services were sought to provide more security until the arrival of reinforcements from the Canadian Forces. Later, Serge would go back onto the streets of Port-au-Prince in an attempt to locate and assist more Canadians in distress.

Surviving for the first three days on raw peanut butter he'd scooped from a half-empty jar and drinking coffee served by the embassy, Serge had his first real meal, an army ration pack, some 60 hours after the initial shock. It was approximately the same time that he had his first shower, which he took at the embassy using a plastic 1-litre water bottle.

In those hours, Serge witnessed plenty of human tragedies, but also upsetting insensitivities. Take this man, who was stuck on the 4th floor of his apartment after the stairs had collapsed. His only chance of survival was to climb down a ladder. After some time, Serge and other rescuers managed to find one long enough for the man and other stranded people to use.

As incredible as it may seem under the circumstances, the man's first priority was to save his laptop, which he insisted Serge catch… four floors down. Could the man value his laptop more than his own life, and even risk injuring a rescuer as the object fell? Yes!

Unfortunately, tales like this one were not uncommon, adding a clear burden on all rescuers, in addition to creating a certain degree of disgust for human selfishness. Dealing with individuals like the man above was truly challenging, and required much integrity and professionalism.

The perils and dangers in Port-au-Prince in the immediate aftermath of the quake were very real. Food was scarce, and millions of desperate people were on the street, some armed with guns and others with makeshift weapons. Venturing out for any reason was a risky endeavour, because no one could predict how desperate, hungry, and thirsty people would react. Therefore, from the time he arrived at the embassy compound and for the next three days, Serge's duties fluctuated between providing security and assisting Canadians in distress.

Outside the secured walls of the embassy, a cacophony of mixed noises could be heard, including people sobbing, dogs barking, roosters crowing, and guns firing. Absolutely exhausted, Serge finally got his first 4-hour sleep nearly three days after the initial earthquake. With continuous aftershocks and the sight of the crumbling Christopher Hotel still fresh in his mind, Serge opted to sleep outside on a cot under the stars, gun belt on his belly. He was simply too apprehensive to sleep under any concrete structures.

Within 24-hours of the tragedy, assistance from the international community began to converge on Haiti, some from as far away as the Middle East. Military and civilian Search and Rescue Teams, medical teams, and aid agencies poured into Haiti, bringing much-needed food supplies and help.

For the next two weeks, Serge and his colleagues would work together under the Canadian contingent flagship. They would provide airport security, armed escort to arriving rescue teams, and convey Canadians to the airport to be safely evacuated home.

Meanwhile, the Haitian National Police was in shambles. All of its members had been somehow victims of the earthquake, with many losing spouses, children, and other loved ones. As a result of the breakdown of MINUSTAH and the HNP, the security on the streets of Port-au-Prince was unofficially delegated to the best organized MINUSTAH contingents. These included Brazil, Canada, and a few others.

For example, Brazil promptly assumed a military presence on the streets, while Canadians and other UNPOL contingents dedicated themselves to the protection of convoys for the distribution of food. These latter duties would turn out to be perilous!

Figure 75: A view of one area of the Hotel Montana after the earthquake. The hotel tumbled onto itself in the space of 35 seconds during the earthquake, killing several Canadians and other international hotel guests. Photo courtesy of Serge Boulianne.

As Serge explained, food distribution after the earthquake was no easy task. As a matter of fact, it was dangerous. Survivors were hungry, thirsty, and desperate. Fights would often break out amongst survivors, many of whom were carrying weapons and trying to steal food rations from each other. Sad traits of human misery could be seen everywhere.

To make matters even worse, crime became the norm for many to survive. The collapse of one of the main prisons enabled over 5,000 prisoners to escape, among them murderers and gang members. The streets of Port-au-Prince became almost instantly a no man's land. Cases of civilian kidnappings, which had been down to almost zero prior to the quake, started to increase over time. There was even a case of three off-duty peacekeepers being robbed at gunpoint in their residence. It was only through the calmness of one of the peacekeepers, a Canadian, that no one got killed.

Approximately two weeks had elapsed before Serge returned to MINUSTAH duties. Lamentably, his workday would only intensify with the constant coming and going of rescue teams from all around the world.

Being a strong leader, Serge had been assigned to the Port-au-Prince Toussaint-Louverture Airport. There, his duties were to ensure the safe arrival and deployment of the incoming Search and Rescue Teams.

By the time Serge had been deployed to the airport, as many as 80 to 90 international Search and Rescue teams had already arrived in Haiti, making the rescue operation one of the largest ever. On a one-to-one country scale, the Haiti rescue efforts were comparable to those undertaken in December 2004, when a tsunami in the Indian Ocean killed nearly 250,000 people across a dozen nations.[373]

To give you an idea of the sheer size of the calamity associated with the Haitian earthquake, official Haitian government counts put the number of deaths at 300,000. That said, these numbers were being challenged by international organizations such as the US Agency for International Development (USAID), whose door-to-door count estimated a maximum death toll of 85,000 people.[374] No matter the numbers, many will agree that the Haitian earthquake brought tremendous suffering and affliction to a nation already in turmoil, and postponed development efforts for many years.

Another of Serge's duties was to ensure the rescue teams' welfare and safety. Many neighbourhoods, such as Cité Soleil, were flourishing with crime prior to the earthquake. Having to send rescue teams into those neighbourhoods was a dangerous endeavour that needed to be closely monitored.

In January in Port-au-Prince, darkness fell by 18:00. It was extremely unsafe for rescue personnel to work by night in collapsed buildings, especially with limited lighting gear. At night, the city streets were taken over by people too scared to live under any type of structure.

Figure 76: The Haiti National Palace built in 1918, seen shortly after the earthquake of January 12, 2010. The second floor has collapsed onto the first under the heavyweight of the roof dome. Photo courtesy of Serge Boulianne.

With a shortage of food and water supplies, in addition to the 5,000-plus prison escapees still roaming in the city, it is no wonder that criminality rose drastically. The echoes of gunshots in the night would soon become an all-too-frequent occurrence.

Very aware of the danger that criminals and desperate people represented to the rescue teams, Serge had to make heart-wrenching decisions. For example, occasionally rescue team leaders would approach Serge late in the afternoon to inform him that survivors had been located in the rubble at a given location. They would urge Serge to provide them with a UN security detail (UNPOL) so that they could go out immediately and start the rescue.

In many instances, Serge had to inform the rescue team leaders that it was too dangerous to undertake relief efforts by night, and as such, had to have them wait until daybreak. These decisions did not go well with many rescue team leaders, who, more often than not, did not understand the potential risks to their teams and the security details if they were to undertake relief efforts at night.

Knowing that his decision would mean that survivors had to wait a few more hours before they had a chance to be saved was morally draining on Serge. Again, he was well aware that his decisions could mean death for many who had been stuck under the debris for several days. With the safety of the UN security details and the rescue teams as a top priority, Serge had no choice but to have them wait until daybreak before going out.

His decisions, however heart-wrenching and difficult as they may have been, were fully supported by his peers and UN management. It is highly possible that some of the trapped victims did not make it as a result of rescue efforts having been delayed; however, there is no doubt that Serge's exacting decisions saved many lives that might otherwise have been lost.

Take this case, for example: a police colleague at a rescue scene called Serge to summon for army backup, as armed thugs were firing in his direction and that of the rescue team. Since the army was unavailable, Serge ordered the member and the team to leave the area immediately. Rescue efforts were abandoned, perhaps costing the life of the individual being rescued. However, if Serge had told the officer to stand his ground and a rescuer or the police officer had been killed, the civilian still wouldn't have been rescued, and an additional person would be dead.

There is much to be thankful for from Serge's strong leadership skills and crisis management ability in this difficult time. Nobody, whether it was a member of a rescue team or a member of a UN security detail, was injured or killed under his command. Although we will never have a clear picture of how many people were saved thanks to Serge's actions, I am almost certain that many more would have perished if his wisdom had not been sought.

Surviving an event like the earthquake in Haiti affects even the strongest people. No one escapes some type of survivor guilt, especially when hundreds of thousands have died all around. Like many of his colleagues, Serge often wondered why he had been spared.

Figure 77: A desperate father and mother with their newborn baby. They have lost all their possessions in the earthquake, but are lucky to be safe and alive! Photo courtesy of Serge Boulianne.

Perhaps he found some of his answers in many of the small projects he undertook after the earthquake. If the Haitian people needed him before the disaster, one could only imagine how manifold that need increased afterwards.

Although he will not admit it openly, Serge is a caring, compassionate, and considerate individual. This is the opinion of him I share with at least 150 other people from a small Port-au-Prince neighbourhood called "Delma 18". People in that residential area lost almost everything after the quake: homes, husbands, wives, and children. Those who survived regrouped together in a small congregation, helping each other to survive.

Having heard about the community's exemplary efforts, Serge became involved with the group, and started to attend many of their reunions. His mere presence at meetings cheered and encouraged the community to move on and rebuild. Understandably, the community's needs were endless: Food, shelter, tools to rebuild, and so on.

What made Serge's visits to that neighbourhood a unique experience was the enthusiasm with which he was received by the community. Although he could not provide them with many of the demands they made, his constant guidance in getting the community to find solutions from within earned him much respect.

With his help, the community was able to get the attention of international Non-Governmental Organizations (NGOs) to seek assistance for reconstruction projects—not a small feat, given the hundreds of thousands of people waiting for assistance at the time.

Then there was Janice, the housemaid. She had been Serge and his roommates' maid since the beginning of their mission. To help her with her family situation (an unemployed husband and a young child of school age), Serge and his buddies sponsored her son's elementary school education. This may seem like nothing, but for Janice and her family, it meant the world!

Well before the quake, with a state lacking in institutional strength and capacity to provide basic services, the educational sector had become increasingly privatized. Therefore, a basic education was only available to those who could afford it.[375] For Serge, the opportunity to sponsor a young person's education, and perhaps contribute to a better future for Haiti, is something that he held dear to his heart.

Another aspect of the Haiti experience that Serge will always remember is to have had the great fortune and pleasure to cross paths with Canada's then-Governor General, Michaëlle Jean. Being of Haitian heritage, Mrs. Jean traveled to Haiti and the Dominican Republic during her official functions in March 2010, and visited the devastated Port-au-Prince. Although his encounter with Mrs. Jean was brief, her charm and philanthropic dedication is something that Serge will remember for a long time.

At the time of this writing, almost nine years had gone by since the fateful earthquake of January 2010. Although much of the rubble has been cleaned and moved outside the city of Port-au-Prince, the infrastructure of the city is still in shambles.

Furthermore, thousands are still living under extremely adverse conditions without electricity or running water, some in makeshift camps they called home. Despite the fact that two new governments have been elected since May 2011, and that hopes for prosperity were initially high, little has changed in that corner of the world, and for the most part, extreme poverty remains the norm.

Figure 78: Then Canada's Governor General, Michaëlle Jean, and her husband, Jean-Daniel Lafond, during an official tour of Port-au-Prince in March 2010. Photo courtesy of Serge Boulianne.

Among the many reasons that prevent Haiti from moving ahead, despite the billions of dollars donated by the international community, is the enduring political instability. The government of former pop-star singer Michel Martelly may have been well-intentioned, but with continuous political in-fighting, activism from former dictators, and other local issues, little did improve. It is the writer's opinion that the government of Jovenel Moise, elected in February 2017, will not be able to do much more than any predecessors. Sadly, Haiti may not be able to get on its feet for years, if not for decades to come.

It is not because Haiti does not have potential. On the contrary! For example, Haiti boasts some of the most beautiful beaches in the Caribbean, potentially helping the country to develop a sustainable tourist industry. And despite its woes with education, Haiti can educate professionals.

In May 2011, I met with medical doctors who had recently graduated from a university in Haiti. These were well-educated young men and women who were ready to contribute to the betterment of their country. The question was whether or not Haiti could make it safe enough for these young professionals to remain in the country, and provide them with an environment to grow and develop their skills.

In the years and decades to come, the prosperity of Haiti will be determined by its ability to become politically stable and, in addition, tackle the high corruption, street violence, and extreme poverty. Whether any professionals that Haiti produces will find it enticing enough for them to elect to stay and help rebuild the country is an area that will need to be monitored.

One of the key attributes to completing a successful and meaningful mission is to be open-minded. To ease into the mission, one should leave behind home standards and make every effort to adapt to local customs.

Figure 79: Doctors' Graduation in Port-au-Prince, May 2011. Some amongst the many dozens of doctors that graduated that day have already left the country for better opportunities. Photo by Ben Maure.

For Serge, what he took away from Haiti was a life lesson. He learned that Haitians could do miracles with very little. For example, he recounted that some Haitian mechanics would repair a broken-down truck with limited or obsolete tools. Nothing was thrown away. The experience made him realize that nothing was impossible, even though the road to success could be arduous.

Though these were some of the most difficult moments of his life, Serge strived to remain enthusiastic. His positive energy was a guiding light for colleagues and a relief to his family and friends thousands of miles away. Nineteenth-century American essayist and poet Ralph Waldo Emerson once said, "Nothing great was ever achieved without enthusiasm."[376] It is clear that Serge's attitude in the face of adversity made the above statement come to life.

Incidentally, one of Serge's best pieces of advice is to strive to remain positive, and to make every effort to turn the page, especially after a period of adversity. For Serge, the Haitian mission was like a book he wrote in every day during his nine-month mission. At the end, he closed the book and placed it in his life's library.

Of course, he may from time to time grab it back from the shelf, peek through it, smile, or grieve. But in the end he understands that it was all worth it, making him an even better person.

On January 10, 2013, almost three years to the day after the Haiti earthquake, Detective Lieutenant Serge Boulianne received an RCMP Commissioner's Commendation for Bravery for his lifesaving and selfless actions during the 2010 earthquake. Detective Lieutenant Serge Boulianne retired in 2012 after 28 years with the SPVM. He now dedicates his time to a new hobby: construction.

Thank you, Serge, for your undisputed contribution to policing and peacekeeping!

11.

Epilogue

BY WRITING THIS book, my main objective was to tell the unique stories of the valiant police peacekeepers introduced herein, so that the world would know what they have accomplished. One mission at a time, they strove to promote world peace through the protection of the rights and human rights of those they served, irrespective of race, nationality, religion, sex, and station of life.

I also wanted the reader to experience what it is like to be a police peacekeeper in those missions. I wished to encourage the reader to go through the same range of emotions, from laughter to tears, hopes to despairs, that some peacekeepers have experienced.

Still, I wanted to do more than just tell stories. I wanted to make this book informative, both from a historical and human experience standpoint. On top of that, it was my intent to provide an inspirational leadership guide, which would plant the seed for someone to discover the world of possibilities that lies inside each of us. I hope I succeeded!

After all, isn't one of the goals in life to grow, to reach one's maximum potential, while helping others to do the same?

The Author,
Ben Maure

APPENDIX A

The Selection Process

LONG BEFORE A police force from a UN member state initiates a candidate selection for a particular mission, a formal request to that member country by the UN Secretary-General in New York will have been made.[377] Such a request will likely have been debated at the UN in the presence of many governments, keeping in mind the specific peacekeeping mandate of the particular proposed mission. During those discussions, a state may informally commit to contributing police officers.[378]

As part of Canada's commitment and desire to participate in international peacekeeping operations, the Royal Canadian Mounted Police (RCMP) has been given the mandate and responsibility to prepare for and deploy Canadian police officers abroad. Although the first priority of the RCMP is its domestic policing needs, it accommodates the deployment of Civilian Police (CIVPOL), nowadays renamed United Nations Police (UNPOL) officers abroad when requests are received from the Department of Foreign Affairs and International Trade (DFAIT).[379]

In the end, the final commitment made on behalf of a member state has to come from its government, with the identification of suitable and available personnel to serve on the specific mission already accomplished. Often, these requests will come to the RCMP on short notice and under conditions of crisis. Since most police officers are engaged in full-time operational duties and may not be replaced if they leave their post, a police organization like the RCMP may have limited flexibility in allowing for an immediate deployment of officers to a particular UN peacekeeping mission.[380] In addition, regular budget allocations seldom allow for such replacement, and thus special financial arrangements need to be made.

Normally, when a request for overseas deployment of police officers comes in, DFAIT will contact the office of the RCMP Commissioner.[381] From there, the RCMP Human Resources and International Peacekeeping Operations departments are involved in reviewing whether or not the demand can be met. For example, language requirements may be imposed, which would limit the number of police officers available for the particular mission.

To assist in meeting some of those requirements and the ever-increasing demand for Canadian police officers overseas, more and more Canadian police agencies (other than the RCMP) have been approached. These forces have also contributed to International Peacekeeping by sending their members abroad.[382]

For example, in Haiti where the primary language spoken is French, Le Service de Police de la Ville de Montréal (SPVM); Sureté du Québec (SQ), the Ontario Provincial Police (OPP), and many other municipal police departments have participated by providing French-speaking officers to the mission.[383]

Next, before a final decision is made as to whether Canada will participate in any given mission, the proposed mandate, living conditions, security arrangements, and medical and health needs of the officers will be evaluated.[384] Further, the type of dangers officers will be facing and the type of support they can expect from a military presence, if any, will be analyzed.[385]

As one can see, Canada will have some say as to what its officers will do on a particular mission. If that were not the case, it could opt not to participate.[386]

Once Canada has deemed it can participate in a mission, the RCMP is in charge of identifying volunteer candidates for the specific mission. Over the years, the RCMP has developed a system for its members whereby International Peace Operations

Missions are advertised on an Intranet and volunteer applications are sought.

Regardless of the mission, once one has volunteered their name for an overseas assignment, being released from regular domestic responsibilities will remain the major obstacle. This is because the officer's regular operational position may not be accommodated by a replacement while they are abroad. Court commitments may also impede availability.

Under the terms of the financial arrangements made by the UN and its member states, the country that hosts police officers to a mission continues to provide the normal salary, benefits, and equipment to the officer.[387]

The UN, on the other hand, will provide a range of expenses, including travel to and from the mission, a Mission Subsistence Allowance (MSA), and other compensations in case of injuries or death.[388]

While Canadian police officers are well paid by nature, such may not be the case for a police officer coming from a developing country. In some instances, the MSA allowance provided by the UN far exceeded the salary earned by a police officer living in a developing country. Therefore, this could result in less-than-qualified candidates being chosen to serve on that mission.[389]

As an example, a certain candidate may be selected if he/she accepts to return a favour (monetary or otherwise) to the government official who made their participation to that mission possible.

As per Canada's lessons learned from operational experience, the candidate selection and training process has developed into a system that can accommodate mission-specific requirements. However, as a base for all Canadian UN police candidates, the individual will need to have a minimum of five years of police experience before they can be considered. The officer will also need to have a good personnel file and police record, demonstrate an ability to get along with others, and be able to work with minimal supervision.[390]

A demonstrated ability to work with people from different races, ethnic backgrounds, and cultures will be given extra consideration. However, the latter element may not be a difficult one to acquire, especially if a candidate comes from a large, multi-cultural city such as Toronto, Montréal, Vancouver, or Halifax.

Of equal importance is the candidate's family support. If a candidate has little or no family support (i.e. from a spouse, children, and/or parents), they have greater chances of being negatively affected by events or situations taking place at home while away.

Next, a candidate who can drive a vehicle with a standard transmission, and who has experience living in areas with few amenities, such as camping in the wild or living in small, isolated communities, would also be given additional consideration. These aptitudes would come in handy in countries where the state of roads is poor, and where living conditions may be less than desirable.[391]

In a final process, candidates who have been identified to go on a particular mission will have to go through a series of medical and physical tests to determine their capability to participate in that mission. These examinations will include a general health probe completed by a recognized physician, as well as an evaluation of the candidate's emotional health.[392]

For example, it would be paramount to screen out a candidate who has problems with alcohol before he was allowed to go.[393] A physical aptitude test, known as the Physical Abilities Requirement Evaluation "PARE" test, is also administered to the candidate before they are given the green light to go on a mission.

The test is a type of obstacle course that involves running, jumping, climbing stairs, vaulting, lifting and pushing weights.[394] All of these must be completed within a certain timeframe, and aims to emulate physical situations in which police officers may find themselves as part of their duty: fighting and arresting a suspect, intervening in family disputes, participating in search and rescues, etc.[395]

If a candidate is successful in all of the above, he will then be required to obtain all the necessary vaccinations and immunizations needed for the area of the world where the mission is located. These may include Hepatitis A & B, Typhoid, Rabies, Tetanus, Cholera, and Malaria vaccines and pills.[396] The candidate is now closer to being mission-ready. The final step is to undertake additional preparation for deployment for the specific mission.

In the end, there are many hurdles to jump and even more qualifications to meet. But many peacekeepers find these obstacles worth the cultural and character experiences they earn abroad. So, Are you ready?

APPENDIX B
Peacebuilding, Peacekeeping, and Peacemaking

THE TERMS PEACEBUILDING, Peacekeeping, and Peacemaking can be confusing to the layperson, especially when these terms are used as interchangeable vocabulary. Let's start with Peacebuilding. The origin and concept go back to 1975, when Johan Galtung, a Norwegian sociologist, published a pioneering essay entitled "Three approaches to Peace: Peacekeeping, Peacemaking, and Peacebuilding". Galtung, who is considered one of the principal founders of the discipline of Peace and Conflict Studies, hypothesized that structures had to be present to remove the cause of wars, in addition to offering alternatives to war.[397]

From there came a definition that described Peacebuilding as a range of approaches targeted to reduce the risk that a country relapse into conflict. Such approaches were to encompass measures to lay the foundation for sustainable peace and development. Peacebuilding would thus include a variety of methods, processes, and activities (e.g. to form and train a new police force; to provide a program to re-insert former rebel fighters into civil society, etc.) to sustain peace over the long-term.[398]

As I understand it, within this framework would come the activities of peacemaking and peacekeeping. The SAGE Encyclopedia of Intercultural Competence provides a definition for both Peacekeeping and Peacemaking.[399] In its simple form, it translates as follows:

1. Peacekeeping: The art of ending attacks and preventing the resumption of fighting in the aftermath of a conflict. It usually requires a strong (neutral) military presence of some sort.

2. Peacemaking: The ability of reaching out to a settlement after a conflict has ended. It often involves a third party as arbitrator (such as the UN).

If we look at my mission in Guatemala, I was sent on a Peacekeeping mission. At least, that was the term used back then. However, the war had ended, and international military presence was minimal. I would argue that the activities I conducted during my mission fell within the greater scope of Peacebuilding. For example, I was monitoring the return of refugees, recording and investigating Human Rights abuses, monitoring the integration of rebel fighters back into society, and so on. Meanwhile, the Guatemalan police was being retrained (with focus on Human Rights) and reformed by Spain.

Based on the above definitions, most missions described in this book, although called Peacekeeping, were more of a Peacebuilding nature. However, calling them Peacekeeping missions does not seem to be wrong either, given today's multi-dimensional peacekeeping operations, which are not only called upon to maintain peace and security, but also promote a fair political process, address Human Rights, review land claim issues, and help demobilize and re-integrate former combatants into civil society.

In conclusion, a measure of uncertainty continues to cloud the definitions of the three terms, perhaps because many people prefer to use the term "peacekeeping" to describe actions and activities that are encompassed in Peacebuilding and Peacemaking. That being said, peacekeeping is generally understood as being efforts to seek lasting peace.

Below is a non-exhaustive list of authoritative websites you may wish to visit to try to get a grasp on the definitions' nuances:

1. Peacemaking, peacekeeping, peacebuilding and peace enforcement in the 21st century. 25 April 2014. https://www.insightonconflict.org/blog/2014/04/peacemaking-peacekeeping-peacebuilding-peace-enforcement-21st-century/

2. UN Peacekeeping, Peacemaking, and Peacebuilding https://www.britannica.com/topic/United-Nations/Peacekeeping-peacemaking-and-peace-building

3. The conceptual origins of peacebuilding http://www.peacebuildinginitiative.org/index34ac.html?pageId=1764

4. Peacekeeping, Peacebuilding, and Peacemaking: Concepts Complication and Canada's Role. 17 May 2004, http://publications.gc.ca/collections/Collection-R/LoPBdP/EB-e/prb0406-e.pdf

APPENDIX C
ABBREVIATIONS & ACRONYMS

AFRC	Armed Forces Revolutionary Council
ANA	Afghanistan National Army
APC	Armoured Personnel Carrier
ATCO trailer	ATCO is a brand of trailer often used as a portable, temporary or permanent mobile office.
AUMS	African Union Mission in Sudan
BBC	British Broadcasting Corporation
CAD	Canadian dollars
CAF	Canadian Armed Forces
CDF	Civil Defence Force
CF	Canadian Forces
CFA	Cease-Fire Agreement
CIA	Central Intelligence Agency
CIMIC	Civil-Military Cooperation
CNS	Camp Nathan Smith
CPA	Comprehensive Peace Agreement
CSIS	Canadian Security Intelligence Service
CIVPOL	Civilian Police
DFAIT	Department of Foreign Affairs and International Trade. As of late 2015, DFAIT had changed its name to Global Affairs Canada (GAC)
DMDC	Defense Manpower Data Center
DPKO	United Nations Department of Peacekeeping Operations
DRC	Democratic Republic of Congo
EPAS	Electronic Performance Appraisal System
EU	European Union
EUPOL COPPS	European Police Coordinating Office for Palestinian Police Support
FIS	Forensic Identification Section
GAP	Government Accountability Project
GoC	Government of Canada
GPS	Global Positioning System
HN	Host Nation
HNP	Haitian National Police
ICC	International Criminal Court
IDP	Internally Displaced Persons

IED	Improvised Explosive Device
IMP	Individual Meal Pack
INTERFET	International Force for East Timor
ISAF	International Security Assistance Force, Afghanistan
JEM	Justice and Equality Movement
JIEDDO	Joint IED Defeat Organization
KAF	Kandahar Airfield
KFOR	Kosovo Force
KLA	Kosovo Liberation Army
Kms	Kilometres
LWOP	Leave Without Pay; Leave of Absence Without Pay
LAV	Light Armoured Vehicle
MIF	Multinational Interim Force
MINUGUA	Misión Naciones Unidas en Guatemala (United Nations Verification Mission in Guatemala)
MINUSTAH	United Nations Stabilization Mission in Haiti
MIPONUH	Mission de Police des Nations Unies en Haiti [English] (United Nations Civilian Police Mission in Haiti)
MOU	Memorandum of Understanding
MSA	Mission Subsistence Allowance
NAFTA	North American Free-Trade Agreement
NATO	North Atlantic Treaty Organization
NDS	National Directorate of Security
NGO	Non-Governmental Organization
NPFL	National Patriotic Front of Liberia
OMLT's	Operational Mentoring Teams
OPP	Ontario Provincial Police
ORQUE	Oficina Regional en Quetzaltenango (Regional Office Quetzaltenango)
PA	Palestinian Authority
PARE test	Physical Abilities Requirement Evaluation test
PCP	Palestinian Civil Police
PFLP	Popular Front for the Liberation of Palestine
PLO	Palestine Liberation Organization
PMT Warhog	Police Mentor Team Warhog
PMT GridIron	Police Mentor Team GridIron
POMLT	Police Operational Mentoring and LiaisonTeam
PSF	Popular Struggle Front
PSS	Police Sub-Station

QRF	Quick Response Force
RCMP	Royal Canadian Mounted Police
RUF	Revolutionary United Front (Sierra Leone)
SEA	Sexual Exploitation and Abuse
SITREP	Situational Report
SLA	Sierra Leone Army
SLM	Sudan Liberation Movement
SPLA	Sudan People's Liberation Army
SPVM	Service de Police de la Ville de Montréal
SQ	Sureté du Québec
SWAPO	South West Africa People's Organization
SWAPOL	South West Africa Police
TAAT	Trans Arabian Air Transport
UK	United Kingdom
UN	United Nations
UNAMET	United Nations Mission in East Timor
UNAMSIL	United Nations Mission in Sierra Leone
UNMIH	United Nations Mission in Haiti
UNEP	United Nations Environment Program
UNGOMAP	United Nations Good Offices Mission in Afghanistan and Pakistan
UNITA	Uniao Nacional para a Independencia Total de Angola, [Portuguese language] (National Union for the Total Independence of Angola), was a movement for the liberation of Angola.
UNMIK	United Nations Interim Administration Mission in Kosovo
UNMIS	United Nations Mission in the Sudan
UNPA	United Nations Protected Area
UNPOL	United Nations Police
UNPROFOR	United Nations Protection Forces (Former Yugoslavia)
UNTAET	United Nations Transitional Authority for East Timor
UNTAG	United Nations Transition Assistance Group, Namibia
UNTMIH	United Nations Transition Mission in Haiti
URNG	Unidad Revolucionaria Nacional Guatemalteca (Guatemalan National Revolutionary Unit)
USAID	US Agency for International Development
USD	United States dollars
VBIED	Vehicle Borne Improvised Explosive Device
WWI	World War I
WWII	World War II

APPENDIX D
ACKNOWLEDGMENTS

AS A READER, I used to skip this section and get right into the substance of a book. Besides, I often thought, I would not know any of the people acknowledged, and would have found the section of little interest. I was wrong! It wasn't until I wrote this book, and realized how crucial and important the assistance and help of others had been in making the book a reality, that I truly understood the value and relevance of this section. Without the people named below, this work would simply not have been. I am truly hoping that you have enjoyed (or will enjoy) all the chapters in this book, and that you will learn something from them that will serve you. So please, don't skip this part: take a minute or two to go over the next paragraphs to get to know the formidable people who helped me put this project together.

First, I am much indebted to the nine Canadian police officers who dedicated their time and shared their most intimate mission experiences and wisdom with me. Since their respective missions, some have been promoted to higher ranks, while others have retired. These are:

Staff Sergeant Major John Buis, with whom I once worked at the Richmond Detachment in British Columbia. John was instrumental in helping me identify peacekeepers willing to participate to this project. Thank you, John, for your incredible support.

Retired Deputy Commissioner Larry Proke, who led the first RCMP contingent to participate in a United Nations mission.

Larry's foresight, diplomacy, experience, and great leadership skills indeed echoed what an officer and a gentleman is all about. Thank you, Larry, for sharing your incredible adventure!

Retired Corporal Chuck Kolot, with whom I started my policing career in Surrey, British Columbia. As a former lawyer, Chuck would often encourage me and my peers to use critical thinking when performing our duties. I am very grateful to you, Chuck, for imparting your wisdom early in my career…and thank you again for sharing the story of your mission.

Sergeant Lorin Lopetinsky. I would like to express my gratitude to you, Lorin, for sharing your tale and giving us an insight into the astonishing powers of networking.

Sergeant Gregor Aitken, featured on the front cover picture, taken in Kandahar, Afghanistan. Through the chronicle of your mission, I gained a deeper understanding of the reasons and the importance for us to be there in Afghanistan. Thank you, Gregor, for broadening my knowledge and for sharing your deepest emotions during your incredible journey.

Superintendent Galib Bhayani. Galib, you have been a long-time friend and a mentor. I continue to admire your strong determination to succeed in whatever you undertake. You have also been a source of motivation for me to complete this book.

Retired Chief Superintendent Rick Taylor. Thank you, Rick, for partaking in this work, and for giving us an intimate look at life in a mission from the perspective of a Team Commander.

Retired Inspector Walt Sutherland. Your insight and work into one of the world's oldest conflict zones was truly informative. Thank you for your wise advice and emphasis on maintaining a healthy balance between work and personal life.

Retired Detective Lieutenant Serge Boulianne. I got to know Serge in 2010 in Haiti, shortly after the devastating earthquake that killed so many. At the time, I was traveling between the Dominican Republic and Haiti once a month as part of my Liaison Officer's duties. When I announced one night that I was in the process of writing a book on United Nations missions, and that I wanted Serge to tell me his story, he did not hesitate for one second! This, despite the fresh memories of the earthquake still haunting him. Thank you, Serge, for sharing your most inner feelings in a deeply engaging narrative.

There have been many other people who have directly influenced my thinking about achievement and success, either in their writings, speeches, or coaching programs over the years. Incorporating their wisdom and capitalizing on their experience has enabled me to produce a unique perspective on the work and lives of the peacekeepers depicted in this book. I am forever grateful to authors and life coaches such as Peter Legge, Brian Tracy, Zig Ziglar, Stephen Covey, Jack Canfield, Jim Rohn, Anthony Robbins, and management thinkers like the great Peter Drucker. Thank you for sharing your wisdom and knowledge.

To my long-time librarian friend, Ana Rosa Blue, who spent countless hours reviewing, correcting, and guiding me through all of my drafts. Thank you for your patience, professionalism, and long-lasting friendship.

BEN J.S. MAURE, M.S.C.

To Nicole Binette, author and spouse of my former colleague in the Dominican Republic, Andre Filiatrault. Thank you, Nicole, for taking the time to have a critical look at the first chapter of my very first draft and steering me in the right direction.

To my content editor, Mary Rosenblum, for her frankness and insight as to what needed to be improved. Despite many corrections to be made, Mary reinforced my faith in the potential of this project.

To Michelle Balfour, my copy editor, whose editing talents were paramount in improving my message and the book as a whole.

To Marla Thompson, the artist responsible for my eye-catching book cover.

To Richard Coles, my proof-reader, for his honesty at identifying weak points and errors I made. I also thank you Richard for helping me further enhance the overall quality of my work.

To Lyda Mclallen, my marketer. Thank you, Lyda, for your wise advice, continuous support, and for helping me promote this work.

To Mr. Ben Coles, CEO; Ms. Heather Westing and Ms. Lauren Olson, author services managers from Cascadia Author Services. Thank you all for your support and for identifying Mary, my content editor, Michelle, my copy editor, Richard, my proof-reader, and Marla, the artist.

To Mr. David Felicissimo, General Counsel of Valnet Inc., copyrights holder of www.WorldAtlas.com maps. Thank you for allowing me a non-exclusive, royalty-free basis for the display of your educative and colourful maps. Being able to use them for this project provided me with a great tool to visually display the location of a country and explain its geo-political situation. Thank you again for your support!

To Andrew Muller, for the permission to use his cool picture of a UN C-130 Hercules plane.

A special "thank you" to retired NYPD Captain and Former United Nations and European Union/United States Department of State Rule of Law Mission Police Chief (in Kosovo), Dr. James F. Albrecht, from Pace University. Jimmy, I am very thankful for the time you took to read my manuscript and for writing a very compelling Foreword.

To the university professors and Chiefs of Police who, despite their extremely busy schedules, accepted to read my manuscript and provide testimonials. Thank you all!

To Mr. Terry Gould, Investigative Journalist and author of *Worth Dying For: Canada's Mission to Train Police in the World's Failing States (2014)*. I would like to express my gratitude to you Terry, for completing a book review of my manuscript and for providing me with wise advice on writing, audience, and publishing.

To my parents, Philippe and Jeannine, for their love, support, and encouragement.

I laboured extensively in order to find the right title for this book. I needed a title that would reflect the experience, the novelty, the dangers, and the leadership skills that many peacekeepers in this book displayed. After some time, I finally found a title that accurately depicted the stories within. Admittedly, I got the idea from Dennis

BEN J.S. MAURE, M.S.C.

N.T. Perkins' book, *Leading at the Edge: Leadership Lessons from the Extraordinary Saga of Shackleton's Antarctic Expedition*.

Although none of the peacekeepers in this book found themselves trapped in the ice like Shackleton's crew did, many stories in this book relate to survival and leadership skills exhibited by the peacekeepers. As an aside, for the reader who loves history, adventure, and who is aspiring to improve leadership skills, Perkins' book is a must-read! By the way, the year 2016 marked the centenary of the safe return of Ernest Shackleton's remarkable expedition to Antarctica.

Finally, I am deeply indebted to my wife, Judy, who has put up over the years with my propensity to get consumed with projects like this. I thank you, Judy, for being my most brutal critic, but yet a truly enduring supporter.

APPENDIX E
ABOUT THE AUTHOR

Figure 80: The author, Inspector Ben Maure, RCMP Federal Policing. Photo courtesy of Ben Maure.

Ben Maure is a serving Peace Officer with the Royal Canadian Mounted Police. He has over 30 years of police experience, most of which have been spent in British Columbia, Canada. Ben's career within the Royal Canadian Mounted Police has been diverse. He started as a uniformed police officer in Surrey, British Columbia, and eventually made his way to Ottawa as an Officer-in-Charge within a federal policing unit. In 1999, Ben completed a one-year secondment tour of duty as a United Nations Peacekeeper in Quetzaltenango, Guatemala. Between 2009 and 2013, Ben acted as a Police Liaison Officer (First Secretary) at the Embassy of Canada in the Dominican Republic. He speaks five languages, and has traveled to more than 26 countries around the world.

BEN J.S. MAURE, M.S.C.

Ben holds a Bachelor of Technology degree from the British Columbia Institute of Technology (BCIT) and a Master of Arts degree in Social Justice from the University of the Fraser Valley (UFV). His interests are international policing and public safety. Ben is also a recipient of the Meritorious Service Cross (M.S.C.). Ben holds membership in Toastmasters International. This is his first book.

Works Cited

Afghanistan. (2012). Retrieved Sep. 10, 2012, from Encyclopaedia Britannica Online: http://www.britannica.com/EBchecked/topic/7798/Afghanistan

Alexander I. (2011). Retrieved Jan. 09, 2011, from Encyclopaedia Britannica Online: http://www.britannica.com/EBchecked/topic/14042/Alexander-I

Amebic Dysentery. (2011). Retrieved Jun. 04, 2011, from Encyclopaedia Britannica Online: http://www.britannica.com/EBchecked/topic/19092/amebic-dysentery

Antimalarial Drugs. (2012A). Retrieved Aug. 25, 2012, from The Free Dictionary: http://medical-dictionary.thefreedictionary.com/Antimalarial+Drugs

Armoured Vehicle. (2016). Retrieved Jun. 11, 2016, from Encyclopaedia Britannica Online: http://www.britannica.com/technology/armoured-vehicle

Battle of Borovo Selo. (2010, Dec. 25). Retrieved Jan. 22, 2011, from Wikipedia: http://en.wikipedia.org/wiki/Borovo_Selo_killings

Battlefield Detectives: The Six Day War [Video]. (2005). Retrieved Jan. 03, 2012, from History Channel on Youtube: http://www.youtube.com/watch?v=v81xG614M5c&feature=related

BBC News. (2001). *1998: US Embassies in Africa Bombed*. Retrieved Sep. 23, 2012, from http://news.bbc.co.uk/onthisday/hi/dates/stories/august/7/newsid_3131000/3131709.stm

BBC News. (2008, Oct. 07). *Darfur Ambush Kills Peacekeeper*. Retrieved Mar. 10, 2014, from http://news.bbc.co.uk/2/hi/7656359.stm

BBC News. (2008). *On This Day April 27, 1961: Sierra Leone Wins Independence*. Retrieved Dec. 19, 2010, from http://news.bbc.co.uk/onthisday/hi/dates/stories/april/27/newsid_2502000/2502411.stm

BBC News. (2006, Mar. 13). *The Charges Against Milosevic*. Retrieved Jan. 12, 2013, from http://news.bbc.co.uk/2/hi/europe/1402790.stm#croatia

BBC News. (2010, Oct. 18). *Timeline: Guatemala*. Retrieved Mar. 20, 2011, from http://news.bbc.co.uk/2/hi/americas/country_profiles/1215811.stm

BBC News. (2010). *Timeline: Sierra Leone*. Retrieved Dec. 26, 2010, from http://news.bbc.co.uk/2/hi/africa/1065898.stm

Bellour, S. (2011, Feb. 15). *EAST TIMOR: Coping with Crocs and Other Hazards*. Retrieved Aug. 25, 2012, from http://www.worldmomsblog.com/2011/02/15/east-timor-coping-with-crocs-and-other-hazards/

Bennett, J. M. (Ed.). (n.d.). *The SAGE Encyclopaedia of Intercultural Competence*. Retrieved Sep. 05, 2016, from https://books.google.ca/books?id=n

Bethlehem, D., & Weller, M. (1997). *The "Yugoslav" Crisis in International Law: General Issues*. Cambridge, United Kingdom: Cambridge University Press.

Braun, T. (Director). (2007). *Darfur Now* [Motion Picture].

Brief History of Palestine. (2011). *In Palestine History.Com*. Retrieved Dec. 31, 2011, from http://www.palestinehistory.com/history/brief/brief.htm#01

British West Africa. (2010). Retrieved Dec. 18, 2010, from Encyclopaedia Britannica Online: http://www.britannica.com/EBchecked/topic/80390/British-West-Africa

Caldwell, W. B., & Finney, N. K. (2011, Feb.). Security, Capacity and Literacy. Military Review.

Camp Mirage. (2012). Retrieved Oct. 27, 2012, from Wikipedia: http://en.wikipedia.org/wiki/Camp_Mirage

Canadian Army. (2016, 01 16). *Light Armoured Vehicle (LAV) III*. Retrieved Jun. 11, 2016, from Canadian Army: http://www.army-armee.forces.gc.ca/en/vehicles/light-armoured-vehicle.

Canoe.ca. (2012). *Nutrition and Fitness: Heat Stroke*. Retrieved Nov. 10, 2012, from http://chealth.canoe.ca/channel_condition_info_details.asp?channel_id=44&relation_id=54611&disease_id=68&page_no=2

Central Intelligence Agency. (2012). *The World Fact Book: Haiti*. Retrieved Feb. 26, 2012, from https://www.cia.gov/library/publications/the-world-factbook/geos/ha.html

Chandler, S. (2008). *100 Ways to Motivate Others--How Great Leaders Can Produce Insane Results Without Driving People Crazy*. Pompton Plains, NJ: Career Press Inc.

Chapell, D., & Evans, J. (1997, Jan. 19). *The Role, Preparation, and Performance of Civilian Police in United Nations Peacekeeping Operations*. Retrieved Apr. 12, 2011, from International Centre for Criminal Law Reform and Criminal Justice Policy: http://icclr.law.ubc.ca/sites/icclr.law.ubc.ca/files/publications/pdfs/Peacekeeping.pdf

Chapter VII of the United Nations Charter. (2012). Retrieved Jan. 21, 2013, from Wikipedia: http://en.wikipedia.org/wiki/Chapter_VII_of_the_United_Nations_Charter

Chesser, S. (2012, Sept. 06). *Afghanistan Casualties: Military Forces and Civilians*. Retrieved Sep. 08, 2012, from Federation of American Scientists: www.fas.org/sgp/crs/natsec/R41084.pdf

Chomsky, N. (2007, Jan. 05). *Audio Interview of Noam Chomsky on Gerald Ford and the Invasion of East Timor*. Retrieved Jul. 01, 2012, from http://www.chomsky.info/audionvideo.htm

Chomsky, N., & Shalom, S. (1999). *East Timor Questions and Answers*. Retrieved Jun. 30, 2012, from https://chomsky.info/199910__02/

Cohen, Roger. (1995, Apr. 12). *U.N. Dismisses Russian from Croatia Peacekeeping Post*. Retrieved Feb. 06, 2011, from The New York Times: http://www.nytimes.com/1995/04/12/world/un-dismisses-russian-from-croatia-peacekeeping-post.html

Colt Canada C7 Rifle. (2012). Retrieved Oct. 14, 2012, from Wikipedia: http://en.wikipedia.org/wiki/Colt_Canada_C7_rifle

Dabangasudan.org. (2016, 07 12). *ICC reports Uganda, Djibouti for not Arresting Al Bashir*. Retrieved 03 18, 2017, from Dabanga.org: https://www.dabangasudan.org/en/all-news/article/icc-reports-uganda-djibouti-for-not-arresting-al-bashir

Dallaire, R. (2003). *Shake Hands with the Devil: The failure of Humanity in Rwanda*. Toronto, Ontario, Canada: Random House.

David Livingstone. (n.d.). Retrieved Jun. 07, 2016, from Wikipedia: https://en.wikipedia.org/wiki/David_Livingstone

Defense Manpower Data Center. (2014, July 31). *U.S. Military Casualties - Operation Enduring Freedom (OEF)*. Retrieved Aug. 02, 2014, from https://www.dmdc.osd.mil/dcas/pages/casualties_oef.xhtml

Democracy Now. (2011, Nov. 14). *East Timor Massacre Remembered: U.S.-Armed Indonesian Troops Kill 270 Timorese 20 Years Ago*. Retrieved Jun. 30, 2012, from http://www.democracynow.org/2011/11/14/santa_cruz_massacre_270_east_timorese

Dengue Fever. (2012B). Retrieved Aug. 25, 2012, from The Free Dictionary: http://medical-dictionary.thefreedictionary.com/dengue+fever

Deutsche Welle. (2010, Nov. 04). *Serbian President Tadic Apologizes for Vukovar Massacre*. Retrieved Jan. 29, 2011, from http://www.dw-world.de/dw/article/0,,6188935,00.html

East Timor. (2009). Retrieved Jun. 17, 2012, from History.com: http://www.history.com/topics/east-timor

East Timor. (2012). Retrieved Jun. 17, 2012, from Encyclopaedia Britannica Online: http://www.britannica.com/EBchecked/topic/596313/East-Timor

East Timor Government. (2012). *History of East Timor*. Retrieved Jun. 24, 2012, from http://www.easttimorgovernment.com/history.htm

Edwards, G. (1997). *Canada and the Bomb: Past and Future*. Retrieved May 18, 2014, from The Canadian Coalition for Nuclear Responibility: http://www.ccnr.org/opinion_ge.html

EU Police Coordinating Office for Palestinian Police Support. (2010, Sep. 10). Retrieved Dec. 27, 2011, from Wikipedia: http://en.wikipedia.org/wiki/European_Union_Police_Mission_for_the_Palestinian_Territories

EUPOL COPPS. (2011, Dec. 27). *EU Police Mission for the Palestinian Territories*. Retrieved Dec. 27, 2011, from http://eupolcopps.eu/en/node/5022

European Union Institute for Security Studies. (2009). *European Security and Defense Policy: The First 10 Years (1999-2009)*. Retrieved Jan. 15, 2012, from www.iss.europa.eu/uploads/media/ESDP_10-web.pdf - France

Foreign Affairs and International Trade Canada. (2011, Mar. 04). *Canada-United States Free Trade Agreement (FTA)*. Retrieved Apr. 25, 2011, from http://www.international.gc.ca/trade-agreements-accords-commerciaux/agr-acc/nafta-alena/index.aspx?lang=eng

François Duvalier. (2012). Retrieved Mar. 10, 2012, from Encyclopaedia Britannica Online: http://www.britannica.com/EBchecked/topic/174718/Francois-Duvalier

French Campaign of Egypt and Syria. (2014). Retrieved Mar. 19, 2014, from Wikipedia: http://en.wikipedia.org/wiki/French_campaign_in_Egypt_and_Syria

Friendship Quotes & Quotations. (2000). Retrieved Jun. 26, 2011, from http://www.indianchild.com/friendship_quotations.htm

Futamura, M., Newman, E., & Tadjbakhsh, S. (2010, Mar. 27). *Towards a Human Security Approach to Peacebuilding.* Retrieved May 19, 2014, from United Nations University: http://unu.edu/publications/policy-briefs/towards-a-human-security-approach-to-peacebuilding.html

Gascoigne, B. (2001-). *History of Afghanistan.* Retrieved Sep. 11, 2012, from History World: http://www.historyworld.net/wrldhis/plaintexthistories.asp?historyid=ad09

Gascoigne, B. (2001-). *History of Assyria.* Retrieved Feb. 18, 2012, from History World: http://www.historyworld.net/wrldhis/PlainTextHistories.asp?historyid=ac26

Gascoigne, B. (2001-). *History of Guatemala.* Retrieved Mar. 20, 2011, from History World: http://www.historyworld.net/wrldhis/PlainTextHistories.asp?historyid=ac12#2353

Gascoigne, B. (2001-). *History of Haiti.* Retrieved Feb. 26, 2012, from History World: http://www.historyworld.net/about/sources.asp?gtrack=pthc

Gascoigne, B. (2001-). *History of Namibia.* Retrieved Sep. 11, 2011, from History World: http://www.historyworld.net/wrldhis/PlainTextHistories.asp?historyid=ad32

Gascoigne, B. (2001-). *History of Sudan.* Retrieved Mar. 18, 2014, from History World: http://www.historyworld.net/wrldhis/plaintexthistories.asp?historyid=aa86

German-Herero Conflict of 1904-07. (2011). Retrieved Sep. 11, 2011, from Encyclopaedia Britannica Online: http://www.britannica.com/EBchecked/topic/1407262/German-Herero-conflict-of-1904-07?anchor=ref1102508

Ginsberg, R. H. (2001). Political Impact of the European Union on Israel, the Palestinians, and the Middle East Peace Process. In *The European Union in international politics: baptism by fire* (pp. 105-180). Lanham, Maryland, USA: Rowman and Littlefield Publishers, Inc.

Globe and Mail. (1994, Dec. 06). Serbs Renege on Pledge Peacekeepers Not Released. p. A.16.

Government Accountability Project. (2012). *Tipping the Scale: Is the United Nations Justice System Promoting Accountability in the Peacekeeping Missions or Undermining it?* Retrieved Sep. 30, 2012, from https://www.whistleblower.org/sites/default/files/FinalTippingTheScales.pdf

Green Line-Israel. (2012). Retrieved Jan. 29, 2012, from Wikipedia: http://en.wikipedia.org/wiki/Green_Line_(Israel)

Guatemala. (2011). Retrieved Mar. 20, 2011, from Encyclopaedia Britannica Online: http://www.britannica.com/EBchecked/topic/701217/Guatemala

Hagan, J., & Rymond-Richmond, W. (2009). *Darfur and the Crime of Genocide.* Cambridge, NY: Cambridge University Press.

Haines, G. (1995). *CIA Historical Review Program.* Retrieved Apr. 02, 2011, from Declassified Document: The CIA and Guatemala Assassination Proposals 1952-1954: https://www.cia.gov/library/readingroom/docs/DOC_0006142929.pdf

Haiti. (2012, Feb. 26). Retrieved Feb. 26, 2012, from Encyclopaedia Britannica Online: http://www.britannica.com/EBchecked/topic/251961/Haiti

Haiti Earthquake of 2010. (2012, Apr. 19). Retrieved Apr. 19, 2012, from Encyclopaedia Britannica Online: http://www.britannica.com/EBchecked/topic/1659695/Haiti-earthquake-of-2010

Haiti Quake Camps Still Home to 500,000. (2012, 01 12). Retrieved May 12, 2012, from CBC News: http://www.cbc.ca/news/haiti-legacy/story/2012/01/08/haiti-quake-camps-reconstruction.html

Haiti: Bodies Outside the Hospital General. (2010, Jan. 16). Retrieved Apr. 18, 2012, from YouTube: http://www.youtube.com/watch?v=DdKvpxcVfHY

Harmon, K. (2010, Jan. 13). *Haiti Earthquake Disaster Little Surprise to Some Seismologists.* Retrieved Feb. 16, 2017, from Scientific American: https://www.scientificamerican.com/article/haiti-earthquake-prediction/

Harvard University Institute of Politics. (1992, Apr. 21). *Massacre in East Timor: A Case Study in U.S. Foreign Policy.* Retrieved Jul. 01, 2012, from http://iop.harvard.edu/forum/massacre-east-timor-case-study-us-foreign-policy

Hezbollah. (2012A, Feb. 11). Retrieved Feb. 11, 2012, from Encyclopaedia Britannica Online: http://www.britannica.com/EBchecked/topic/264741/Hezbollah

Hezbollah. (2012B, Feb. 08). Retrieved Feb. 11, 2012, from Wikipedia: http://en.wikipedia.org/wiki/Hezbollah

History of East Timor. (2012). Retrieved Jun. 24, 2012, from Wikipedia: http://en.wikipedia.org/wiki/History_of_East_Timor

History of Guatemala. (2011). Retrieved Mar. 20, 2011, from Wikipedia: http://en.wikipedia.org/wiki/History_of_Guatemala

History of Haiti. (2012). Retrieved Feb. 26, 2012, from Wikipedia: http://en.wikipedia.org/wiki/History_of_Haiti

History of Sierra Leone. (2010). Retrieved Dec. 19, 2010, from History World: http://www.historyworld.net/wrldhis/PlainTextHistories.asp?historyid=ad45

Ignatieff, M. (2000). *Virtual War: Kosovo and Beyond.* New York, NY: Metropolitan Books.

Indian Ocean Tsunami of 2004. (2012, Apr. 19). Retrieved Apr. 19, 2012, from Encyclopaedia Britannica Online: http://www.britannica.com/EBchecked/topic/1027119/Indian-Ocean-tsunami-of-2004

Individual Meal Pack. (2011, Dec. 05). Retrieved Dec. 10, 2011, from Wikipedia: http://en.wikipedia.org/wiki/Individual_Meal_Pack

International Committee of the Red Cross. (2001). *Cluster Bombs and Landmines in Kosovo: Explosive Remnants of War.* Retrieved Jan. 08, 2013, from https://www.icrc.org/eng/assets/files/other/icrc_002_0780.pdf

International Crisis Group. (1999). *Kosovo Briefing - The Albanian Refugee Crisis.* Retrieved Jan. 06, 2013, from http://reliefweb.int/report/albania/kosovo-briefing-albanian-refugee-crisis

International Force for East Timor. (2012). Retrieved Aug. 05, 2012, from Wikipedia: http://en.wikipedia.org/wiki/International_Force_for_East_Timor

Jacobson, S., & Colon, E. (2006). *The 911 Report: A Graphic Adaptation.* New York: Hill and Wang.

Jerusalem. (2012). Retrieved Jan. 29, 2012, from Encyclopaedia Britannica Online: http://www.britannica.com/EBchecked/topic/302812/Jerusalem

Johnson, H. (2012, Sep. 28). *GAP Releases Report on UN Justice System in Peacekeeping Missions: Daily Whistleblower News.* Retrieved Sep. 28, 2012, from https://www.whistleblower.org/blog/094322-gap-releases-report-un-whistleblower-cases

Judah, T. (2000). *Kosovo War and Revenge.* New Haven, USA: Yale University Press.

Kanwal, G., Wapenyi, F., Becchi, F., & Rubino, A. (1990, Mar.). UNTAG Journal. Windhoek, Namibia.

Karsner, L. (2001). *The Long Distance Romance Guide: Stay close whenever apart.* Lincoln, NE: IUniverse.

Kenny, S. (2006, Mar. 11). *The Charges Against Milosevic.* Retrieved Jan. 12, 2013, from http://www.guardian.co.uk/world/2006/mar/11/warcrimes.milosevictrial

Khapalwak, R. (2006, Mar. 06). *Canadian Soldier Injured by Ax-Wielding Afghan Youth.* Retrieved Oct. 13, 2012, from The New York Times: http://www.nytimes.com/2006/03/05/international/asia/05cnd-afghan.html?_r=0

Khedivate of Egypt. (2014). Retrieved Mar. 19, 2014, from Wikipedia: http://en.wikipedia.org/wiki/French_campaign_in_Egypt_and_Syria

Koerner, B. (2005). *Who Are the Janjaweed?* Retrieved Mar. 21, 2014, from Slate.com: http://www.slate.com/articles/news_and_politics/explainer/2004/07/who_are_the_janjaweed.html

Kosovo. (2012, Dec. 21). Retrieved Jan. 03, 2013, from Wikipedia: http://en.wikipedia.org/wiki/Kosovo#Disintegration_of_Yugoslavia

Landmines and Cluster Munition Monitor. (2009). *Namibia: Mine Ban Policy.* Retrieved Oct. 03, 2011, from http://www.the-monitor.org/index.php/publications/display?url=lm/1999/namibia.html

Laurie, D. (2008, Apr. 15). *Kosovo to Scrap its Main Exports.* Retrieved Feb. 11, 2013, from BBCNews: http://news.bbc.co.uk/2/hi/business/7346055.stm

League of Nations. (2011). Retrieved Sep. 11, 2011, from Encyclopaedia Britannica Online: http://www.britannica.com/EBchecked/topic/405820/League-of-Nations

Legge, P. (2012). *365 Days of Insights.* Burnaby, British Columbia: Eaglet Publishing.

Legge, P. (2013). *If Only I'd Said That, Volume VI.* Burnaby, British Columbia: Eaglet Publishing.

Legge, P. (2005). *The Runway of Life.* Burnaby, British Columbia: Eaglet Publishing, Peter Legge Management Co., Ltd.

Legge, P., & Ziara, T. (2009). *The Power to Soar Higher.* Burnaby, British Columbia: Eaglet Publishing.

Lonely Planet. (2009). *Western Balkans.* Oakland, USA: Lonely Planet.

Luzincourt, K., & Gulbrandson, J. (2010). *Education and Conflict in Haiti: Rebuilding the Education Sector after the 2010 Earthquake.* Retrieved May 28, 2012, from United States Institute of Peace: www.usip.org/files/resources/sr245.pdf

MacQueen, K. (2013, Jan 07). *Rewiring Trevor Greene's Brain.* Retrieved Jun. 02, 2013, from Maclean's: http://www2.macleans.ca/2013/01/07/rewiring-trevor-greenes-brain/

Madonik, R. (2011, Jul. 16). *Trevor Greene: My Thoughts.* Retrieved Oct. 13, 2012, from The Toronto Star: http://thestar.blogs.com/photoblog/2011/07/trevor-greene-and-me.html

Malaria:. (2011). Retrieved Dec. 04, 2011, from Encyclopaedia Britannica Online: <http://www.britannica.com/EBchecked/topic/359534/malaria>.

Malone, D. (2004). *The UN Security Council: from the Cold War to the 21st Century.* Boulder, CO: Lynne Rienner Publishers.

Martinez Almanzar, J. (1996). *Manual de Historia Critica Dominicana.* Santo Domingo, Republica Dominicana: 9 de Octubre.

Miller, J. (1999, Sep. 06). Radio Broadcast on Pacifica Radio: Situation in East Timor September 6, 1999. (Amy Goodman for Democracy Now, Interviewer)

Mills, E. (1932). *Census of Palestine 1931, Population of Villages, Towns and Administrative Areas.* Retrieved Dec. 02, 2012, from http://www.archive.org/details/CensusOfPalestine1931.PopulationOfVillagesTownsAndAdministrativeAreas

Mine Action. (2014). Retrieved Mar. 22, 2014, from Wikipedia: http://en.wikipedia.org/wiki/Mine_action

MINUGUA-Final Report. (2011). Retrieved Mar. 20, 2011, from Wikisource: http://en.wikisource.org/wiki/MINUGUA_-_Final_report

MINUSTAH. (2012). *United Nations Stabilization Mission in Haiti*. Retrieved Mar. 17, 2012, from http://www.un.org/en/peacekeeping/missions/minustah/background.shtml

MINUSTAH. (2012, Feb. 08). *United Nations Stabilization Mission in Haiti*. Retrieved Feb. 25, 2012, from http://www.un.org/en/peacekeeping/missions/minustah/

Mitchell, G. (2008, Oct. 22). *US Role in Israeli-Palestinian Conflict. [video]*. Retrieved Dec. 29, 2011, from Encyclopeadia Britannica Online: http://www.britannica.com/EBchecked/topic/439645/Palestine/45071/The-early-postwar-period

Mojsilovic, J. (1995, Jun. 01). Hostages not mistreated, Serbs assure the West: [FINAL Edition]. *The Gazette* , p. A.15.

Montgomery, S. (2010, Feb. 26). No word for search on two Quebec men; Ottawa mom: Buried in rubble of Montana Hotel. *The Gazette* , p. A.4.

Mount Holyoke College. (2004). *History and Conflicts in East Timor*. Retrieved Jun. 24, 2012, from http://www.mtholyoke.edu/~rgwhitma/classweb2/history%20and%20conflict.htm

Moya Pons, F. (2008). *Manual de Historia Dominicana*. Santo Domingo, Republica Dominicana: Caribbean Publishers.

Mulatto. (n.d.). Retrieved Mar. 10, 2012, from Dictionary.Com: http://dictionary.reference.com/cite.html?qh=mulatto&ia=luna

Namibia. (2011 A). Retrieved Sep. 10, 2011, from Wikipedia: http://en.wikipedia.org/wiki/Namibia

Namibia. (2011 B). Retrieved Sep. 10, 2010, from Encyclopaedia Britannica Online: http://www.britannica.com/EBchecked/topic/402283/Namibia

Nartens, J. (2009). Dilemmas of promoting "local Ownership": The case of postwar Kosovo. In R. Paris, & T. Sisk, *The Dilemmas of Statebuilding: Confronting the Contradictions of Postwar Peace Operations*. New York: Routledge.

National Defence and the Canadian Forces. (2012, Oct. 02). *Fallen Canadians*. Retrieved Nov. 05, 2012, from http://www.forces.gc.ca/en/honours-history-fallen-canadians/index.page

National Defence and the Canadian Forces. (2008, Nov. 28). *Operation Quartz*. Retrieved Apr. 03, 2011, from http://www.cmp-cpm.forces.gc.ca/dhh-dhp/od-bdo/di-ri-eng.asp?IntlOpId=116&CdnOpId=136

Nationsonline.Org. (2012). *History of Afghanistan*. Retrieved Sep. 22, 2012, from http://www.nationsonline.org/oneworld/History/Afghanistan-history.htm

NATO. (2012). *Afghanistan International Security Assistance Force (ISAF)*. Retrieved Oct. 06, 2012, from http://www.isaf.nato.int/history.html

NATO. (2001, Sep. 24). *Results of Recent Examinations of German Foreign Office Staff for Contamination with Depleted Uranium in Kosovo*. Retrieved Feb. 03, 2013, from http://www.nato.int/du/docu/d010917a.htm

NATO. (n.d.). *UN Security Council Resolutions (NATO's Role in Bringing Peace to Fomer Yugoslavia)*. Retrieved Jan. 22, 2011, from http://www.nato.int/ifor/un/un-resol.htm

Nelson, S. S. (2008). *National Public Radio: Afghans Frustrated by Slow Pace of Development*. Retrieved Oct. 06, 2012, from http://www.npr.org/templates/story/story.php?storyId=90536577

Operation Enduring Freedom. (2014, July 31). Retrieved Aug. 02, 2014, from iCasualty.org: http://icasualties.org/OEF/Fatalities.aspx

Our Africa. (2014, Mar. 10). *Sudan, Geography and Wildlife*. Retrieved Mar. 10, 2014, from http://www.our-africa.org/sudan/geography-wildlife

Pacheco, D., & Kumar, R. (2007). *The Balkan Peace Process*. Retrieved Feb. 05, 2011, from Partition Conflicts and Peace Process: http://www.partitionconflicts.com/partitions/regions/balkans/peace_process/05_05_01/

Paiva Cietto, R. (2012). *Combating the Good Combat-How to Fight Terrorism with a Peacekeeping Mission*. Retrieved Mar. 19, 2017, from http://cdn.peaceopstraining.org/theses/cietto.pdf

Pakistani Defence. (2012). *Pakistani Police Serving with the UN Found Guilty of Sexual Abuse*. Retrieved Sep. 29, 2012, from http://www.defence.pk/forums/pakistan-army/165317-pakistani-police-serving-un-found-guilty-sexual-abuse.html

Palestine. (2011). Retrieved Dec. 30, 2011, from Encyclopaedia Britannica Online: http://www.britannica.com/EBchecked/topic/439645/Palestine

Palestinian Territories. (2011, Dec. 23). Retrieved Dec. 30, 2011, from Wikipedia: http://en.wikipedia.org/wiki/Palestinian_territories

Paris, R. (2004). *At War's End: Building Peace After Civil Conflict.* Cambridge, United Kingdom: Cambridge University Press.

Permanent Court of Arbitration. (2012). *Boundaries in the Island of Timor, Netherlands vs. Portugal 1914.* Retrieved Jun. 24, 2012, from http://www.worldcourts.com/pca/eng/decisions/1914.06.25_Netherlands_v_Portugal.pdf

Petra. (2012, Jan. 26). Retrieved Feb. 11, 2012, from Wikipedia: http://en.wikipedia.org/wiki/Petra

ProCons.Org. (2011). *Palestine: Arab and Jewish Population Chart (1914-1946).* Retrieved Jan. 02, 2012, from http://israelipalestinian.procon.org/view.resource.php?resourceID=000636#graph3

Public Safety Canada. (2016, 11 20). *Currently Listed Entities.* Retrieved Mar. 18, 2017, from https://www.publicsafety.gc.ca/cnt/ntnl-scrt/cntr-trrrsm/lstd-ntts/crrnt-lstd-ntts-en.aspx

RAID. (2011, Mar. 07). Retrieved Jul. 20, 2011, from Wikipedia: http://en.wikipedia.org/wiki/Raid_(insecticide)

RCMP Officers Quit Haiti UN Reimposes Sanctions: [Final Edition]. (1993, Oct. 14). *Waterloo Region Record* , p. A1.

Rezak, D. (2003). *The Frog and the Prince--Secrets of Positive Networking to change your life.* Vancouver, Canada: Friesens.

Rice, C. (2006). *Oprah Winfrey on TIME.COM.* Retrieved Jun. 19, 2011, from http://content.time.com/time/specials/packages/article/0,28804,1975813_1975846_1976560,00.html

Richler, N. (2012). *What We Talk About When We Talk About War.* Fredericton, NB: Goose Lane Editions.

Rickard, J. (2012). *Military History Encyclopedia on the Web: Third Afghan War, 1919.* Retrieved Sep. 15, 2012, from http://www.historyofwar.org/articles/wars_afghan3.html

Robert Pickton. (2013). Retrieved Feb. 23, 2013, from Wikipedia: http://en.wikipedia.org/wiki/Robert_Pickton#Trial

Robinson, G. (2010). *"If you Leave Us Here We Will Die" How Genocide was stopped in East Timor.* Princeton, New Jersey: Princeton University Press.

Roehner, N. (2011). *UN Peacebuilding : Light Footprint or Friendly Takeover?* Boca Raton, Florida: Universal Publishers.

Royal Canadian Mounted Police. (2006). *Core Values of the RCMP*. Retrieved Sep. 15, 2012, from http://www.rcmp-grc.gc.ca/about-ausujet/mission-eng.htm

Royal Canadian Mounted Police. (2011). *International Peace Operations: West Bank UNPOL COPPS*. Retrieved Jan. 15, 2012, from http://www.rcmp-grc.gc.ca/po-mp/missions-curr-cour-eng.htm#israel

Royal Canadian Mounted Police. (2011, Feb. 09). *PARE - Physical Abilities Requirement Evaluation*. Retrieved Apr. 23, 2011, from http://www.rcmp-grc.gc.ca/en/prepare-for-pare

Rutledge, L. (1994, Aug. 10). Letter from Krajina. *The Peace Arch News* , p. A.3.

Schulz, M. (2009). The EU's Intervention in the Israeli-Palestinian Conflict. In K. Aggestam, & A. Bjorkdahl, *War and Peace in Transition: Changing Roles of External Actors* (pp. 72-89). Lund, Sweden: Nordic Academic Press.

September 11 Attacks. (2012). Retrieved Sep. 23, 2012, from Encyclopaedia Britannica Online: http://www.britannica.com/EBchecked/topic/762320/September-11-attacks

Severo, R. (1972, Jan. 28). Impoverished Haitians Sell Plasma for Use in the U.S. *New York Times* , p. 2.

Sharia. (2014). Retrieved Mar. 22, 2014, from Encyclopaedia Britannica Online: http://www.britannica.com/EBchecked/topic/538793/Shariah/68927/Development-of-different-schools-of-law

Shephard, M. (2014, Oct. 31). How Canada Has Abandoned Its Role As Peacekeeper. Toronto, Ont: The Toronto Star.

Slobodan Milošević. (2013A). Retrieved Jan. 05, 2013, from Encyclopaedia Britannica Online: http://www.britannica.com/EBchecked/topic/383076/Slobodan-Milosevic

Slobodan Milošević. (2013B). Retrieved Jan. 12, 2013, from Wikipedia: http://en.wikipedia.org/wiki/Slobodan_Milo%C5%A1evi%C4%87#The_Hague_trial

Sotiropoulou, A. (2002). *The Role of Ethnicity in Ethnic Conflicts: The Case of Yugoslavia*. Retrieved Jan. 10, 2011, from https://www.files.ethz.ch/isn/26506/PN04.02.pdf

South African Court Rules Failure to Detain Omar al-Bashir was Disgraceful. (2016, 03 16). Retrieved Mar. 18, 2017, from The Guardian: https://www.theguardian.com/world/2016/mar/16/south-african-court-rules-failure-to-detain-omar-al-bashir-was-disgraceful

South Sudan. (2014). Retrieved Mar. 10, 2014, from Encyclopaedia Britannica Online: http://www.britannica.com/EBchecked/topic/1779607/South-Sudan/300724/Resumption-of-civil-war

Soviet War in Afghanistan. (2012). Retrieved Sep. 22, 2012, from Wikipedia: http://en.wikipedia.org/wiki/Soviet_war_in_Afghanistan#1980s:_Insurrection

Srivastava, G. (1990, March). An Indian's Namibian Odyssey. *UNTAG Journal , 3* . (M. G. Kanwal, Ed.) Windhoek, Namibia.

Stern, L. (1994, Dec. 09). Canadian Peacekeepers: All's Well at Home as 55 Are Freed; Phone Lines Hum as Families Rejoice in Men's Release:. *The Ottawa Citizen* , p. A.1.

Stone & Stone Second World War Books. (1999). *Afghanistan During World War II.* Retrieved Sep. 22, 2012, from http://stonebooks.com/history/afghanistan.shtml

Suez Canal Authority. (2008). *Canal History.* Retrieved Mar. 19, 2014, from http://www.suezcanal.gov.eg/sc.aspx?show=8

Tel Aviv. (2012). Retrieved Jan. 22, 2012, from Wikipedia: http://en.wikipedia.org/wiki/Tel_Aviv

The Anglo-Egyptian Condominium. (2014). Retrieved Mar. 19, 2014, from Wikipedia: http://en.wikipedia.org/wiki/Anglo-Egyptian_Sudan#Union_with_Egypt

The Battle of Vukovar. (2011). Retrieved Jan. 29, 2011, from Wikipedia: http://en.wikipedia.org/wiki/Battle_of_Vukovar

The Christian Science Monitor. (1999, Jul. 02). *Grand Hotel Pristina: Where Guests Tote Guns, Cameras.* Retrieved Jan. 13, 2013, from http://www.luciankim.com/archives/balkans/grand-hotel-pristina-where-guests-tote-guns-cameras/

The Churchill Centre. (2014). Retrieved Mar. 01, 2014, from http://www.winstonchurchill.org/learn/speeches/quotations/quotes-faq

The Conceptual Origins of Peacebuilding. (2008). Retrieved Sep. 05, 2016, from Peacebuildinginitiative.org: http://www.peacebuildinginitiative.org/index34ac.html?pageId=1764

The Crusades. (2011, Dec. 29). Retrieved Dec. 31, 2011, from Wikipedia: http://en.wikipedia.org/wiki/Crusades

The History of Israel: A Chronological Presentation. (2009). Retrieved Jan. 14, 2012, from History-of-Israel.org: http://history-of-israel.org/history/chronological_presentation21.php

The International Criminal Court. (2013). *President of the Assembly Regrets Visit of Sudanese President to Chad.* Retrieved Mar. 21, 2014, from http://www.icc-cpi.int/en_menus/icc/press%20and%20media/press%20releases/Pages/pr874.aspx

The International Criminal Court. (2014). *The Prosecutor v. Omar Hassan Ahmad Al Bashir.* Retrieved Mar. 21, 2014, from http://www.icc-cpi.int/EN_Menus/ICC/Situations%20and%20Cases/Situations/Situation%20ICC%200205/Pages/situation%20icc-0205.aspx

The Louverture Project. (2010). *Slavery in Saint-Domingue.* Retrieved Feb. 27, 2012, from http://thelouvertureproject.org/index.php?title=Slavery_in_Saint-Domingue#Treatment_of_slaves

The Louverture Project. (2009, Feb. 27). *Treaty of Ryswick.* Retrieved Feb. 27, 2012, from http://thelouvertureproject.org/index.php?title=Treaty_of_Ryswick

The Sierra Leone Web. (2010). *Peace Agreement Between the Government of Sierra Leone and the United Revolutionary Front.* Retrieved Dec. 25, 2010, from http://www.sierra-leone.org/lomeaccord.html

The Special Court For Sierra Leone. (2016). Retrieved Dec. 26, 2016, from https://www.files.ethz.ch/isn/26506/PN04.02.pdf

The Sunday Times. (2010, Jun. 13). *Is this the world's worst hotel?* Retrieved Jan. 13, 2012, from http://www.thesundaytimes.co.uk/sto/travel/weekends/Places_to_stay/article295269.ece

The Taliban. (2012). Retrieved Sep. 23, 2012, from Encyclopaedia Britannica Online: http://www.britannica.com/EBchecked/topic/734615/Taliban

The Tarnak Farm Incident. (2012). Retrieved Nov. 11, 2012, from Wikipedia: http://en.wikipedia.org/wiki/Tarnak_Farm_incident

The Trial of Charles Taylor. (2008). *Former Child Soldier Describes the Atrocities Committed by the RUF and the AFRC.* Retrieved 12 19, 2010, from http://www.charlestaylortrial.org/2008/05/05/former-child-soldier-describes-the-atrocities-committed-by-the-ruf-and-the-afrc/

The Vancouver Sun. (2012, Sep. 27). *UN Peacekeeping Misconduct Goes Mostly Unpunished "bad apples" Remain: Study*. Retrieved Sep. 28, 2012, from Retrieved from Canadian Newsstream Ebrary: http://www.vancouversun.com/news/peacekeeping+misconduct+goes+mostly+unpunished+apples+remain/7311365/story.html

Tonton Macoutes. (2012). Retrieved Mar. 10, 2012, from Wikipedia: https://en.wikipedia.org/wiki/Tonton_Macoute

Tracy, B. (2011). Time Management Made Simple 12-CD Program. Gildan Media Corp.

Tremblay, S. (1998). *Crime Statistics in Canada*. Retrieved May 23, 2011, from Statistics Canada: www.statcan.gc.ca/pub/85-002-x/85-002-x1999009-eng.pdf

Tristam, P. (2012). *History of the Taliban: Who They Are, What They Want*. Retrieved Sep. 23, 2012, from http://middleeast.about.com/od/afghanistan/ss/me080914a.htm

Turkish Toleration. (2011). In The American Forum.

UN Works. (2008). *What's Going On? Child Soldier in Sierra Leone*. Retrieved 12 19, 2010, from https://archive.org/details/UnworksVideo: https://archive.org/details/UnworksVideo

UNAMSIL. (2005). *United Nations Mission in Sierra Leone*. Retrieved December 26, 2010, from http://www.un.org/en/peacekeeping/missions/past/unamsil/background.html

United Nations. (2012). *Afghanistan & the United Nations*. Retrieved Sep. 23, 2012, from http://www.un.org/News/dh/latest/afghan/un-afghan-history.shtml

United Nations. (2003A). *Completed Peacekeeping Operations: MINUGUA (Jan.-May 1997)*. Retrieved Apr. 03, 2011, from http://www.un.org/en/peacekeeping/missions/past/minugua.htm

United Nations Department of Peacekeeping Operations. (2003). *United Nations Mission in Haiti-UNMIH*. Retrieved Mar. 17, 2012, from http://www.un.org/en/peacekeeping/missions/past/unmih.htm

United Nations Development Program. (2007). *Human Development Report*. Retrieved January 01, 2011, from http://hdr.undp.org/en/media/HDR_20072008_EN_Complete.pdf

United Nations Development Programme. (2007). *Informe Estadistico de la Violencia en Guatemala.* Retrieved May 22, 2011, from http://centralamericasecurity.thedialogue.org/articles/informe-estadistico-de-la-violencia-en-guatemala

United Nations. (2002, May.). *East Timor UNTAET Background.* Retrieved Jul. 01, 2012, from http://www.un.org/en/peacekeeping/missions/past/etimor/UntaetB.htm

United Nations. (1996, Aug. 31). *Former Yugoslavia-UNPROFOR.* Retrieved Jan. 15, 2011, from http://www.un.org/Depts/DPKO/Missions/unprof_p.htm

United Nations. (1994, Dec. 09). *General Assembly 83RD Planetary Meeting.* Retrieved Jan. 24, 2011, from http://www.un.org/documents/ga/res/49/a49r043.htm

United Nations. (2003B). *Guatemala-MINUGUA Background.* Retrieved Mar. 18, 2011, from http://www.un.org/en/peacekeeping/missions/past/minuguabackgr.html

United Nations. (2005). *Guidelines for Civilian Police Officers on Assignment with the United Nations Assistance Mission in Afghanistan (UNAMA).* Retrieved Apr. 23, 2011, from www.inprol.org/files/unamaguidelinescivpolonassignment.pdf

United Nations. (2012). *Haiti: Three UN peacekeepers repatriated for sexual abuse.* Retrieved Sep. 29, 2012, from http://www.un.org/apps/news/story.asp?NewsID=41538&Cr=Haiti&Cr1

United Nations Interim Administration Mission in Kosovo. (1999). *Resolution 1244 (1999).* Retrieved Jan. 06, 2012, from http://www.unmikonline.org/Pages/1244.aspx

United Nations. (2012). *MINUSTAH-United Nations Stabilization Mission in Haiti.* Retrieved FEB. 25, 2012, from http://www.un.org/en/peacekeeping/missions/minustah/

United Nations Peacebuilding Support Office. (2016). Retrieved Sep. 05, 2016, from http://www.un.org/en/peacebuilding/pbso/faq.shtml

United Nations Peacekeeping. (2011). *Namibia-UNTAG Background.* Retrieved Sep. 17, 2011, from http://www.un.org/en/peacekeeping/missions/past/untagFT.htm

United Nations Peacekeeping Operations. (1997). *United Nations Verification*

Mission in Guatemala. Retrieved Apr. 03, 2011, from http://www.un.org/Depts/DPKO/Missions/minugua.htm

United Nations. (1968). *Resolution Adopted Without a Reference to a Main Committee.* Retrieved August 15, 2016, from Official Documents System of the United Nations: https://documents-dds-ny.un.org/doc/RESOLUTION/GEN/NR0/240/62/IMG/NR024062.pdf?OpenElement

United Nations. (2005). *Security Council Resolution 1590.* Retrieved 03 30, 2014, from http://www.un.org/press/en/2005/sc8343.doc.htm

United Nations. (2012, Dec. 31). *United Nations Interim Administration Mission in Kosovo--UNMIK.* Retrieved Jan. 02, 2013, from http://www.un.org/en/peacekeeping/missions/unmik/mandate.shtml

United Nations. (2016). *United Nations Peacekeeping.* Retrieved August 13, 2016, from United Nations Mission in South Sudan: https://unmiss.unmissions.org/mandate

United Nations. (1997A). *United Nations Security Council Resolution (1094) 1997.* Retrieved Mar. 18, 2011, from http://www.un.org/Docs/scres/1997/scres97.htm

United Nations. (1997B). *United Nations Verification Mission in Guatemala.* Retrieved Mar. 18, 2011, from http://www.un.org/Depts/DPKO/Missions/minugua.htm

United Nations. (2014). *UNMIS United Nations Mission in the Sudan.* Retrieved Mar. 22, 2014, from http://www.un.org/en/peacekeeping/missions/past/unmis/background.shtml

United States Memorial Holocaust Museum. (2011). *Deadly Medecine: Creating the Master Race.* Retrieved Mar. 18, 2017, from https://www.ushmm.org/information/exhibitions/traveling-exhibitions/deadly-medicine

Vanden Brook, T. (2012, Jan. 26). *IED Attacks in Afghanistan Set Record.* Retrieved Nov. 05, 2013, from USA Today: http://usatoday30.usatoday.com/news/world/story/2012-01-25/IEDs-afghanistan/52795302/1

Wapenyi, F. (1990, March). Elections in Damaraland. *UNTAG Journal*, 3. (M. G. Kanwal, Ed.) Windhoek, Namibia.

War in Darfur. (2014). Retrieved Mar. 20, 2014, from Wikipedia: http://en.wikipedia.org/wiki/War_in_Darfur

War on Terror. (2012). Retrieved Sep. 29, 2013, from Wikipedia: http://en.wikipedia.org/wiki/War_on_Terror

Warfare and Conflict Between Kosovar Albanians and Serbs Since 1912. (2011, Oct. 29). Retrieved Jan. 04, 2013, from Historyguy.com: http://www.historyguy.com/kosovar_serb_warfare.html

Warnica, R. (2011). *Kosovo: Independent, but a Basket Case, the Economy is Dead, Corruption is Rampant, and Serbia Remains Hostile.* Retrieved Feb. 11, 2013, from Macleans.ca: http://www2.macleans.ca/2011/09/21/independent-but-a-basket-case/

Water for South Sudan. (2011). *A Brief History of Modern Sudan and South Sudan.* Retrieved Mar. 20, 2014, from http://www.waterforsouthsudan.org/

Yugoslavia. (2011). Retrieved Jan. 09, 2011, from Encyclopaedia Britannica Online: http://www.britannica.com/EBchecked/topic/654783/Yugoslavia

End Notes

1. (Namibia, 2011 B)
2. (Namibia, 2011 A) (Namibia, 2011 B)
3. (Namibia, 2011 B)
4. (Namibia, 2011 B)
5. (Namibia, 2011 B)
6. (German-Herero Conflict of 1904-07, 2011); (Gascoigne, History of Namibia, 2001-); (Namibia, 2011 A); (United States Memorial Holocaust Museum, 2011)
7. (Namibia, 2011 B)
8. The League of Nations was a result of the 1919 Paris Peace Conference. The term was coined to describe international cooperation between the victorious Allied powers, namely Britain and the United States, at the end of WWI. The League of Nations was replaced in 1946 by the United Nations, which inherited many of its purposes, methods, and structure. Ref: (League of Nations, 2011)
9. (Gascoigne, History of Namibia, 2001-)
10. (Gascoigne, History of Namibia, 2001-)
11. (Gascoigne, History of Namibia, 2001-)
12. (Gascoigne, History of Namibia, 2001-)
13. (Gascoigne, History of Namibia, 2001-)
14. (United Nations, 1968)
15. (United Nations Peacekeeping, 2011)
16. (United Nations Peacekeeping, 2011)
17. (Paris, 2004)
18. (United Nations Peacekeeping, 2011)
19. (Wapenyi, 1990)
20. (Srivastava, 1990)
21. An ATCO trailer is the name given to a type of portable mobile office, whether temporary or permanent.
22. Canadian Military rations, also known as Individual Meal Packs (IMPs) come in a variety of 5 breakfasts, 6 lunches, and 6 dinners (i.e. Macaroni, Shepherd's Pie, etc.). The main meals are pre-cooked and ready to eat. Reference: (Individual Meal Pack, 2011).
23. (Malaria:, 2011).
24. (Malaria:, 2011)
25. (Malaria:, 2011)
26. (United Nations Peacekeeping, 2011) (Kanwal, Wapenyi, Becchi, & Rubino, 1990)

27 (Landmines and Cluster Munition Monitor, 2009)

28 UNITA (National Union for the Total Independence of Angola—in Portuguese Uniao Nacional para a Independencia Total de Angola) was a movement for the liberation of Angola.

29 FaceTime is an audio-video communication application associated with Apple products. Skype is another type of voice-over-Internet instant messaging program that can be downloaded onto smartphones, computers, and other devices.

30 (United Nations, 1996)

31 (Yugoslavia, 2011)

32 (Yugoslavia, 2011)

33 (Yugoslavia, 2011)

34 (Sotiropoulou, 2002). Note that Serbs, Montenegrins, and Macedonians are of Eastern Orthodox religion. Croats and Slovenes are of the Roman Catholic faith, while a sizeable Muslim population lives in Bosnia-Herzegovina.

35 King Alexander I was a Serbian prince who distinguished himself as a Serbian Army commander in the Balkan wars and WWI. He proclaimed the creation of the new Kingdom of Serbs, Croats, and Slovenes in 1918. Ref. (Alexander I, 2011).

36 (Alexander I, 2011)

37 (Alexander I, 2011)

38 (Yugoslavia, 2011)

39 (Yugoslavia, 2011)

40 (Yugoslavia, 2011)

41 (Sotiropoulou, 2002)

42 Zvornik is a Bosnian town that lies on the border of Serbia. During the Bosnian War of Independence, it is estimated that 1,000 Zvornik citizens of Bosniak heritage were abused and killed by ethnic Serbians. As a note, 100,000 people are believed to have been killed in the conflict between Bosnia-Herzegovina and Serbia. Ref: (Yugoslavia, 2011).

43 (Yugoslavia, 2011)

44 (Yugoslavia, 2011)

45 (United Nations, 1996)

46 (NATO, n.d.)

47 (United Nations, 1996)

48 The UNPA's were divided into four sectors: Sector North, Sector South, Sector East (including the town of Ilok where John Buis was posted), and Sector West.

49 (United Nations, 1996)

50 (United Nations, 1996)

51 (United Nations, 1994)

52 The City of Vukovar is located in north-eastern Croatia. On or about November 18, 1991, Serb militia, assisted by the Yugoslavian Army, bombarded the city and

took control of it in a process that levelled the entire city. In addition to the Croat population being expelled from the area, an estimated 200 Croats fell victim to persecution, torture, and murder at the hands of the Serbian forces. These latter acts led to War Crimes charges being laid against Yugoslav President and Serb leader Slobodan Milosevic. Reference: (Deutsche Welle, 2010); (The Battle of Vukovar, 2011)

53 (Bethlehem & Weller, 1997)

54 (Bethlehem & Weller, 1997)

55 (Rutledge, 1994)

56 Quote from: http://www.un.org/News/Press/docs/2004/sgsm9579.doc.htm

57 The shooter in this incident was sentenced to life imprisonment in 1980. He was released on parole in 1992. Although John was able to return to work after three months' convalescence, he would have to endure a total of seven major reconstructive leg surgeries over a period of 10 years. In October 2017, John underwent another surgery to try to remove the last 18 shotgun pellets that were still in embedded in his leg.

58 (Cohen, Roger, 1995)

59 (Mojsilovic, 1995)

60 (Globe and Mail, 1994)

61 Portable radios were the only available mode of communication available to the peacekeepers. Although UN Headquarters was aware that John and his colleagues were safe at the UN Russian base, the information never made it to Canada.

62 (Stern, 1994)

63 (United Nations, 2003B) URNG is a Spanish acronym which stands for *Unidad Revolucionaria Nacional Guatemalteca*.

64 (Guatemala, 2011)

65 (Gascoigne, History of Guatemala, 2001-)

66 (Gascoigne, History of Guatemala, 2001-), (Guatemala, 2011)

67 (History of Guatemala, 2011)

68 (Gascoigne, History of Guatemala, 2001-)

69 (Guatemala, 2011)

70 (Gascoigne, History of Guatemala, 2001-)

71 (Gascoigne, History of Guatemala, 2001-), (Haines, 1995)

72 (Gascoigne, History of Guatemala, 2001-) (Haines, 1995)

73 (Gascoigne, History of Guatemala, 2001-)

74 (Gascoigne, History of Guatemala, 2001-), (History of Guatemala, 2011)

75 (United Nations, 2003A) (United Nations, 2003B; United Nations, 2005)

76 (United Nations, 2003B)

77 (National Defence and the Canadian Forces, 2008)

78 (National Defence and the Canadian Forces, 2008)

79 (National Defence and the Canadian Forces, 2008), (United Nations, 2003A)
80 (National Defence and the Canadian Forces, 2008)
81 (National Defence and the Canadian Forces, 2008), (MINUGUA-Final Report, 2011)
82 (Foreign Affairs and International Trade Canada, 2011)
83 (Legge, The Runway of Life, 2005)
84 (United Nations Development Programme, 2007)
85 (Tremblay, 1998)
86 For more details on the 12 Peace Accords and their contents, please visit the United States Institute of Peace at http://www.usip.org/publications/peace-agreements-guatemala
87 Note that when I first arrived in Quetzaltenango, the Italian police officer in town was Giuseppe Constantini. Officer Constantini's tour of duty ended soon after my arrival, and he was replaced by Carabinieri officer Paolo Belligi.
88 (Rice, 2006)
89 For those interested in the work of World Vision, I have reproduced a hyperlink to its website: http://www.worldvision.org
90 (United Nations, 2012)
91 (Kosovo, 2012)
92 (Warfare and Conflict Between Kosovar Albanians and Serbs Since 1912, 2011),
93 (Warfare and Conflict Between Kosovar Albanians and Serbs Since 1912, 2011)
94 (Slobodan Milošević, 2013A)
95 (Ignatieff, 2000). Note that the term "Kosovars" should encompass all ethnicities living in Kosovo. However, in much literature, the term has come to describe the ethnic Albanian majority (Judah, 2000).
96 (Ignatieff, 2000)
97 (Ignatieff, 2000), (Judah, 2000)
98 (Ignatieff, 2000),
99 (Ignatieff, 2000). Under Chapter VII of the UN Charter, the UN Security Council is granted with decision-making powers to determine the existence, if any, of threats to the peace or acts of aggression against or by a state, and to take appropriate actions (military and non-military) in order to restore international peace and security. Ref: (Chapter VII of the United Nations Charter, 2012).
100 (Judah, 2000) (Ignatieff, 2000)
101 (Judah, 2000) (Ignatieff, 2000)
102 (International Committee of the Red Cross, 2001)
103 (United Nations, 2012), (United Nations Interim Administration Mission in Kosovo, 1999)
104 (United Nations, 2012)
105 RCMP members are generally encouraged to seek transfers and/or perform

different duties throughout their police careers. Although there are no guarantees, a transfer or a change of duty may contribute to enhancing one's career by learning something new or providing a promotional opportunity.

106 In reference to Figure 23, The Grand Hotel Prishtina, the photo is used here under the terms of the GNU Free Documentation License, with no Invariant Sections, no Front-Cover Texts, and no Back-Cover Texts. https://en.wikipedia.org/wiki/GNU_Free_Documentation_License Accessed on June 5, 2016.

107 (Rezak, 2003) An excellent resource and reference on the powers of networking is found in Darcy Rezak's book *The Frog and the Prince: Secrets of Positive Networking*. This easy-to-read and humorous best-seller is recommended reading for anyone wishing to enhance both business and personal life skills.

108 (Rezak, 2003)

109 (Rezak, 2003)

110 Kosovo scrap metal exports were indeed a booming industry in the early 2000s. Crushed up vehicles were believed to account for up to half of Kosovo's export value, according to the UNDP. Rusting, dilapidated old cars and trucks lay at the roadside everywhere, waiting to be scrapped. Whether the scrap metal business boom had anything to do with the numerous accidents is unknown. What is known, however, is that many Kosovar were unable to afford new cars. Thus, for many years, they would import old ones (15-20 years) from Western Europe. Ref. (Laurie, 2008)

111 (NATO, 2001)

112 (NATO, 2001)

113 A mission lockdown is an emergency procedure intended to secure and protect occupants who are in the proximity of an immediate threat. A lockdown can be performed by controlling entry, exit, and movement of personnel within a facility. Lorin was affected by the procedure, which prevented his UN roommate from returning from his Boston holiday until the condition was lowered, several weeks later.

114 (Nartens, 2009)

115 (Nartens, 2009)

116 (Nartens, 2009)

117 (East Timor, 2012)

118 (East Timor, 2012), (East Timor Government, 2012)

119 With the Treaty of Lisbon in 1859, the eastern part of the island officially became a Portuguese colony, while the western half remained in Dutch possession. (East Timor, 2012)landed in the national uts.

120 (East Timor Government, 2012) (History of East Timor, 2012)

121 (East Timor Government, 2012)

122 (East Timor Government, 2012)

123 (East Timor Government, 2012)

124 (East Timor Government, 2012)
125 (Chomsky, Audio Interview of Noam Chomsky on Gerald Ford and the Invasion of East Timor, 2007)
126 (East Timor, 2012), (Harvard University Institute of Politics, 1992)
127 (East Timor Government, 2012) (East Timor, 2012)
128 (East Timor Government, 2012
129 (Harvard University Institute of Politics, 1992)
130 (Democracy Now, 2011), (Harvard University Institute of Politics, 1992; German-Herero Conflict of 1904-07, 2011; German-Herero Conflict of 1904-07, 2011)
131 (East Timor Government, 2012)
132 (East Timor, 2012)
133 (United Nations, 2002)
134 (United Nations, 2002)
135 (United Nations, 2002)
136 (United Nations, 2002)
137 (United Nations, 2002)
138 (East Timor Government, 2012)
139 (United Nations, 2002)
140 (United Nations, 2002)
141 (United Nations, 2002) (Chomsky, Audio Interview of Noam Chomsky on Gerald Ford and the Invasion of East Timor, 2007), (Chomsky & Shalom, East Timor Questions and Answers, 1999)
142 (East Timor, 2009), (United Nations, 2002)
143 (United Nations, 2002)
144 (United Nations, 2002)
145 (East Timor Government, 2012)
146 (United Nations, 2002),
147 (International Force for East Timor, 2012)
148 (International Force for East Timor, 2012)
149 To clarify a point, Rick's title in Dili was that of Canadian Contingent Commander. As such, he supervised 19 Canadian peacekeepers scattered throughout the country. The position of Contingent Commander is always decided by the country that sends its peacekeepers, and not by the UN.
150 UNTAET was established on October 25, 1999 to administer the Territory, exercise legislative and executive authority during the transition period. It also supported capacity-building for self-government. It was preceded by UNAMET which lasted from June 11, 1999 until the pogrom of September 1999.
151 Money and duty-free for East Timor. www.worldtravelguide.net

152 (United Nations, 2002)

153 (Dallaire, 2003)

154 In reference to Figure 32, I took photos of this modified trailer unit while on the compound of the Canadian Embassy in Port-au-Prince, Haiti, in 2012. It served as emergency and temporary housing to staff and guests.

155 Aviation Standards for Peacekeeping and Humanitarian Air Transport Operations. www.un.org

156 (Antimalarial Drugs, 2012A)

157 (Dengue Fever, 2012B)

158 East Timor became the first new sovereign state of the 21st century on May 20, 2002. Reference: (East Timor, 2012), (East Timor, 2009).

159 At the time of this writing, UN post allowance could reach amounts of up to $5,000.00 USD per month, depending on the location. This could be considered a fortune for peace officers coming from developing countries, some of whom could earn a meagre $300.00 USD a month or less.

160 (The Vancouver Sun, 2012; The Vancouver Sun, 2012) (Johnson, 2012) Note that the report referred to all peacekeepers, whether they were military, civilian staff, or civilian police.

161 (Johnson, 2012)

162 (Johnson, 2012)

163 (Pakistani Defence, 2012), MINUSTAH (United Mission Stabilization Mission in Haiti).

164 (Pakistani Defence, 2012) (United Nations, 2012)

165 (Karsner, 2001)

166 The RCMP Core Values can be summed up as a set of guiding principles for employees, which aim to create and foster an environment of individual safety, well-being and development. These principles include attributes such as integrity, honesty, professionalism, compassion, respect, and accountability. Reference (Royal Canadian Mounted Police, 2006).

167 (Encyclopaedia Britannica on-line, 2010)

168 (History World, 2010)

169 (History World, 2010)

170 (History World, 2010)

171 (History World, 2010)

172 (History World, 2010)

173 (BBC News, 2008)

174 (Encyclopaedia Britannica on-line, 2010)

175 (History World, 2010)

176 (History World, 2010)

177 (The trial of Charles Taylor, 2008)
178 (UN Works, 2010)
179 The peace accord was named Lome because the negotiations took place in Lome, the capital city of Togo.
180 (The Sierra Leone Web, 2010)
181 (The Sierra Leone Web, 2010, Article IX).
182 (Malone, 2004)
183 (Malone, 2004)
184 (BBC News, 2010)
185 (UNAMSIL, 2005)
186 (UNAMSIL, 2005)
187 (BBC News, 2010)
188 (The Special Court For Sierra Leone, 2010)
189 Note that this Proceeds of Crime expertise was initially sought since the state contemplated the seizure of the ill-gained assets of some of the worst violators.
190 (The Special Court For Sierra Leone, 2010)
191 I have known Chuck for nearly 27 years, and have had the pleasure of working with him when I was a patrol officer in Surrey, British Columbia. However, I will admit that he can be intimidating at times…so I understand why Little Franklin may have been scared!
192 (United Nations Development Program, 2007)
193 (South Sudan, 2014)
194 The Byzantine Empire is also referred to as the Eastern Roman Empire, which fell to the Ottoman Empire in 1453. Ref: (The Anglo-Egyptian Condominium, 2014)
195 (Khedivate of Egypt, 2014) A Khedivate is an autonomous tributary state under the Ottoman Empire. A Khedive is its ruler, and is the equivalent of a British viceroy running a colony.
196 (The Anglo-Egyptian Condominium, 2014)
197 (The Anglo-Egyptian Condominium, 2014)
198 (Gascoigne, History of Sudan, 2001-)
199 (Gascoigne, History of Sudan, 2001-)
200 (South Sudan, 2014)
201 The agreement that was abrogated was the 1972 Addis Ababa Agreement (Addis Ababa is the capital city of Ethiopia where the agreement was signed), which allowed more autonomy for South Sudan.
202 (Water for South Sudan, 2011) (Gascoigne, History of Sudan, 2001-)

203 The Sharia law is an Islamic legal code systematized during the 2nd and 3rd centuries of the Muslim era. Ref: (Sharia, 2014).

204 (Water for South Sudan, 2011)

205 (Gascoigne, History of Sudan, 2001-)

206 (Water for South Sudan, 2011)

207 (Koerner, 2005)

208 (Braun, 2007)

209 (United Nations, 2005)

210 Mine action refers to a domain within humanitarian aid that aims to reduce the social, economic, and environmental impact of landmines and explosive remnants of war. Ref: (Mine Action, 2014).

211 (United Nations, 2014)

212 The Richmond RCMP was a very progressive police detachment of approximately 200 officers, located in Richmond, British Columbia. It was led by now retired Superintendent Ward Clapham. I owe Superintendent Clapham much credit for providing myself and others with many developmental opportunities.

213 (The Churchill Centre, 2014)

214 Refer to Appendix B for an additional definition of the term "peacebuilder".

215 David Livingstone was a 19th Century British explorer of Scottish descent, who was one of the first Westerners to make a transcontinental journey across Africa in 1854-56. Ref: (David Livingstone in Wikipedia, the Free Encyclopedia)

216 Watch a one-minute YouTube video of a haboob in Khartoum in April 2007 at http://www.youtube.com/watch?v=hKsF1Vto5Pw

217 The waivers Galib signed were like ownership slips for the equipment. For instance, if Galib lost or damaged a radio that was given to him, he was to pay for it. A $500.00 USD damage deposit was deducted from his first paycheque and held for the duration of the mission. Not having lost or damaged any equipment, Galib was refunded at the end of his mission.

218 Note that Galib did not provide details as to the quality of the meat nor its hygiene—but given the general sanitation in the area, I suspect it was not very high…

219 In Sudan and many Asian and sub-Saharan countries, the squat toilet is preferred to the conventional western-style toilet.

220 Soccer fields were amongst the safest places to land mainly because of the frequency of adults and children playing soccer, thus making it more difficult for rebels to plant landmines or other explosives.

221 (Hagan & Rymond-Richmond, 2009)

222 (Hagan & Rymond-Richmond, 2009)

223 (BBC News, 2008)

224 (The International Criminal Court, 2014; The International Criminal Court, 2013) (Dabangasudan.org, 2016; Theguardian, 2016). There are 122 countries that are party to the Rome Statutes of the ICC, including 34 countries on the African continent. Parties to the statute have an obligation of cooperation to arrest, detain,

and send to The Hague any war criminal wanted by the ICC. Unfortunately, this obligation is not enforceable, as noted with the case of Chad in February 2013. Furthermore, South Africa in 2015, Djibouti and Uganda in 2016 all failed to arrest Al-Bashir during state visits to those countries.

225 (Our Africa, 2014)

226 The SPLA was a South Sudan guerrilla movement that was founded in 1983. It became the Army of the Republic of South Sudan in 2011, when the country gained its independence from Sudan. Ref: (South Sudan, 2014).

227 There are some excellent books and audio programs commercially available that can help one enhance their time management and leadership skills, as well as assist development of goal-setting methodology. For example, Stephen Covey's *The 7 Habits of Highly Effective People*, Brian Tracy's books *Time Management* and *Psychology of Achievement*, Peter Legge's *The Power to Soar Higher*, and Richard Templar's *The Rules of Work*, only to name a few, are collections by well-known authors that can help one become a better and more effective individual.

228 (United Nations, 2014)

229 (United Nations, 2016)

230 (EU Police Coordinating Office for Palestinian Police Support, 2010)

231 (EUPOL COPPS, 2011)

232 HAMAS was still considered a Terrorist Organization at the time of this writing in March 2017. Ref: (Public Safety Canada, 2016)

233 (Ginsberg, 2001)

234 (Palestinian Territories, 2011)

235 (Palestinian Territories, 2011)

236 (Palestinian Territories, 2011)

237 (Palestinian Territories, 2011)

238 (Palestine, 2011)

239 (Gascoigne, History of Assyria, 2001-)

240 (Palestine, 2011)

241 (Palestine, 2011)

242 (Palestine, 2011)

243 (Brief History of Palestine, 2011)

244 The Crusades were a series of religious wars blessed by the Clergy (between 1095-1291CE) and led by military units from all over Western Europe (though predominately French-speaking Western Christians). These had come together to fight the Islamic invasion of Europe, as well as restore Christian access to the Holy Land near Jerusalem. Of interest, Jews and Muslims fought together to defend Jerusalem from the Crusaders on or about 1099 CE. They were unsuccessful, and most were killed. Ref: (The Crusades, 2011)

245 (Brief History of Palestine, 2011), (Turkish Toleration, 2011)

246 (Brief History of Palestine, 2011)

247 (ProCons.Org, 2011) , (Mills, 1932) and (The History of Israel: A Chronological Presentation, 2009). Note that by 1931, the Arab population in Palestine was approximately 858,708 inhabitants.

248 The Western Wall is sacred to Jews because it is the only remnant of the second temple of Jerusalem. It is sacred to Muslims because the wall forms part of a larger wall that surrounds the Al-Aqsa Mosque. Ref: (Palestine, 2011)

249 (Palestine, 2011)

250 (Brief History of Palestine, 2011), (Palestine, 2011) Some of the terrorist groups formed by extremist Jews were the LEHI (in Hebrew: Lohamei Herut Israel, meaning Fighter for the Freedom of Israel) and the IRGUN.

251 (Palestine, 2011)

252 (Palestine, 2011)

253 (Palestine, 2011)

254 (Palestine, 2011), (Battlefield Detectives: The Six Day War [Video], 2005

255 (Palestine, 2011)

256 The Intifada is an armed revolt of Palestinians against the Israeli occupation of the West Bank and Gaza Strip. Ref: Merriam-Webster Dictionary. www.Merriam-webster.com/dictionary/intifada

257 (Palestine, 2011)

258 (Palestine, 2011)

259 (Schulz, 2009)

260 (Schulz, 2009)

261 (EUPOL COPPS, 2011)

262 (EUPOL COPPS, 2011), (Royal Canadian Mounted Police, 2011)

263 (Royal Canadian Mounted Police, 2011), (European Union Institute for Security Studies, 2009)

264 (Tel Aviv, 2012)

265 (Jerusalem, 2012).

266 (Green Line-Israel, 2012)

267 Hezbollah, meaning Party of God, is a political Islamic militia group that has operated in Lebanon since 1982. Hezbollah has received funding from Iran and Syria, and has aspired to eliminate Israeli influence from Lebanon. Hezbollah is also considered a terrorist entity by the United Kingdom, the United States, the Netherlands, Australia, and Canada. Ref: (Hezbollah, 2012A) (Hezbollah, 2012B).

268 (Petra, 2012)

269 (Afghanistan, 2012)

270 (United Nations, 2012)

271 (Afghanistan, 2012)

272 (Gascoigne, History of Afghanistan, 2001-)

273 (Gascoigne, History of Afghanistan, 2001-)

274 (Gascoigne, History of Afghanistan, 2001-)

275 (Gascoigne, History of Afghanistan, 2001-)

276 (Gascoigne, History of Afghanistan, 2001-)

277 (Gascoigne, History of Afghanistan, 2001-) The emir's name was Abd Al-Rahman

278 (Afghanistan, 2012) (Gascoigne, History of Afghanistan, 2001-)

279 (Gascoigne, History of Afghanistan, 2001-)

280 (Gascoigne, History of Afghanistan, 2001-)

281 (Stone & Stone Second World War Books, 1999), (Nationsonline.Org, 2012).

282 (Gascoigne, History of Afghanistan, 2001-)

283 (Gascoigne, History of Afghanistan, 2001-) (Soviet War in Afghanistan, 2012). The Cold War is a term coined to refer to the rivalry that developed after WWII between the United States and the Soviet Union, along with their respective allies.

284 (Soviet War in Afghanistan, 2012)

285 (Gascoigne, History of Afghanistan, 2001-) (Soviet War in Afghanistan, 2012)

286 (Gascoigne, History of Afghanistan, 2001-)

287 (Gascoigne, History of Afghanistan, 2001-) (United Nations, 2012)

288 (Afghanistan, 2012)

289 (Tristam, 2012)

290 (Afghanistan, 2012) (Tristam, 2012)

291 (Afghanistan, 2012) (Tristam, 2012)

292 (Gascoigne, History of Afghanistan, 2001-) (Tristam, 2012)

293 (The Taliban, 2012), (Afghanistan, 2012) (Gascoigne, History of Afghanistan, 2001-) (BBC News, 2001) After the Afghan war, Osama bin-Laden became disenchanted with Saudi Arabia and the United States, which he accused of supporting enemies of Islam, among a series of other charges. Bin-Laden and al-Qaeda were thus attributed several pre-September 2001 terrorist attacks against United States interests. These were namely: the 1993 bombing of the World Trade Center in New York; the 1998 simultaneous bombing of US Embassies in Kenya and Tanzania; and the bombing of the United States warship "USS Cole" in Yemen in 2000.

294 (Jacobson & Colon, 2006)

295 (Jacobson & Colon, 2006). Note that the fourth airliner, United Airlines flight 93, was believed to be heading towards Washington, DC, where it was to crash into a target building. Learning of the previous attacks, some courageous passengers attempted to regain control of the aircraft, which ended up diving and blowing up in a field in Pennsylvania. The heroic actions of the passengers likely saved the lives of hundreds of people in the nation's capital.

296 (September 11 Attacks, 2012) (Gascoigne, History of Afghanistan, 2001-)

297 (September 11 Attacks, 2012) (War on Terror, 2012). "The Global War on Terror" is a term coined for an international military campaign led by the United States and its allies against al-Qaeda and other militant organizations, with the ultimate goal of eliminating them.

298 Operation Enduring Freedom is the official name used by the United States government for the war in Afghanistan. Ref: (War on Terror, 2012).

299 (Nationsonline.Org, 2012)

300 (United Nations, 2012)

301 (United Nations, 2012)

302 (United Nations, 2012)

303 (Gascoigne, History of Afghanistan, 2001-) (United Nations, 2012)

304 (The Taliban, 2012) (United Nations, 2012)

305 (Afghanistan, 2012) (United Nations, 2012) (NATO, 2012)

306 (NATO, 2012)

307 (Nelson, 2008)

308 (Chesser, 2012) (NATO, 2012)

309 Gregor has high esteem for some colleagues, friends, and American troops, whom he credits with making his mission as safe as could be. They are: Gary Hollender, Roger Caron, Peter Hart, Andrew Turnbull, and Dimitris Harris, only to name a few.

310 (Khapalwak, 2006), (Madonik, 2011), (MacQueen, 2013). The officer who was savagely attacked was Captain Charles Trevor Green of the Canadian Forces. Once condemned to a life in an institution after his severe brain injury, Green's determination to recover has astounded everyone. Defying the limits of science, Green's brain is recovering in ways that rehabilitation specialists once thought impossible. For his determination to overcome almost insurmountable adversities, Green is a national hero, and an example to all of us.

311 The C-7 is a 30-round magazine military assault rifle that has semi-automatic and fully automatic fire modes. The weapon is manufactured by Colt Canada and used by the Canadian Forces. Ref: (Colt Canada C7 Rifle, 2012)

312 Note that even though the standard for government air travel is economy class at the lowest fare, Canadian Government Travel Directives allow for business class airfare when continuous air travel exceeds nine hours. Since Gregor's travel exceeded that time, he fell under those directives.

313 A Light Armoured Vehicle (LAV) is an Infantry Fighting vehicle fitted with partial- or full-armour plating for protection against bullets, shell fragments, and other projectiles. The LAV is built in Canada. A LAV can have approximately 10 occupants (7 passengers & 3 crew members). Ref: (Canadian Army, 2016) and (Armoured Vehicle in Encyclopaedia Britannica, 2016)

314 Although the RCMP Officer and CF colleagues riding in vehicles behind the one that exploded were not hurt, they put their own lives on the line to remove the

bodies of their comrades (some being close friends and teammates) from the LAV and loaded them onto a responding helicopter. The bravery and emotional stress these people went through cannot be emphasized enough.

315 Camp Nathan Smith was a former fruit factory that was rebuilt in 2003 by the American Army. The camp was turned over to the Canadian Armed Forces in 2005 and renamed Camp Nathan Smith, in honour of the Private from the Princess Patricia Canadian Light Infantry regiment who was killed in Afghanistan. In 2002, Smith and three other CF members were inadvertently killed by friendly fire during a mission. The deaths were the first suffered by Canada in the war in Afghanistan. Ref: (The Tarnak Farm Incident, 2012).

316 (Tracy, 2011) The comrade who sat in the LAV and reassured Gregor on his way from Kandahar Airfield to CNS would later become a solid mentor to him.

317 (Tracy, 2011)

318 In reference to Figure 60, ground guiding is an essential component of moving military vehicles in restricted visibility and restricted terrain conditions. Ground guiding can be extremely dangerous if either the vehicle or the ground guide do not follow or execute proper procedures. Each year in the US military, soldiers are seriously injured or killed in ground guiding accidents. Ref. https://safety.army.mil

319 At the time of Gregor's mission, the illiteracy rate among members of the Afghan National Security Forces, which included the ANP police, stood at nearly 80%. Ref: (Caldwell & Finney, 2011)

320 (National Defence and the Canadian Forces, 2012)

321 (Defense Manpower Data Center, 2014)

322 (Operation Enduring Freedom, 2014)

323 Heatstroke is a thermic fever that happens when the body's mechanisms for controlling its temperature fails. Heatstroke is a life-threatening emergency that requires immediate treatment. Treatments for heatstroke include removing the victim from the heat source (i.e. sun, warm clothing) and immersing the victim in cool water. Ref: (Canoe.ca, 2012)

324 (Legge, 365 Days of Insights , 2012)

325 (Legge, 365 Days of Insights , 2012)

326 (Legge, 365 Days of Insights , 2012)

327 (Legge, 365 Days of Insights , 2012)

328 Creating S.M.A.R.T. Goals http://topachievement.com/smart.html Accessed December 3, 2016

329 (United Nations, 2012)

330 (Haiti, 2012) (Central Intelligence Agency, 2012)

331 (Martinez Almanzar, 1996) (History of Haiti, 2012)

332 (History of Haiti, 2012) (Martinez Almanzar, 1996)

333 (Haiti, 2012)

334 (Haiti, 2012)

335 (Haiti, 2012)

336 The Treaty of Ryswick, named after the town (Risjwijik) in the western Netherlands where peace negotiations took place, was a treaty signed between France and the nation alliance of Spain, England, and the Holy Roman Empire. In the part of the treaty dealing with French interests in the Caribbean, Spain ceded the western third of the island of Hispaniola to France. Ref: (The Louverture Project, 2009).

337 (Haiti, 2012)

338 A Mulatto is an individual whose ancestry is a mixture of Negro and Caucasian. Ref: (Mulatto, n.d.), (Haiti, 2012)

339 (History of Haiti, 2012)

340 (The Louverture Project, 2010)

341 (Gascoigne, History of Haiti, 2001-)

342 (Gascoigne, History of Haiti, 2001-)

343 (Martinez Almanzar, 1996)

344 (Martinez Almanzar, 1996)

345 (Martinez Almanzar, 1996) (Gascoigne, History of Haiti, 2001-)

346 (Martinez Almanzar, 1996)

347 (Gascoigne, History of Haiti, 2001-), (Martinez Almanzar, 1996)

348 (Gascoigne, History of Haiti, 2001-)

349 (History of Haiti, 2012), (Gascoigne, History of Haiti, 2001-)

350 (Gascoigne, History of Haiti, 2001-), (François Duvalier, 2012)

351 (Gascoigne, History of Haiti, 2001-) (François Duvalier, 2012)

352 The "Tontons Macoutes" or "Bogeymen" were a Haitian militia created by Dictator Francois Duvalier. They were responsible for terrorizing, kidnapping, and assassinating dissidents and opponents to Duvalier's dictatorship. In all, they are believed to have murdered over 30,000 Haitians. Ref: (Tonton Macoutes, 2012).

353 (François Duvalier, 2012)

354 (Gascoigne, History of Haiti, 2001-)

355 (Gascoigne, History of Haiti, 2001-), (François Duvalier, 2012)

356 (MINUSTAH, 2012)

357 (RCMP Officers Quit Haiti UN Reimposes Sanctions: [Final Edition], 1993)

358 (Haiti, 2012)

359 (Gascoigne, History of Haiti, 2001-)

360 (History of Haiti, 2012), (MINUSTAH, 2012)

361 (MINUSTAH, 2012) MIPONUH is a French acronym that stands for *Mission de Police des Nations Unies en Haiti.*

362 (United Nations Department of Peacekeeping Operations, 2003)

363 (Haiti, 2012)

364 (MINUSTAH, 2012)

365 These are only three of the several mandates MINUSTAH had set up. Please refer to http://www.un.org/en/peacekeeping/missions/minustah/background.shtml or (MINUSTAH, 2012) for a more exhaustive list.

366 (MINUSTAH, 2012)

367 More than 500 SPVM police officers have participated in 13 international peacekeeping missions since 1995. In 2008, a protocol was signed between the RCMP and SPVM for the latter to have 50 officers ready for deployment at any time until 2011. Ref: http://www.spvm.qc.ca/en/Pages/Discover-SPVM/Who-does-what/International-Missions

368 (MINUSTAH, 2012), (Harmon, 2010)

369 (MINUSTAH, 2012)

370 (MINUSTAH, 2012)

371 (MINUSTAH, 2012)

372 (MINUSTAH, 2012)

373 (Indian Ocean Tsunami of 2004, 2012)

374 (Haiti Earthquake of 2010, 2012)

375 (Luzincourt & Gulbrandson, 2010)

376 (Chandler, 2008)

377 (Chapell & Evans, 1997)

378 (Chapell & Evans, 1997)

379 As this book was being completed, the Department of Foreign Affairs and International Trade had been renamed as Global Affairs Canada (GAC)

380 (Chapell & Evans, 1997)

381 (Chapell & Evans, 1997)

382 (Chapell & Evans, 1997)

383 (Chapell & Evans, 1997)

384 (Chapell & Evans, 1997)

385 (Chapell & Evans, 1997)

386 (Chapell & Evans, 1997) As the reader will have discovered in the chapter on the Former Yugoslavia, the sending of UN Peacekeepers to Sarajevo (Bosnia-Herzegovina) in 1994 may have been a mistake, as some were eventually taken hostage by rebel forces.

387 (Chapell & Evans, 1997)

388 (Chapell & Evans, 1997)

389 (Chapell & Evans, 1997) Author's note: Although this book does not intend to critique selection practices of other UN Member States, some of the chapters have unavoidably identified shortcomings related to poor candidate identification procedures.

390 (Chapell & Evans, 1997)
391 (Chapell & Evans, 1997)
392 (Chapell & Evans, 1997)
393 (Chapell & Evans, 1997)
394 (Royal Canadian Mounted Police, 2011)
395 (Royal Canadian Mounted Police, 2011)
396 (United Nations, 2005; United Nations, 2005)
397 The Conceptual Origins of Peacebuilding, 2008)
398 (United Nations, 2016)
399 (Bennett)

Manufactured by Amazon.ca
Acheson, AB